The Advertising Law Guide

◆ ◆ ◆

The Advertising Law Guide

◆ ◆ ◆

A Friendly Desktop Reference for
Advertising Professionals

LEE WILSON

ALLWORTH PRESS
NEW YORK

05   04   03   02   01   00   5   4   3   2   1

Published by Allworth Press
An imprint of Allworth Communications
10 East 23rd Street, New York, NY 10010

Cover design by Douglas Design Associates, New York, NY

Page composition/typography by SR Desktop Services, Ridge, NY

Library of Congress Cataloging-in-Publication Data
Wilson, Lee, 1951–
    The advertising law guide: a friendly desktop reference for advertising
professionals / by Linda Lee Wilson.
        p.   cm.
    Includes index.
    ISBN: 1-58115-070-9
    1. Advertising laws—United States.   I. Title.
KF1614.Z9 W55   2000
343.73'082—dc21
                                                            00-059436

Printed in Canada

◆ ◆ ◆

This book is dedicated to the memory of Miss Geneva Dillard, who taught me, and several generations of other second graders, how to read. This book is also dedicated to my sister, Patricia Wilson Bowers, who continues the useful work of lovingly shaping the minds of young children. For these women, and others like them, every literate person should be grateful.

◆ ◆ ◆

CONTENTS

Preface

I N A FORMER LIFE, AND FOR MORE THAN FIVE YEARS, I WAS THE CREATIVE
director for a national marketing corporation. I met with clients; designed campaigns and programs; wrote ad copy, newsletters, manuals,
and trade press articles; worked elbow-to-elbow with graphic designers,
art directors, and photographers; attended photo sessions; proofed
bluelines; produced radio spots and advertising jingles in dark little recording studios and pretty good television spots in studios and on location;
hired and fired freelancers and other talent; answered to the CEO when a
deadline was missed; and learned to eat pencils instead of lunch. I had prepared for my brilliant career in advertising by majoring in English litera-
ture in college and working, during one brief, shining moment in the
annals of journalism, as a reporter for a daily newspaper.

When I left my glamorous job in advertising for the drudgery of law
school, I supported myself, badly, as a freelance writer. Today I am an intel-
lectual-property lawyer. Over the nearly twenty years I have practiced law,
I have represented design studios, advertising agencies and advertising production companies, photographers, artists, and writers. Because I used to do
what you do, I have a good idea of the daily concerns of advertising people and of the problems you face. Because I am now a lawyer, I also know
that you have problems that you don't even know you have.

Until I began studying law, I knew far too little about the areas of law
that concern advertising. I never stepped on anyone's rights during my
tenure in advertising, more through instinct than through knowledge. That
was very dangerous—for me and my job and for the company that
employed me. Even well-meaning, honorable people can get into trouble

without the right information. That's what this book is about—giving you the information you need to stay on the right side of the law and to protect what you create and the interests of your clients.

A word about the audience for this book. This book is primarily addressed to advertising agency creative staffs and graphic designers. Most of the examples used illustrate advertising agency and design studio situations. However, because advertising and design job categories don't always represent neat divisions of labor, but instead often have floating, overlapping boundaries (most agency account executives routinely participate in advertising creative decisions, for instance, and many small graphic design studios produce ads for some clients), this book is potentially useful to everyone who works in advertising or graphic design in any capacity, whether full-time or just sometimes.

This book will also be useful to freelancers and other creative professionals, such as photographers, copywriters, illustrators, graphic designers, broadcast producers, Web site designers, jingle composers, and public relations people. Freelancers often do not have the information and support available to people who have similar jobs at agencies and design studios. It will even be useful to people who work in the in-house agencies of corporations that have in-house legal departments that review ads and advise creative personnel regarding legalities. Time is always a problem in such settings and no one can ever know too much about his or her job.

My thanks to the last real man in America who cooks dinner, my very good friend Dane Bryant, who offered me unfailing aid and comfort during the often tedious process of writing this book; to my old friend Todd Waterman, who gave me the same moral support during law school and who helped me edit parts of the manuscript for this book; and to my good friend and former co-worker, Eric Stein, the most vicious grammarian in captivity, who read every single word I wrote and complained, justifiably, about usage, punctuation, and sentence structure.

—LEE WILSON
Nashville, Tennessee
January 2000

CHAPTER 1

Legal Issues in Advertising

THIS BOOK IS A HANDBOOK FOR STAYING OUT OF TROUBLE. YOU CAN view it, if you choose, like a map guiding you around the hazards on the road to professional success. It won't teach you how to write more intriguing copy or shoot more arresting photographs or design more attractive packaging. It won't help you attract more clients or get a promotion or win an Addy. The information this book does contain, however, *is* necessary for career advancement in a very fundamental way: If you are ignorant of the topics it discusses and can't answer the questions it raises, you may not *have* a career for long.

If you earn your living by creating advertising, you need a good working knowledge of false advertising law (two varieties), libel law, the law of privacy and the law governing the right of publicity, copyright law, trademark law, and contract law. That's true whether you work for an ad agency, own your own design studio, or freelance out of your spare bedroom. In fact, as an art director, creative director, account executive, producer, copywriter, illustrator, graphic designer, photographer, Web site designer, jingle composer, or marketing or public relations professional, you really need to know more about these narrow but important areas of U.S. law than most lawyers, because every day your professional activities involve copyright decisions, trademark decisions, and questions involving false advertising law, libel law, privacy and publicity issues, and contract law—whether you know it or not.

For example:

- If you proclaim in your new advertising campaign that your kitchen cleaner is "More Effective at Killing Household Bacteria Than Any Other Brand" can the manufacturer of a competing cleaner sue you, and if so, why?

- If you substitute nice, big chunks of beef for the puny ones that came out of your client's can of vegetable beef soup before you photograph the soup for a magazine ad, will the Federal Trade Commission notice? What will the FTC do to you or your client if it does notice?
- Is it libel to say in a political campaign ad that your client's opponent has the worst voting record on environmental issues of any member of the legislature? What about saying that he takes bribes if you have good reason to believe that he does but can't prove it?
- Can you use a letter from a consumer to your client complimenting your client's laundry detergent in an ad? If you do, can you use the consumer's name and address?
- If you find a photo of Meryl Streep wearing your client's wristwatch, can you feature the photo in an ad? Do you need Ms. Streep's permission if you have permission from the photographer to use the photo?
- If you use a photograph of a sunrise from your files for the package you design for a client's vitamin tablets without asking for or receiving permission from the photographer, can the photographer sue you? Can he sue your client? If he does, can he win? What will the court do to you if he does?
- If an agency hires you to come up with a new logo for a restaurant chain and you do and they like it but it looks a whole lot like the Coca-Cola logo, is the Coca-Cola Company going to cause trouble, and who's in hot water, you or your client?
- If you offer a job to a freelance writer who was really your second choice for the project and then find out your first-choice writer is available after all, can you retrieve the project from your second-choice writer, and if you do, can that writer claim that you owe him the fee you promised for the work he now won't do?

If you don't know the answers to these questions you are, at best, simply ignorant of the law in several matters that may be crucial to your professional advancement. At worst, you may be a sitting duck for lawsuits, unemployment, and financial disaster.

When did things get so complicated?

Advertising, and the laws governing it, became complicated when technology made it possible to reach millions of people in one minute on network television. Over the last forty years, the rules have become much more complex and the stakes exponentially higher for anyone who creates any communication that is disseminated by any of our sophisticated, far-reaching communications media. That means that even if you only swim occasionally in the vast river of information that flows daily into almost every household in the country, you must know how not to drown.

If you expect either to protect and profit from what you create or to avoid infringing the rights of others, you cannot ignore questions of false advertising, libel, privacy, publicity, copyright, trademark, and contract law. If you do, you risk losing valuable rights, the trust of your clients, your job, or even worse, being sued. All it takes to put a small agency or studio out of business or you out of a job is one medium-sized lawsuit. Even if you win the lawsuit you've lost money spent in legal fees and the respect of your client or employer.

The good news is that you don't have to be scared of learning what you need to know. Anybody who is smart enough to design an ad or create a television spot can easily learn enough to stay on the right side of the law and out of lawsuits, as well as profit from knowing more. Raises, new clients, and fat paychecks come to those who know what they need to know; those who don't know what they need to know face the real possibility of a lot of unnecessary trouble. Read on. Knowledge is power.

This book would weigh about forty pounds and consist of several fat volumes if it contained *all* there is to know about the eight areas of the law that it discusses. And you wouldn't read it. Or if you did, you'd be an overworked law student who needed to cut back on caffeine. Consequently, we're going to consider only enough of each area of law to give you a fairly good idea of the terrain and the rough spots in it. Then, because you are a sharp and savvy person who knows the dangers inherent in trying to become your own lawyer, you'll take the questions you encounter to a real lawyer and pay his or her fee for the advice you need. Then you will do what your lawyer advises. And you'll be happy to do so. You will have avoided several awful potential consequences of failing to educate yourself about advertising law: lawsuits, being fired, losing clients, and losing face. And you won't have to go to law school yourself or depend on your own, possibly inadequate, analysis of your dilemma. After all, these are the burdens you will have paid your lawyer to assume.

Now for a flyby of the eight areas of law that impinge daily on the lives of people who create advertising for any medium. With the exception of the discussions of copyright and trademark law, each of the other fields of law is discussed at length in later chapters of the book. The *whole* of copyright law and *everything* you always wanted to know about trademark law are beyond the scope of this book. Instead, the very basic principles of copyright law and trademark law are reviewed below. The chapter on copyright later in this book gives you the basic information you need to avoid infringing the copyrights of others. Similarly, the chapters on trademark law that follow it deal only with the important task of choosing registrable, and protectable, trademarks and the big hazard of infringing existing, established trademarks. For a detailed discussion of all aspects of copyright ownership, registration, infringement, and exploitation, see *The Copyright Guide* by Lee Wilson, from Allworth Press. For a detailed discussion of all aspects of trademark ownership, registration, infringement, and proper use, see *The Trademark Guide* by Lee Wilson, also from Allworth Press. You can also obtain some good but limited information about both copyrights and trademarks by consulting the Copyright Resources and Trademark Resources sections of the appendix of this book and ordering the very reliable *free* pamphlets offered by the Copyright Office and the Trademark Office. (Don't worry about patent law; there's a very brief discussion of it below, but that is included mostly to distinguish it from copyright and trademark law, which are the other two most common forms of intellectual property.)

A Short Course in Intellectual-Property Law

A rose is a rose is a rose, but a copyright is not a patent or a trademark, even though all three terms name varieties of "intellectual property" (valuable intangible products of the imagination), which, in this country, have their origins in our Constitution.

The makers of the United States Constitution lived in an era during which science and philosophy bore exotic fruit—inventions and ideas that changed forever the way men and women lived their lives and viewed their condition. Because of this important explosion of thought and technology, the men who wrote our Constitution provided for the encouragement and reward of the thinkers and creators in the new American nation.

In Article I, Section 8, Clause 8 of the Constitution, the authors empowered Congress to "promote the Progress of Science and useful Arts, by securing, for limited Times to Authors and Inventors, the exclusive Right to their respective Writings and Discoveries." The theory was that Americans would write great books and invent useful inventions if they were rewarded for their efforts by being made the only ones entitled to profit from their creations. This provision of the Constition is the source for both the U.S. copyright statute and the U.S. patent statute.

United States trademark law has its origins in an entirely different section of the Constitution, the "commerce clause," in which Congress is given the power to regulate interstate commerce. As commerce in the nation grew, Congress realized that legislation was needed to protect consumers from confusion as to the sources of the goods they bought and to allow manufacturers to profit from their own good commercial reputations without interference from unscrupulous imitators, so it passed a trademark statute. The current federal trademark statute was passed in 1946. Each state also has a trademark statute.

This boring stuff really isn't boring, if you think about it. If you live in the United States, you are a part of the world's largest free enterprise society and should be concerned about having and preserving the ability to profit from your own commercial activities unimpeded by anyone who wants a free ride on your commercial coattails. That's trademark law. And whether you create photographs, print ads, broadcast ads, jingles, or illustrations, if you earn your living by what you create, you need to know what rights the law gives creators. That's copyright law. Further, anyone who creates copyrights or trademarks must know how to avoid infringing the trademark and copyright rights of others.

Patents

A patent is a monopoly granted by the U.S. Patent Office for a limited time to the creator of a new invention. A utility patent may be granted to a process, a machine, a manufacture, a composition of matter, or an improvement of an existing idea that falls into one of these categories. For example, a utility patent would be granted to the inventor of a new industrial or technical process or a new chemical composition. Utility patents endure twenty years after the application for a patent is filed. Plant patents are issued for new asexually or sexually reproducible plants and last seventeen years from the date of issue. Design patents are granted for ornamental designs used for nonfunctional aspects of manufactured items. An example of this would be a lamp base in the shape of a caryatid; the caryatid would visually enhance the appearance of the lamp but would not improve the function of the lamp base, e.g., to elevate the bulb and shade portions of the lamp. A design patent lasts fourteen years from the date it is issued. An inventor must meet very strict standards before the Patent Office will grant a patent for his or her invention. Then, the inventor can stop everyone else from manufacturing the invention without permission or even importing an infringing invention into the United States, even if the infringer of the patent independently came up with the same invention.

No product name is protectable by patent law; a product name is a trademark and trademark protection is, as we shall see, earned in the marketplace rather than being awarded like a patent. And no song, story, painting, or play can be patented; copyright gives writers and artists the right to keep others from copying their works, but not a complete monopoly on the creation or importation of similar works. If you create advertising, there is almost no chance that your daily work will require that you know any more about patents than you can learn in this very short discussion. The same is not true of copyrights and trademarks.

(For a more detailed discussion of patent law, see *The Patent Guide* by Carl Battle, from Allworth Press.)

Copyright Law 101

A copyright is like the "deed" to a literary or artistic work. The owner of a copyright has the exclusive right to copy or reproduce the work, to prepare alternate or "derivative" versions of the work, to distribute and sell copies of the work, and to perform or display the work publicly. The only way someone else can legally exercise one of these rights is by permission of the copyright owner or by becoming the owner of one or more of these rights. Any unauthorized exercise of any of these rights is copyright infringement.

On January 1, 1978, a new U.S. copyright statute came into effect. For any copyrightable "work," that is, for any photograph, poem, musical composition, or other original product of the imagination, created on or after that date, the law is very different from what it was for works created earlier. The first thing to know about copyright law is that, for any work created after December 31, 1977, copyright exists at the moment the work is "fixed in any tangible form." Although a copyright is, itself, a set of intangible legal rights that are entirely separate from any physical object that embodies the work, under the new law the existence of copyright is triggered by the reduction of the work to a tangible form that allows the work to be perceived by the senses.

This means that when your pen leaves the paper, when your camera clicks, you own the copyright in what you have created. This is true even if you never publish your work, or put a copyright notice on it, or register the copyright in it. Your copyright rights automatically begin the moment you "fix" your work.

You own the copyright in what you create *unless:*

- You copied someone else's copyrighted work. That is copyright infringement, and the law does not grant you rights in something you wrongfully took from someone else.
- You work full time for someone else and create your photograph or copy or jingle for them as a part of your regular duties. Then your creation is considered to be a "work-for-hire" and your employer owns the copyright in it from the beginning.
- You have created something that is not protectable under copyright law. There are only a few categories of works that are not copyrightable. They include blank forms, slogans, titles, raw information, ideas, methods, and systems.

If you remember nothing else about copyright law, remember this most basic concept: copyright protects not ideas but only *particular expressions of ideas.*

You can grasp this concept, which confuses even lawyers and sometimes judges, by remembering a simple example. If a dozen photographers took simultaneous photographs of the same still-life arrangement of fruit and flowers, each photograph would be a separate expression of the same idea—the idea of an image of a still-life arrangement of fruit and flowers. There would be variations in the photographs because of the photographers' individual approaches to angle and composition, and because of their varying choices of cameras, film, and filters. But even if, by some chance, two of them independently took identical photographs of that one still-life arrangement, both of the identical photographs would be copyrightable.

"Copyright protection" means the protection the law gives copyright owners from unauthorized use of their works. The period during which the law protects a particular work is called the "term of copyright." The term of copyright for works created after December 31, 1977 has recently generally been extended by twenty years. Copyrights in works created by individuals now endure for a period of the author's life plus seventy years. Copyrights created jointly by two or more people now will endure until seventy years after the death of the last of the co-authors. The term for a work created as a work-for-hire, anonymously, or under a fictitious name has been similarly extended; these now endure either one hundred and twenty years from the date the work was created or ninety-five years from the date of publication, whichever period expires first.

Reliable free pamphlets on copyright and copyright registration forms are available from the Copyright Office; information on these pamphlets and registration forms and how to obtain them is given in the Copyright Resources section of the appendix of this book.

Trademarks for Beginners

A trademark represents the commercial reputation of a product or service as embodied in a design (a logotype) or a word or name. Trademark law is a variety of the law of unfair competition. This means that trademark law prohibits certain trade practices that are considered unfair, such as the imitation of another's trademark in order to profit from consumers' mistaken belief that the imitation trademark and the product it names are the real thing. That is trademark infringement.

Trademark law also exists to protect consumers. It ensures, for instance, that when you buy a pair of running shoes marked with the Nike name, they are of the high quality you have come to expect in Nike products because they are, indeed, manufactured by Nike.

The two things that advertising creative people need to know about trademarks are how to choose them and how to use them.

Choosing a new product name is not a simple undertaking, and shouldn't be. Certain kinds of names are not registrable as trademarks with the U.S. Patent and Trademark Office, and the knowledgeable person who christens a new product must take these restrictions into account, since federal registration is, or should be, the goal of every trademark owner. The other major consideration in choosing a trademark is picking one that no one else is using. This process is called trademark clearance. You ignore it at your peril, since adopting and using someone's established trademark, even innocently, is trademark infringement, and trademark infringement can result in lawsuits that are expensive to settle and hopelessly expensive to defend.

In the United States, trademark ownership accrues by use of the trademark in commerce. Unless a trademark is used in the marketplace, there *is* no trademark, because there is no commercial reputation that can be exemplified by the word or symbol. Roughly speaking, trademark owners earn the right to prevent others from using the same symbol or word to represent or name a product or service similar to theirs in direct proportion to the extent of their use of that name or symbol, geographically and otherwise.

The owner of the four Bonet's Boutique ladies' clothing stores in northeast Idaho can probably keep other retailers from calling new clothing stores of any kind by the Bonet's Boutique name, or any name that is confusingly similar to Bonet's Boutique, only within the same general area—that is, within the geographic area where the commercial reputation of Bonet's Boutique has spread.

The longstanding fame of Bloomingdale's, however, allows Bloomingdale's to stop the use of that name or any confusingly similar name of a department or specialty clothing store anywhere in the United States, even in areas geographically remote from the famous New York store (or any of its outposts). This is because, although the famous store is physically located in New York City, its reputation has spread across the United States, and U.S. trademark law prohibits competitors anywhere in the country from competing with it unfairly by appropriating its name.

Once a trademark is "cleared for takeoff" and is in use, *how* the mark is used is very important. For example, if a trademark is used as a noun rather than as an adjective ("Winkles" rather than "Winkles toy trucks"), it can lose its status as a trademark. That's what happened to "aspirin," "cellophane," and "escalator," all of which once named particular brands of the products for which they are now the generic names. And if the ® symbol is not used properly in conjunction with a federally registered trademark, the trademark owner's right to collect money damages in a lawsuit against a trademark infringer may be diminished.

In the abstract, these may seem like niggling considerations; in actuality, proper trademark usage can be crucial to the overall health of the company that owns the mark since the company trademark may represent the most valuable asset of the company, its goodwill. The Xerox Company thinks so, at least. Otherwise it would not run thousands of dollars worth of ads every year pointing out that photocopiers are not "xerox machines" and that their machines are "Xerox brand photocopiers."

Xerox doesn't want to end up like the once-famous Escalator Company, which, ironically, lost its fame because of the popularity and success of the moving stairways marketed under the same name. When the name "Escalator" became a generic term applicable to all moving stairways, the Escalator moving stairway faded into the woodwork, so to speak, becoming so famous it became anonymous.

A very reliable free pamphlet on federal trademark registration is available from the U.S. Patent and Trademark Office. Information on this pamphlet as well as on how to obtain forms for state trademark registration is given in the Trademark Resources section of the appendix of this book.

False Advertising

"False advertising" refers to two separate kinds of trouble that are of special concern to advertising creative people since the genesis of both kinds of false advertising claims is the content, both visual and verbal, of advertising.

The Lanham Act, the federal trademark statute, contains one section, Section 43(a), that has given rise over the years to a body of case law that has little to do with trademarks. Section 43(a) allows people who feel they have been harmed by misrepresentations made in someone else's advertising to sue for false advertising. Usually the people who feel they have been harmed and who sue are the competitors of the company that places the allegedly false ad, and usually they sue for significant false claims made about the advertised products. However, Section 43(a) also allows suits to be brought because of false claims made about the products of the *competitors* of the advertiser.

The other kind of false advertising claim is not a private suit like a Section 43(a) claim but is, rather, an action taken by the Federal Trade Commission (FTC) because it believes that an ad transgresses its regulations governing advertising and is "materially misleading" to consumers. The FTC may decide that an ad is materially misleading either because of specific claims made in the ad or because of omissions of information that could, if included, influence a consumer's purchasing decision.

In other words, if you are not very careful to tell the *whole* truth in advertising materials you create, including the photos and the copy and the fine print, you and your client may end up, because of the content of one ad, fending off both your client's angry competitors and the federal government. As with the other areas of law discussed in this book, false advertising claims present a danger even to honest people who can't depend simply on their good intentions to shield them from the ire of competitors or the righteous indignation of the federal government.

Libel, Privacy, and Publicity

Like copyright, trademark, and patent law, libel, privacy, and publicity law are related but very different areas of the law. Advertising creative people can avoid most of the tedious disputes and enormous problems that may result from even an unintentional trespass upon someone's right of privacy or publicity or a defamation (libel) of someone by learning enough about these three areas of the law to recognize the red flags that signal a possible lawsuit.

Unlike learning about copyright and trademark law, getting up to speed about libel, privacy, and publicity law will not reward you directly. Your only reward for not stepping on someone's legal toes by libeling them, invading their privacy, or infringing their right of publicity is that you will stay out of lawsuits. This may seem like small benefit to some, but if you have ever been close to such a lawsuit, you know that virtue, in these areas of the law, is its own reward.

To "defame" someone is to damage his or her reputation by spreading false statements about him or her. Slander is *speaking* defamatory statements. Libel, which is probably the only sort of defamation of any real concern to advertising creative people, occurs when defamatory information is spread by written or printed materials (photographs, newspaper or magazine ads, etc.) or, in most jurisdictions, broadcast over the airwaves (any sort of broadcast advertising). Lately, libel has also been possible by other media, including Internet ads and communications.

The right of privacy is the right of every U.S. citizen to be left alone, to live a life uninterrupted by intrusions into private matters or living areas, and to be free from unwilling exposure to public scrutiny or participation in the commercial process. There are four kinds of invasion of privacy:

- "False light" invasion of privacy, which is a sort of cousin to defamation, is the placing of someone in a "false light" before the public, usually by publishing a photograph or story that portrays that person in a misleading way that is offensive to him or her.

- "Intrusion" invasion of privacy involves some invasion of a person's private space or solitude. The invasion of privacy does not have to result from a *physical* invasion of private space; eavesdropping on private conversations and taking photos of someone through a window with a long-range lens are examples of this sort of invasion of privacy.
- "Public disclosure of private facts" invasion of privacy involves the publication of true but private information about an individual, such as details about the person's sex life or health or finances.
- "Misappropriation" invasion of privacy is the unauthorized use of a person's name or likeness for commercial purposes, such as in an ad, and represents the most common sort of privacy lawsuit involving advertising creative people.

The infringement of someone's right of publicity consists of the exploitation of someone's name or image in some commercial context without his or her permission. Unlike invasion of privacy, which is related to the right of private people to be left alone, the right of publicity is more in the nature of a property right of a famous person to exclusively exploit his or her own fame. The right of publicity is really the flip side of the right of privacy, since a violation of someone's right of publicity is a violation of his or her right to be the only one to make use of the "publicity value" of his or her name, and a private individual's name usually has no such publicity value.

That is not to say that the name and photograph of a private individual would never be used without permisson by a manufacturer in an endorsement for the company's products, but the usual lawsuit for infringement of someone's right of publicity involves a famous person who is suing because someone has used his or her name or picture to imply such an endorsement or to attract consumers' attention. In other words, people concerned with preserving their right of publicity are usually well known.

Contracts

Contract law is the underpinning of much of American commerce, although it is sometimes all but invisible if everything is going well. This is because experienced businesspeople learn to offer, negotiate, and execute contracts as facilely as a pro ball player handles a ball. If you are to prosper in advertising, you also need to know something about contracts: how they arise, what constitutes a contract, the effect of the provisions in contracts you are likely to encounter, what you can do if you want out of a contract, and what someone else can do to you if you fail to live up to your part of the bargain.

A contract is a set of legal rights and responsibilities created by the mutual agreement of two or more people or companies. A contract is the agreement itself, not the paper document that records the agreement. In fact, some contracts don't even have to be in writing to be valid, although written contracts are almost always a good idea.

In advertising, one of the more common sorts of contracts that arise is a contract for the services of a freelance photographer, illustrator, copywriter, jingle writer, or graphic designer. When you offer to engage the services of a freelancer, you have set in motion a sequence of events that may result in a contract. If the freelancer is willing to perform the job for the amount you offer and will do so by the deadline you name, he or she can create a contract with you by simply stating his or her agreement to your terms. However, if you make an offer to someone who turns it down, that person cannot later try to accept it and create a contract from your offer. The same is true of counteroffers. If you offer to hire someone's services for "$800 a day" and that person responds, "Sorry, but I won't do the job for less than $1,000 a day," he or she has rejected your offer by making an alternate offer, or counteroffer. The counteroffer becomes the offer of a new agreement, which you can then accept if you choose.

Contracts for someone's personal services over long periods of time, for sizeable amounts of money, or for the sale of land have to be in writing to be valid under the law. So do agreements that transfer ownership of copyrights. But you don't really need to learn the rules about the varieties of contracts that must be written, because if you aspire to be a shrewd businessperson you will document almost *every* agreement you enter. Except for simple short-term contracts that don't involve a lot of money, practically every contract can benefit from written documentation. And although people usually don't realize it, the process of working out the language in written agreements allows them to refine the terms of their arrangement, which in turn eliminates many of the problems that can arise during the life of an agreement.

If you have read this far, you may be worried that you haven't understood and absorbed everything you have read. Don't worry. We have the rest of this book to consider the two sorts of false advertising law, libel law, privacy law, publicity law, and contract law at a more leisurely pace and in more detail. Remember, the whole of copyright law and trademark law are beyond the scope of this book. However, we will discuss several important copyright and trademark topics concerning the largest threats of lawsuits faced by advertising creative people.

We will also take a look at how each of these eight areas of law works and, especially, how each impacts your work. We will learn how to recognize problems and how to avoid or solve them, often without the advice of a lawyer. By the time you get to the end of this book, you will have a good working knowledge of the pertinent areas of the law as they relate to your job and, better still, some confidence that you can deal with questions that you are likely to encounter. You'll find it well worth the effort.

These are not the most important questions in the world. However, your knowledge of the law that is applicable to your professional activities does affect one of the most important things in *your* world: your competence in your work. And if you are competent in what you do, your work will be better and your work life will be happier. Listen up, so you can whistle while you work.

CHAPTER 2

Avoiding False Advertising Challenges from Other Marketers

THERE ARE TWO MAJOR WAYS A COMPANY CAN GET INTO TROUBLE FOR false advertising. One is a private suit under Section 43(a) of the Lanham Act; that is, a suit brought by an individual or another company for violations of that section of the federal trademark statute. The other is an investigation or litigation by an agency of the federal government, the Federal Trade Commission, because of a claimed violation of the Federal Trade Act or FTC Trade Regulation Rules. Generally speaking, an egregious enough misrepresentation in an ad will result in one or both of these varieties of false advertising trouble, along with headaches, enormous legal fees, and lots of time spent getting nowhere.

False advertising litigation is generally brought against the advertiser. This is mostly because truth in advertising is more the responsibility of the advertiser than of the agency or studio that creates the ad. However, it is not at all uncommon for an ad agency to be named in a false advertising suit and enjoined by the court from further actions that the court finds are violations. Whether you work for the advertiser or an outside agency, merely being in the same room when an ad is created that is later the focus of a lawsuit can earn you a pink slip from your employer or demerits from your client. Advertisers in this country spend more money each year to create and produce advertising than most countries spend to run their armies. It only makes sense that you should do everything in your power to see that the production budgets for which you are responsible aren't spent to create ads that later have to be pulled. That means doing your best to stay out of false advertising briar patches.

It isn't all that hard, usually. All you have to do is squelch your cleverness long enough to ask yourself if Abraham Lincoln would say it or photograph it in the same way, had he been lucky enough to be you instead of the sixteenth president of the United States. Then you have to look at it through the eyes of a seventy-year-old widow living on a pension who is intimidated by the thought of not having enough insurance, or those of a four-year-old who believes everything he sees on television. If your ad passes these tests, you can send it to the printer. If it doesn't, call your lawyer.

In almost every case, the only goal for a defendant in either a Section 43(a) or an FTC suit is to get out of it as quickly as possible, which may be difficult. The only really quick way to avoid trouble from false advertising litigation is to stay out of it entirely in the first place. Avoiding trouble means knowing where the quicksand is. This chapter, as well as the next, will serve as a map guiding you through the treacherous terrain of false advertising law.

Section 43(a)

You might not expect to find a false advertising pitfall lurking in the middle of the federal trademark statute, but there it is. Section 43(a), the scourge of exaggerators and fabricators, was originally meant to provide a means of recourse against several forms of unfair competition, including false advertising. It allowed a company that had been harmed by some "false description or representation" made by a competitor about that competitor's goods or services to bring a federal suit to have the practice stopped. In other words, if your competitor lied about the merits of its products, you could sue to challenge the misrepresentations.

Some years ago, Section 43(a) was revised to enlarge the bases upon which a plaintiff can bring a Section 43(a) false advertising suit. Plaintiffs can now also sue competitors for making false statements of fact about the plaintiffs' products; this was not originally possible under the provision. This means that now Section 43(a) prohibits any advertising claim that misrepresents the nature, characteristics, qualities, or origin of another company's or person's goods, services, or commercial activities.

The revised text of Section 43(a) of the Lanham Act pertaining specifically to false advertising reads as follows:

(a) Any person who, on or in connection with any goods or services, or any container for goods, uses in commerce any word, term, name, symbol, or device, or any combination thereof, or any false designation of origin, false or misleading description of fact, or false or misleading representation of fact, which in commercial advertising or promotion, misrepresents the nature, characteristics, qualities, or geographic origin of his or her or another person's goods, services, or commercial activities shall be liable in a civil action by any person who believes that he or she is or is likely to be damaged by such act.

It is important to understand that a Section 43(a) suit is more than just a nuisance. Like a copyright or trademark infringement action, it is a suit that claims a violation of federal law and it is brought, and fought, in federal court, which is not small claims court. A winning plaintiff in a false advertising suit can recover the defendant's profits from the false advertising, the damages suffered by the plaintiff, the plaintiff's costs, and, sometimes, the plaintiff's attorneys' fees. In addition the court may enjoin further publication or broadcast of the offending ad and, sometimes, require corrective advertising.

So. The four elements of a Section 43(a) claim are: (1) *A false statement of fact made (usually in an ad) by the defendant;* (2) *about either the defendant's products or those of the plaintiff;* (3) *which has actually deceived a substantial number of the people to whom the ad is addressed or has the capacity to deceive them;* and (4) *which constitutes a material deception that is likely to influence purchasing decisions.*

Except for a few particulars, which we will consider below, that's it.

False Statements of Fact

The requirement that a Section 43(a) false advertising claim be based on a statement of fact is like the principle in defamation that opinions are not actionable. Nobody will sue your client for publishing an ad that quotes several satisfied consumers who sent fan letters about your client's new bathroom cleaner. However flattering the statements of those consumers, they are only opinions of those particular people and are not actionable even if they are incorrect. But try stating that "98 percent of housewives surveyed prefer new Dazzle cleanser" when your research really reported that 98 percent of the housewives surveyed preferred Dazzle over Rustaway, but only 34 percent preferred Dazzle over Daisy, the other leading cleanser. Your client may find himself staring down the barrel of a Section 43(a) false advertising suit.

An advertising "statement" can be visual or aural, as well as verbal. In fact, given the power of visual representations and the great care with which advertising illustrations are created and photographs are edited or altered these days, visual statements may be potentially even more misleading than verbal ones. Designers and art directors must pay special attention to the implications of their visual representations of products to detect false implications.

Television spots and Internet ads or Web pages are especially dangerous because they may combine verbal, aural, *and* visual messages. Because
ads in these media can be so powerful, any misleading representation in a
television spot, Internet ad, or Web page is not likely to go unchallenged by
competitors. One television spot for an expensive car that ran a few years
ago contained an implication that was so objectionable to the competitor
of the advertiser automaker that the competitor sued immediately. The spot
was pulled from the air after only nine days, under a court injunction.

The Defendant's Products or the Plaintiff's

A plaintiff in a Section 43(a) false advertising suit may sue because of false
statements made either about the defendant's goods or services or those of
the plaintiff. It isn't hard to figure out if the defendant made the statement
about its own products or services; the ad itself tells you that. It may be
harder, however, to tell if a false statement made in an ad is about the products or services of the plaintiff. Again, an analogy may be drawn to defamation law. A false statement about the plaintiff's products may be implied by
an ad or may refer to the plaintiff only by virtue of some outside facts not
contained in the ad. "The only toothpaste sold in America scientifically
proven to stop tartar!" implies that no other American toothpaste can stop
tartar without ever mentioning any other toothpaste by name. Similarly,
"Start-Up Batteries outperform every other leading brand of auto batteries" includes in its scope, by reference, the other leading battery brands and
thus is "about" them.

Actual or Potential Deception

The false statement must have actually deceived or have the capacity to
deceive a substantial segment of the ad's audience. In other words, if only
your gullible Uncle Mark and other people who don't get out much are
going to believe that "Eating Crunchies for breakfast makes you hand-
somer!" the makers of Sweeties cereal will not have a valid ground for a
Section 43(a) false advertising suit. Obviously, most false advertising suits
involve statements that are much more likely to deceive a substantial segment of the audience for the ad.

People who design and write ads often use such subtle visual signals
and language that evaluation of the possibility for deception is often difficult. The sophistication of the audience (or lack of sophistication) is a big
factor in evaluating the possibility for deceptiveness. Certain groups, such
as children and elderly people, are presumed to be more easily deceived
than other groups. Often, the audience for any particular ad is not mono-
lithic. A particular ad can be aimed at Mom and Dad *and* the kiddies.

Furthermore, even though ads accused of being misleading are evaluated according to whether the supposedly false statement concerns an

important enough feature of the product (in other words, is "material") to influence a purchasing decision, the people who write the checks do not necessarily make up the audience for the ad that prompts them to do so. Doting parents often make purchasing decisions because their tots have previously decided, due to a persuasive ad aimed at children, that they can't live another month without a glow-in-the-dark dinosaur gumball machine. In situations like this, the parents are not the audience for the ad even though they do make the ultimate purchase. If your ad for the flourescent dino implies that the toy is a veritable perpetual supply of tasty gumballs when in fact the gumballs are not included, you may be in trouble with your competitors who want that segment of the dinosaur gumball machine market for themselves and are willing to sue to stop you from co-opting it by deception.

Material Deception

It isn't always easy to gauge whether a statement in an ad is "materially mis-leading." Materially misleading statements come in two sizes, Plausible Falsehoods and Stir-Fried Truth. Each variety of misleading statement represents a separate hazard for anyone who has any role in creating advertising. You don't have to worry too much about whether you can get into trouble by employing a Plausible Falsehood in an ad. You can. If you are so foolish as to create an ad that contains any false statement of fact, be it verbal or visual or aural, your client's competitor will file a suit, in federal court, accusing your client of false advertising. Once again, good business judgment and garden-variety common sense dictate that avoiding the issue is far preferable to having it decided in court. That means scrutinizing the ads you create to eliminate any false representation, made directly or by implication, about either your own client's products or those of competitors.

This doesn't mean that you have to abandon the use of humorous exaggeration or obvious tall tales. Remember that your client can't be sued successfully unless the false representation is a big one and is likely to be believed. Courts look at what your ad actually means to the people to whom it is addressed. The late, great Joe Isuzu told the biggest whoppers ever seen on TV outside of political campaigns, but nobody sued Isuzu because nobody believed Joe. And nobody in America has ever known how all those fancy cars are supposed to have landed on top of those picturesque western buttes, but no automaker has ever been sued for implying that its automobiles could fly there.

Puffery

What the law calls "puffery" in ads is not actionable. Puffery is flattering, sometimes exaggerated, sales rhetoric that consumers are not likely to rely upon when making a purchase. ("The most generous auto dealer in

Bangor!" or "Eat the biggest T-bones in Texas at Ethel's Surf and Turf Lounge.") But it is dangerous to rely too much on this exception to "material deception.""The most skilled auto mechanics in the world work for us" may be non-actionable puffery; "The best auto mechanics in Peoria" may not be. Since the burden of proving that an extravagant statement is puffery is on the defendant in a Section 43(a) suit, it is better to be safe than sorry.

The really hard part of avoiding Section 43(a) false advertising accusations is determining when a true statement can get you in trouble. Theoretically, telling the truth should never result in a false advertising suit. The tricky part is telling the truth in such a way that no one is misled. Otherwise, what you end up with is Stir-Fried Truth, which can land you in a lawsuit as quickly as any false statement.

In some cases, all of this comes down to a matter of semantics and implications and interpretation. There is a line of cases known irreverently as "The Aspirin Wars" resulting from suits between two major American pharmaceutical companies over what most people would consider innocent representations of the relative merits of several brands of analgesics. These lawsuits were fought so long and so fiercely that they, collectively, wore out more Ivy League lawyers than can dance on the head of a pen. All because reasonable companies differed about the truth regarding their products.

The moral of this tale of life in a litigious society is that, past a certain point, determining the truth of statements made in ads is something that really is not in your bailiwick. You are not a research chemist, you did not conduct the survey, you did not test the product. You, personally, do not know if it does cut grease faster or is preferred by nine out of ten doctors or does last longer than any other comparably priced battery.

You must rely on your client or employer for this information. And you must be very careful to present the information you receive as accurately as possible, without implying that an ingredient of the sunscreen can prevent (rather than diminish the chance of) skin cancer, without exaggerating the number of almonds in the cereal, without distorting the survey results through clever manipulation of the English language.

Examples

The following examples will help you understand a little better the kinds of advertising representations that can result in Section 43(a) lawsuits.

- You create a snazzy television spot for your client the orange juice manufacturer, a company named Sunjuice. The spot features a well-known former Olympic swimming medalist, who squeezes fat oranges and pours the freshly-squeezed juice into a Sunjuice carton, all the while extolling the "wonderful fresh-squeezed taste" of Sunjuice orange juice. Two weeks after the debut of the ad,

Sunjuice's major competitor, the Liquid Gold Company, files a Section 43(a) suit, claiming that it has been harmed by Sunjuice's misrepresentation that Sunjuice's orange juice is fresh-squeezed orange juice, when in fact it is reconstituted from concentrate and is sometimes frozen before packaging.

Sunjuice's lawyers argue at trial that no one is likely to believe that orange juice is simply packaged fresh-squeezed juice and that therefore Sunjuice's spot is not actionable under Section 43(a). You were the creative director for the spot and, sitting in the Sunjuice cheering section in court on the day that Sunjuice makes this argument, you are hopeful that the judge will buy it. He doesn't.

The judge rules that the squeezing/pouring section of the Sunjuice spot, especially when coupled with the spokesman's comments, constitutes a material misrepresentation of fact by its powerful implication that Sunjuice sells fresh-squeezed orange juice in its cartons. He enjoins the further broadcast of the television spot. The Liquid Gold Company is happy. Sunjuice is very unhappy. So are you, because you lose the Sunjuice account.

- Your mail order marketing company client asks you to help him design materials to advertise and sell a "K-Tel" type collection of World War II—era pop music. Your client has obtained permission from the record companies that own the original master recordings of the thirty songs included in the two-cassette package to repackage and sell the recordings by mail. The cassettes include songs by various popular artists of the era, the most famous of whom is Frank Sinatra, who sings two selections. You decide to capitalize on the fact that Frank Sinatra recordings are included when you create the Sunday supplement newspaper ad for the package, which is called "Forties Favorites." Prominently displayed in the ad is the headline "Forties Favorites from Frank Sinatra (and Other Artists)."

The "Forties Favorites" ad results in record sales . . . and a federal lawsuit, filed by the estate of Frank Sinatra against your client's company. Mr. Sinatra's estate claims that the use of his name in your client's ad was more prominent than the content of the cassette collection justifies and that this over-attribution of the "Forties Favorites" to Mr. Sinatra is material misrepresentation of the contents of the cassettes and constitutes false advertising under Section 43(a). The suit asks for an injunction against any further use of the misleading ad and damages for the previous publication of the ad.

Your client voluntarily pulls his ad, not wanting to add fuel to the flame by disputing the claims of Mr. Sinatra's estate, among which are a claim for infringement of the estate's interest in Mr. Sinatra's right of publicity. Your client's lawyer tells him that the

Sinatra estate's claims are justified and your client settles the lawsuit. You design a new, more accurate newspaper ad for your client but he stops returning your phone calls and hires another agency. (Section 43(a) claims often result from situations where the contribution or role of a famous person is overstated in ads for some entertainment product. In such cases, they may be joined with right of publicity claims, which are similar, though not identical.)

- You have a small dairy product manufacturer client, based in Wisconsin. Your client wants you to help it develop packaging for its new product, a packaged gelato, produced in Wisconsin from authentic Italian recipes. You decide to emphasize the Italian angle, figuring that the gelato will appeal to sophisticated buyers if it appears to be made somewhere besides the Midwest.

  You recommend to your client that the new product be called "Buono" and you design packaging for the gelato that features the Italian flag prominently. As a further clever device, you also advise your client to print the label information in both English and Italian. Under the product name on the carton you use the slogan "A genuine Italian gelato." Your client loves the name, the copy, and the packaging. The product is launched and breaks all sales records for the company within the first month of marketing in the three Midwest states where it is introduced.

  Then your client is sued by its competitor, who claims that the packaging for your client's gelato is materially misleading in that it falsely states that the product is made in Italy. Your client is outraged by the temerity of its competitor and fights the lawsuit, unfortunately to no avail.

  The court says that your clever packaging is an obvious effort to lead consumers to believe that your client's gelato is made in Italy. It ignores the arguments of the lawyers for your client that no sophisticated buyer of the product would believe this actually to be the case. It says that very few grocery shoppers are likely to know that the packaging for a real imported product would state that the product was manufactured elsewhere, and, in any event, that it is not reasonable to expect such a close reading of the label from a grocery shopper.

  The plaintiff wins. Your client gets a lawyer who is knowledgeable about Food and Drug Administration labeling regulations and false advertising law to review the gelato packaging. The lawyer makes a few copy changes and eliminates the Italian flag and Italian-language ingredients list. You find out all this by reading the new gelato carton at the grocery store, because your client ditched you the day the court ruled in favor of its competitor.

If you manage to steer clear of any violations of Section 43(a), you will probably also stay out of trouble with the Federal Trade Commission, affectionately known as the FTC. Staying out of FTC trouble is the subject of the next chapter.

◆ ◆ ◆

Marketers who have never run afoul of an indignant competitor (and its lawyers) may underestimate the ire of competing marketers who feel they have been diminished in the eyes of consumers by what they think are unwarranted claims in ads. A very good example of this is the lawsuit brought by one venerable behemoth bookseller, Barnes & Noble, against another giant bookseller of somewhat more recent vintage, Amazon.com. The following is taken from a May 1997 *Publishers Weekly* article about the suit:

B&N Suing Amazon Over Ad Claim

Barnes & Noble has filed a suit against Amazon.com contesting the online bookseller's advertising claim that it is "The Earth's Biggest Bookstore." The suit also takes issue with Amazon's contention that it stocks more books than B&N, and B&N adds that any book Amazon can get, B&N can get too. As well as unspecified damages, B&N is seeking to bar Amazon from running the ads that make these claims and to have Amazon issue "corrective" ads. In addition, the suit maintains that Amazon "isn't a bookstore at all.... It is a book broker making use of the Internet exclusively to generate sales to the public."

Apparently, Barnes & Noble didn't think for a minute that Amazon's claims were mere "puffery." It also quite obviously felt that they painted a less than-accurate portrait of Barnes & Noble's role in the bookselling industry. As we know, this suit did not stop Amazon's ambitious efforts to become *the* online bookseller, but it did slow it down a bit. Who won the suit? Or was it settled out of court? Was there a big damages award? Or did Amazon pay to settle? None of these questions really matters. Because the suit, like most lawsuits, didn't produce anything new, didn't solve any problem, cost a lot to bring and to defend, and consumed far too much of the valuable time of executives of both the plaintiff and the defendant, whoever "won" in reality won only a Pyrrhic victory. The moral of this fable? Even if your conscience doesn't keep your ads honest, your competitors will, at great expense to you and at some inconvenience.

◆ ◆ ◆

CHAPTER 3

Avoiding Trouble with the Federal Trade Commission

F YOU STAY OUT OF SECTION 43(A) SUITS, YOU MUST STILL WORRY ABOUT avoiding trouble with the Federal Trade Commission. The FTC is the federal agency that enforces the Federal Trade Commission Act, which is a federal law that regulates, among other things, advertising. The Federal Trade Commission Act prohibits unfair methods of commercial competition and unfair or deceptive trade practices and empowers the FTC to initiate proceedings to stop such methods or practices. One of the unfair methods of competition prohibited is false advertising, which the statute defines as follows:

> The term "false advertisement" means an advertisement, other than labeling, which is misleading in a material respect; and in determining whether an advertisement is misleading, there shall be taken into account (among other things) not only representations made or suggested by statement, word, design, device, sound, or any combination thereof, but also the extent to which the advertisement fails to reveal facts material in the light of such representations or material with respect to consequences which may result from the use of the commodity to which the advertisement relates under the conditions prescribed in said advertisement, or under such conditions as are customary or usual.

This short section of the statute is the basis for many court decisions in suits brought by the FTC against advertisers accused of false advertising, and for innumerable "consent decrees" between advertisers and the FTC, which are like settlement agreements reached after the FTC has challenged the advertisers' practices as misleading. This extensive body of case law is the source for almost all law that deals with advertising compliance with the Federal Trade Commission Act.

The difference between being the defendant in a Section 43(a) suit and having the FTC investigate and prosecute you is the difference between the "plaintiffs" in these two sorts of actions. Your competitor (or the competitor of your client) can cause a lot of trouble and expense with its Section 43(a) suit, but it probably will not be able to wield the clout the FTC has, even if it wins.

Due to cyclical changes in the prevailing political climate in Washington, the FTC becomes less fierce during certain periods and leaves most American capitalists alone. During these periods of relative dormancy, the FTC goes after only the really bad guys and leaves a lot of the quibbling over the fine points of advertising language and visuals to the capitalists themselves, who enthusiastically file Section 43(a) suits whenever one thinks another has made an unfounded claim in an ad. However, even though the FTC is sometimes seemingly dormant, it has by no means lost its teeth. This means that you need a good working knowledge of FTC false advertising standards in order to help your clients or your employer avoid FTC challenges to the ads you create. The first thing to know is the FTC's definition of a deceptive ad.

Materially Misleading

The FTC says that an ad is deceptive if it contains a material representation or a material omission that is likely, if reasonably interpreted under the circumstances, to mislead consumers and affect their decisions with regard to purchasing the product. If you think this sounds familiar, you get points for paying attention when you read the previous chapter, because the FTC standard for a deceptive ad is, with one notable exception, essentially the same standard as that for a Section 43(a) false advertising claim.

Like Section 43(a), the FTC considers false statements actionable if they are material. (A claim is "material" if it pertains to important characteristics of the product, such as performance, quality, cost, and function, so that the claim is likely to affect the consumer's purchasing decision.) And the FTC standard for "reasonable interpretation" of the ad is pretty much the same as that for Section 43(a) claims; that is, the FTC takes into account the sophistication of the audience for the ad and the likelihood that anyone will believe the false claim.

The difference is that the FTC will act to halt advertising that is deceptive because it omits information that would, if disclosed, affect the consumer's purchasing decision. There is no such provision in Section 43(a); those suits are brought because of specific claims. In other words, under Section 43(a) you can get into trouble because of what you say; but in an FTC suit, you may incur the wrath of the FTC for what you say *or* for what you don't say.

Prior Substantiation

There is one other important difference between FTC law and Section 43(a). The FTC requires that advertisers have "prior substantiation" for specific claims made in ads. A Section 43(a) defendant may try to prove at trial that the alleged false claims in the ad are not false, but there is no requirement that a defendant have compiled evidence of the truth of the claim before making it. This is not the case with the FTC. The FTC prior substantiation doctrine simply requires that an advertiser have a reasonable basis for making any important objective claims about its products before disseminating any ad containing those claims. Inability to supply such substantiation may result in even *true* statements being enjoined by the FTC.

This makes sense, if you think about it. The FTC's whole goal with regard to its false advertising activities is to protect consumers from unscrupulous and less-than-careful marketers who make unfounded claims for their products. If the FTC allowed companies to try to verify their claims *after* making them in ads, consumers would be subjected to far more false advertising and the FTC would have to become an even bigger agency to handle the complaints that would result. The agency wisely decided to shut the barn door before the cow gets out, by requiring companies to figure out in advance whether they are telling the truth and to be able to show the evidence of the truth of their claims.

Generally speaking, the more specific and material the advertising claim, the higher the level of substantiation required by the FTC. The same goes for implied claims. ("New, improved Sparkle window cleaner cuts grime 25 percent faster than before" implies that tests have been conducted that reached this determination.) As with Section 43(a) claims, mere "puffery" is not actionable. You don't have to become a window cleaner tester in order to do your job for your clients. The prior substantiation of advertising claims is your clients' responsibility, or your employer's. Your job is merely to let your employers or your clients know that they should be able to prove what they claim.

Hypothetical Examples of Violations of FTC Standards

The following hypothetical examples illustrate the sorts of actions that violate FTC standards for acceptable advertising:

- Your client Ernie tells you that he intends to begin marketing a baldness remedy through the mail, in addition to his other existing far-
fetched ventures. He brings you information that he wants included
in a newspaper ad for his Hair Today Miracle Baldness Cure, which
consists of an ointment that Ernie makes, from "all natural ingredients," in his basement. You produce the ad in time for him to mail it
off to the *National Enquirer* and when he comes to pick it up you
question his substantiation for a couple of the claims he makes in the
ad copy. You ask him about "New Hair Growth in Only Seven
Days!" and "Laboratory tests prove Hair Today works!" Ernie tells you
that you worry too much and races to the post office with his ad.

  Ernie's mail-order empire never gets off the ground. You hear in
a few months that, after several consumer complaints, the FTC
launched an investigation of Ernie and his baldness remedy. When
Ernie couldn't supply the substantiation for his extravagant claims
about Hair Today, he entered a consent decree with the FTC to
forestall any further action by the agency. In the consent decree he
promised, among other things, to cease making any unfounded
claims for his product, which of course means no claims at all, since
Ernie has no evidence that his product cures baldness and can't
come up with any. In addition, since he failed to comply with the
regulations of the Food and Drug Administration governing labeling for all sorts of products intended to be used on or in the body,
including his ointment, he is in trouble with the FDA. The last you
hear, Ernie is thinking of re-labeling the tins of ointment that fill
his garage and selling the rejuvenated concoction as a shoe water-
proofing product.

- A local plastic products company comes to you for help in developing advertising and packaging materials for an addition to its line
of toys. The new product is the Space Cadet Ray Gun, which
proves to be a sparkly silver plastic "space pistol" with a red lens in
the end of the barrel and a flashlight battery to power the "death
ray," which is activated when the trigger of the pistol is pulled.

  You "test market" the toy by taking a pair of pistols to your
nephews. They like the gun, but beef up its effect by yelling "Zap!"
whenever they aim and fire. You design a color ad for the gun that
consists largely of a photo of young boys, dressed as spacemen,
dueling with a pair of the toys. To emphasize the "death ray" feature of the gun, you retouch the photo to add red flares from the
ends of the pistols. You also scatter a cloud of "Zap!" sound effects
around the heads of the models, in the time-honored manner of
superhero comics. The packaging for the toy includes most of the
same elements you used for the ad.

Your client loves both the ad and the packaging and sales of the toy are high. So, unfortunately, are complaints from parents of space cadets. It seems that a large percentage of children are very disappointed to find, upon receiving the gun, that it neither annihilates enemies with a red flare nor makes a "Zap!" noise. The next piece of bad news is that the FTC has sent your client a letter informing it that the FTC is considering investigating your client for misleading advertising. Your client, on the advice of a lawyer, immediately mails to all its dealers stickers for affixation to all Space Cadet Ray Gun packages. The stickers state that the gun has no red flare and makes no noise when "shot." You are called upon to alter the ad artwork and the artwork for future packaging of the toy. In the art for both, you eliminate the red flare and replace it with a representation of a red glow from the end of the gun, which is a more accurate depiction of the product's abilities. You also change the floating "Zap!" sound effects to cartoon balloon dialogue coming from the models, clarifying the source of the sound effects.

The FTC is satisfied with your client's efforts to remedy the failings of your ad and packaging and enters a consent order with it. You don't lose your client because you are good at what you do. However, you are also more careful in the future about the implications of the visual elements of your ads, especially those aimed at children, because you hope to avoid being zapped again by the FTC.

- A young entrepreneur named Sonia comes to you with an interesting assignment. After running a successful catering business from her home for several years, she has begun to sell some of her more popular recipes in grocery stores. She needs labeling and ads for her line of soups, called, of course, Sonia's Soups, and wants you to design both.

Being efficient, Sonia has already arranged for guidance from a lawyer knowledgeable about the Food and Drug Administration's labeling regulations. You submit the label roughs and copy to him and begin on the newspaper ads for Sonia's Soups. Sonia has supplied you with information about the nutrients in each variety of her soup. Since several of the soups are very high in fiber, you decide that this is a selling point and make this the focus of one whole segment of the ad campaign. Under the headline, "Sonia's Soups Are High in Healthy Fiber," you use a very nice photo of a bowl of Sonia's Soup. You had planned to use a bowl of navy bean soup, since that soup has a very high fiber content, but you couldn't come up with any way to make a bowl of it look interesting, so you use instead a tasty-looking bowl of gazpacho, with sprigs of parsley floating in it. Sonia likes the ad. The state attorney general's office does not. It complains in a letter to Sonia that the ads are misleading because they make a claim ("High in Fiber") that is not true about the soup illustrated. Sonia pulls the offending ad, at some cost and inconvenience, and also her account. She now has the fastest-growing business in the state, but you don't have any of it, because she also has a long memory.

FTC Actions and Penalties

The alternative to complying with FTC advertising law is not a pretty sight. Acting on complaints from either consumers or competitors, or on its own initiative, the FTC can, after an investigation, enter a "cease and desist order" against any company that has arguably transgressed its regulations. A cease and desist order is in the nature of an injunction that prohibits an accused false advertiser from further dissemination of specified offending ads. Monetary penalties may be levied against companies that fail to abide by FTC cease and desist orders.

In addition to cease and desist orders, the FTC can ask, in federal court, for a whole laundry list of other remedies, including preliminary and permanent injunctions, civil and criminal penalties, and various forms of consumer relief, such as corrective advertising, refunds, and invalidation of contracts with affected consumers. Either before or after the FTC files a complaint in federal court, the FTC and the advertiser that is the subject of the FTC's investigation can enter a "consent decree," which is like a settlement agreement. More than 75 percent of all FTC investigations end with consent orders, probably because most accused advertisers know that the FTC is the government and they are not, and wisely settle.

Furthermore, to protect consumers from really bad guys whom the FTC does not trust to abide by the law, the FTC can, through the federal courts or through consent orders, ban certain individuals from certain industries (sometimes permanently) or require them to post bonds before engaging in certain business activities. Acting on complaints brought by the FTC, federal courts also sometimes require advertisers to repay consumers who have been bilked by misleading ads or make other amends for dishonest advertising (this remedy is also sometimes used in FTC consent orders). If advertisers fail to heed cease and desist orders in FTC actions, civil penalties may be imposed by federal courts.

In federal court cases where defendants ignore orders of the court, penalties for civil or criminal contempt may be imposed, including, for criminal contempt, prison terms.

While the Federal Trade Commission ordinarily holds the advertiser responsible for advertising it deems deceptive, it will also sue the agency involved in the preparation of the offending ad if the agency knew or should have known that the ad was deceptive. While the agency does not itself have to substantiate the claims the advertiser makes in order to avoid responsibility for false claims, it cannot ignore patent flaws and obvious exaggerations in information supplied by the advertiser, including tests designed to substantiate claims the advertiser makes. Sometimes other parties in the chain of distribution of products for which overly optimistic, unfounded claims are made are also held responsible. This group includes catalog marketers, retailers, and infomercial producers who make or disseminate deceptive claims about the performance of a product.

Real FTC Cases

The following examples of actual FTC cases illustrate some of the kinds of ads the FTC is likely to challenge. If you thought that creating advertising was a nice, safe job that couldn't get you in trouble—except maybe with a dissatisfied client or boss—you may change your mind after reading this list of summarized FTC cases. It will convince you that there are people out there watching the ads *you* create and evaluating them to figure out whether you have done something that needs to be brought to the attention of a judge. Many of these people work for the government.

These cautionary tales are in the form of short synopses of the facts in cases involving advertisements challenged by the FTC for their content or presentation or both. Notice that the remedies imposed by the FTC or the courts include not only abandonment of questionable advertising claims, but also money damages, corrective advertising, complying with promises and representations made to consumers and other forms of consumer redress, consumer education, bans from the industry for egregious offenders, bonds imposed to guarantee compliance with court orders, and the production of further or better substantiation for claims made. Pin this list over your drawing table or desk to remind yourself that good advertising is more than cleverness, and to discourage yourself from the sorts of actions that create trouble for advertisers and the people who create their ads.

- The FTC challenged American Honda Motor Corporation, Kubota Tractor Corporation, The Stanley Works (a tool, hardware, and home-building supply manufacturer), Johnson Worldwide Associates (a marketer of consumer recreation products), USDrives Corporation (a manufacturer of CD-ROM drives), and Rand International Leisure Products (a wholesaler of imported bicycles and accessories) for using "Made in America" or "Made in USA" language and logos in and on ads, labels, and packaging for their products because, the FTC alleged, the products were not "all or virtually all" made in the United States, since a substantial portion of the components of the products were made in other countries. The proposed settlements in these cases prohibited the corporations from misrepresenting the extent to which their products were manufactured in the United States.

- After the FTC challenged its claims, Eggland's Best, Inc., a marketer of eggs, was required by the terms of a consent order it entered to label its packaging for one year with a notice correctly stating the effect of eggs on serum cholesterol to counteract prior misleading statements.

- Phaseout of America, Inc., the marketer of a device advertised as being able to reduce the health risks of smoking, agreed in a consent order to notify purchasers that its product had not been proven to reduce the risk of diseases related to smoking.

- To settle FTC charges that it made misleading claims about its gasoline's ability to clean engines and reduce maintenance costs, the Exxon Corporation agreed in a consent order to undertake a consumer education campaign about the actual attributes of its products, including television ads and a brochure.

- A multi-level marketing corporation, New Vision International, and its affiliate companies and the principals of those companies, agreed to settle an FTC complaint that it made unsubstantiated claims in ads for nutritional supplements called "God's Recipe." One of its major distributors, in a separate agreement, agreed to stop claiming that the supplements could cure Attention Deficit Disorder or Attention Deficit Hyperactivity Disorder.

- The marketer of Winston "No Additives" cigarettes, R.J. Reynolds Tobacco Company, agreed in a consent order to disclose in future ads that "No additives in our tobacco does NOT mean a safer cigarette."

- When the FTC challenged the representations it made, Blenheim Expositions, a producer of franchise trade shows, agreed in a consent order to distribute a copy of the FTC pamphlet "Consumer's Guide to Buying a Franchise" for five years to as many as five hundred people attending each trade show promoted by the company.

- The marketer of Terminate, a termite bait system, agreed to change its ads and promotional materials after the FTC and the attorneys general of eight states charged that they were deceptive and unsubstantiated. The system was promoted as "the first do-it-yourself termite home defense system."

- In *FTC v. National Clearing House, Inc.,* the principals in a fraudulent charitable fundraising scheme were permanently banned from prize-promotion telemarketing.

- Third Option Laboratories, Inc., the marketer of the cider beverage "Jogging in a Jug," agreed in a consent order to disclose that there is no scientific evidence that the product provides any health benefits. The FTC had also challenged the representation that the beverage was approved by the U.S. Department of Agriculture. Third Option also agreed in the consent order to pay $480,000 in redress.

- After the FTC charged that the ads for a pre-mixed Kahlua White Russian cocktail falsely claimed that the cocktail was low in alcohol content, Allied Domecq Wine USA agreed not to represent any drink containing 5.9% alcohol by volume as a low alcohol beverage and to refrain from misrepresenting the alcohol content of its other products.

- Apple Computer, Inc. agreed in a consent order to honor its representations in ads that "Apple Assurance" customers would receive free support for as long as they owned their Apple products. The FTC had challenged the company's practice of charging computer owners for technical support despite having made representations in ads that such services would be free.

- After the FTC challenged its claims, the American Urological Corporation, the marketer of Väegra (not the legitimate erectile-disfunction treatment, Viagra), a dietary supplement advertised as effective in treating impotence, was permanently enjoined from further such advertising and a six-million-dollar bond was imposed by the court to guarantee its compliance with the injunction.

- A 2.4-million-dollar civil penalty was assessed against the General Nutrition Corporation after the marketer of dietary supplements violated a previous FTC order requiring that it be able to furnish substantiation for disease-prevention, weight-loss, and muscle-building claims made in ads for its products.

- The FTC challenged the deceptive claim that an iron marketed by Black and Decker (U.S.), Inc. had received the endorsement of the National Fire Safety Council because that group does not have the requisite expertise to evaluate appliance safety. The claims were settled by a consent order.

- Gateway 2000 agreed to pay $290,000 to the U.S. Treasury to settle FTC charges that its "money-back-guarantee," "full-refund," and "on-site-service" representations in ads for its products were false. Gateway agreed not to misrepresent its money-back-guarantee policy and to disclose that certain deductions would be made before a customer received a refund, and that there were limitations to the "on-site service" it offers.

- After the FTC charged that the Unocal Corporation had made unsubstantiated performance claims for its higher octane fuels, the corporation entered a consent order that required the company to mail corrective notices to credit card holders who had received the ads that made the unsubstantiated claims.

- In *FTC* v. *Pantron I Corporation,* the federal court held that consumer satisfaction surveys and studies demonstrating the placebo effect were not sufficient to meet the FTC standard of competent and reliable scientific evidence for the substantiation of claims of health benefits from the use of advertised products.
- FTC charges that the marketer for Doan's Pills made unsubstantiated claims that the pills were more effective in relieving back pain than other over-the-counter analgesics were upheld by a judge. The judge ordered Novartis Corporation, the marketer of Doan's Pills, not to make claims of superiority without reliable scientific support for such claims, including at least two clinical studies substantiating them.
- Toyota Motor Sales, U.S.A., Volkswagen of America, and the advertising agencies for American Honda Motor Corporation, Mitsubishi Motor Sales of America, and Mazda Motor of America agreed to enter settlement agreements with the FTC after the FTC charged that their advertisements offering auto leases and credit misrepresented the actual terms available by failing to disclose or to adequately disclose additional fees consumers were expected to pay and essential terms of the agreements. Among other provisions of the settlements, the automakers agreed to refrain from misrepresenting the total amounts of all payments due from the consumer at the time a lease was entered, and from misrepresenting any payments due from the consumer by portraying them less prominently (by using small type in print ads or by displaying them only briefly in television ads).
- Honeywell, Inc. agreed to settle FTC charges that its ads made unsubstantiated claims for the efficiency of and allergy relief available from Honeywell Air Purifiers. In the settlement agreement, Honeywell agreed to refrain from making any claims about the efficacy, benefits, or performance of any air cleaning product unless it possessed substantiating scientific evidence for such claims at the time of making them.
- Weight Watchers International agreed to settle with the FTC after the FTC charged that it had too little substantiation for its claims of success in maintaining weight loss in users of the Weight Watchers program. Weight Watchers agreed to include additional disclosures about the actual experiences of its customers when making weight-maintenance claims and to include the statement "For many dieters, weight loss is temporary" in its ads. The company must also include information about typical or expected weight loss when reporting incidences of atypical weight loss.

- Schering-Plough Healthcare Products, which markets Coppertone Kids sunscreen products for children, agreed to settle with the FTC after the FTC charged that its advertisements for one of its children's suncreens were deceptive and lacked substantiation. The settlement agreement prohibited any deceptive claims about the effectiveness or length of protection that any children's sunscreen provides and required Schering-Plough to produce and distribute 150,000 consumer education brochures to alert parents to the need for sunscreens for children and to the fact that such products must be reapplied after activities or towel drying.
- Zales, the largest jewelry retailer in the country, was accused by the FTC of deceptively advertising its "Ocean Treasures" imitation pearl jewelry as being manufactured from cultured pearls. In settling with the FTC, Zales agreed to refrain from any such deceptive advertising of pearls, to clearly and prominently display in ads the nature of the pearl jewelry it sold, including characterizing it as "artificial," "imitation," or "simulated" if it was not composed of real pearls and as "cultured" or "cultivated" if it was. In addition, Zales agreed to display information in its stores and furnish flyers to inform consumers about the meanings of the terms used to describe its pearls.

It is informative that many of these targets for FTC actions were large corporations that, presumably, had access to experienced and skilled advertising agencies and reliable legal counsel. This supports the point made earlier that almost *any* advertiser can run afoul of the FTC. In almost every instance, the goal of the company is to settle as quickly as possible, which may be difficult. Remember, the most efficient way to extricate yourself from false advertising challenges is to avoid them in the first place by creating ads carefully.

Advertising to Children
Unless you are the sort of person who is willing to tell clever lies to exaggerate the benefits of a product, in which case you are not likely to be reading this book, you probably will have little trouble with either Section 43(a) claims or FTC challenges. If you make a sincere effort to tell both the visual and the verbal truth in the ads you create and to pay some attention to the particulars of the Better Business Bureau Code of Advertising reproduced in the appendix of this book, it is unlikely, in most cases, that your ads will be challenged as false advertising. However, there is one fairly common sort of ad that can be challenged more readily than others for making misleading statements because of the audience for this kind of ad. These are ads that are addressed primarily to children or that include children in their audience.

An ad for spark plugs is an ad that will attract the attention of adults. Few children are ever likely to even read it and none will consider its claims before buying new spark plugs. The same can be said for ads for many consumer products that hold no interest for even precocious children. However, the situation is exactly reversed with ads for any toy, candy or snack product, soft drink, sports equipment, or other product designed to appeal primarily to children. Even if the product is expensive enough that a child is not likely to be able to buy it, such ads do create in children the desire to own the advertised product, and prompt the child to ask (or demand) that his or her parents buy it. Anyone acquainted with children knows that, in many cases, a child's desire for a product is almost automatically translated into a purchase of that product, even if the child must compel an adult to buy it.

Because of children's greater susceptibility to advertising claims, the FTC scrutinizes ads aimed at children with special care. An advertising claim that would have no particular effect on an adult may produce an automatic response in children, and the FTC, seeking to treat this class of consumers as fairly as any others, prohibits advertising claims that dupe children. As with some other sorts of advertising representations, the desire to tell the truth in ads addressed to children may be insufficient to keep the advertiser out of trouble, since children may read into otherwise honest claims representations that are not explicitly stated or even intended.

The best way to avoid trouble with ads addressed to children is to read and refer to the Self-Regulatory Guidelines for Children's Advertising promulgated by the Children's Advertising Review Unit (CARU) of the National Advertising Review Council, an alliance between the advertising industry and the Council of Better Business Bureaus. These guidelines, prefaced by a short explanation of the role of the organization that gave rise to them, are reprinted in the appendix of this book. Read them, and use them whenever you create an ad for any product that children are likely to want.

And if you or one of your clients operate a Web site aimed at children, you need to be aware of new FTC rules that implement the Children's Online Privacy Protection Act of 1998. These rules, which became effective on April 21, 2000, apply to commercial Web sites that are aimed at children under thirteen or are likely to be visited by such children.

The FTC rules govern what notice the Web sites must give about their information collection practices, how Web sites treat personal information they obtain from children under thirteen, and what rights parents have regarding the collection and use of such information. The rules are easy enough to understand and compliance with them is mandatory for any affected Web site operator. The FTC's guidelines for complying with the Children's Online Privacy Protection Act are reproduced in the FTC Resources section of the appendix. Read 'em if you need 'em.

Other Challenges

There are special marketing circumstances that may require you to pay attention to FTC regulations for certain sorts of advertising. Depending on the nature of your business or your clients, you may never encounter any of these circumstances. However, it is equally likely, depending on your business or clients, that you may encounter one or more of these special circumstances routinely. Some of these are: advertising loans, using endorsements and testimonials in ads, conducting sweepstakes, making environmental claims in advertising, advertising product warranties, and advertising tobacco, down and feather products, jewelry, diamonds, or fur products, among numerous other special advertising circumstances. Peruse the long list of FTC publications in the FTC Resources section of the appendix. If you see a publication that deals with a product, service, or activity that you encounter in your professional life, such as telemarketing or direct mail, order it and read it to learn how to stay out of FTC trouble.

As bad as FTC trouble can be, you should understand that the FTC and your client's competitors are not necessarily the only people who will pounce if your employer's or your client's ads are not truthful. There are a lot of other politicos and bureaucrats scattered over the American landscape who also believe that free enterprise means fair competition. One of the most vigilant groups of late has been the National Association of Attorneys General (the NAAG), a group of law enforcers who bring false advertising suits under the consumer protection laws of their various states. (State consumer protection laws vary but generally seek to prevent the same unfair trade practices that bother the FTC.) The NAAG has become very active in the past decade or so, acting as a clearinghouse for information about unfair trade practices, including false advertising, among other activities. In short, if the feds don't get you, the "generals" will.

There is also a whole bowlful of alphabet-soup federal agencies that regulate certain kinds of advertising. Some of these agencies are: the Bureau of Alcohol, Tobacco and Firearms (BATF), the Consumer Product Safety Commission (CPSC), the Department of Transportation (DOT), the Environmental Protection Agency (EPA), the Federal Communications Commission (FCC), the Federal Reserve Board (FRB), the Food and Drug Administration (FDA), the Securities and Exchange Commission (SEC), the Internal Revenue Service (IRS), and the U.S. Postal Service. The kinds of advertising these agencies regulate is, in the case of some, pretty obvious. Others are more surprising. The IRS, for instance, regulates some political advertising. Further, many of these federal agencies share jurisdiction with the FTC over the sorts of advertising they regulate. Further, your competitors or those of your clients may appeal to the standards divisions maintained by all the major television networks, or complain to the National

Advertising Division of the Council of Better Business Bureaus (a self-regulatory group created by the advertising industry) if they don't like your ads.

The best way to make sense of the many product-specific regulations set and enforced by the federal government is to refer to the Other Federal Agencies list in the appendix of this book to find out which kind of product advertising each regulates. Then, search the Web site for each agency to find and download the official guidelines and publications that explain the agency's regulations for any products or services for which you may prepare ads. Starting a reference file of this sort is an inexpensive way to insure against "unwelcome advances" from a federal enforcer who has a problem with your ads.

Your Role and That of Your Lawyer

You have a responsibility to help your clients stay out of false advertising trouble of any sort. To start with, you can advise them that there is such a thing as false advertising. You can point out that making false claims about their own products or services can result in tedious and expensive lawsuits brought by their competitors or an investigation or litigation by the FTC, the NAAG, or another federal agency. You can tell them that false statements about other companies' products or services are likely to result in Section 43(a) suits. You can let them know that even what they don't say can attract the attention of the FTC or some other federal agency, if their omissions are serious ones. You can inform them that they have a legal responsibility to substantiate their claims about their products or services before they begin making those claims in their ads. You can avoid turning the substantiated facts about their products into Stir-Fried Truth in the process of creating persuasive ads.

And you can tell them that even though you are familiar with the major features of the false advertising landscape, you are not a lawyer. The rules and standards applied by the FTC and others to determine if an ad passes muster legally are too specific and the transgressions of these rules and standards can be too subtle for you or your client to depend entirely on your own interpretations. Correctly interpreting these rules and standards requires informed judgment.

The single most effective way to avoid false advertising claims of any sort, besides telling the truth, is to have a lawyer knowledgeable about false advertising law review ads for possible Section 43(a) and FTC problems *before* publication. And not just any lawyer will do. Most real estate, divorce, and criminal lawyers know practically nothing about false advertising law and are content to leave things that way. Remember that in this age of e-mail and fax machines and overnight couriers, the lawyer you hire doesn't have to have an office down the street. It is not uncommon for lawyers who deal with advertising and its content to live in different area codes than their clients, who get their advice over the phone and send materials for review by fax or FedEx or even e-mail. Look for this sort of lawyer in large cities. You can also find an advertising lawyer via the Internet by means of various lawyer locater services and can check out the Web sites of some of the more prominent advertising law firms, all from your own desk. You wouldn't hire a dermatologist to take out your appendix, so insist that advertising law is one of the primary areas of practice of any lawyer who may be hired to review your ads. Or ask if you can hire a lawyer on behalf of your client or employer and pass the bill on.

You don't need to worry about every ad you produce. But any ad that makes specific claims about your client's or employer's products or those of another company, or is addressed to children or concerns any industry or product that is, or may be, regulated by the government or any state, should be reviewed. Legal fees are a necessary evil for many advertisers. With regard to some types of ads, you almost have no choice—you can either pay now, for ad review, or later, for litigation. You choose.

The appendix contains information on free publications offered by the Federal Trade Commission that can aid you in staying on its good side. It also contains the complete texts of the Better Business Bureau Code of Advertising, which will help you create ads that are not misleading, and the CARU Guidelines for advertising to children, which will enable you to decide whether your ads to children are likely to cause problems. There is also information about the three units of the Council of Better Business Bureaus that monitor national advertising with the voluntary participation of advertisers. These three units are the National Advertising Division (NAD), the Children's Advertising Review Unit (CARU), and the National Advertising Review Board. These various organizations and agencies are set up to help you stay on the right side of the law. View their addresses and the publications and other resources they offer as important tools of your profession. What have you got to lose? If you fix an ad that would otherwise have caused trouble for your employer or client, you'll look like a hero for knowing where to turn for information. If you fail to fix that ad, there'll be plenty of blame to go around, and some of it may stick to you.

◆ ◆ ◆

All Publicity Is *Not* Good Publicity

The next time you are tempted to stretch the truth in an ad, think how you'd like to end up as the subject of a Federal Trade Commission press release such as the one that follows, which was posted on the FTC's Web site as well as distributed to more traditional media. Then rethink your ad so that the FTC will approve of it.

For Release: April 15, 1999

Internet Mall Promoters Settle FTC Charges
Earnings Claims For Internet-Based Businesses Were False

Internet commerce site iMall and two former principals have agreed to pay $4 million to settle Federal Trade Commission charges that they made false earnings claims for Internet-based businesses they promoted and that they violated the Franchise Rule. Craig R. Pickering and Mark R. Comer, two past presidents of iMall, also would be barred for life from selling any Internet or pay-per-call business opportunity; barred for ten years from selling franchises; required to post a $500,000 bond before selling certain types of business opportunities; and barred from violating the Franchise Rule. iMall would be permanently barred from violations of the Franchise Rule and from misrepresenting material facts about any business opportunity it promotes.

iMall operates an Internet shopping mall and hosts sellers of a variety of goods and services.

"A deceptive claim is a deceptive claim, whether it's on the Internet or in your local newspaper," said Jodie Bernstein, Director of the FTC's Bureau of Consumer Protection. "This case sends two important messages: Marketers, back up your earnings claims. It's the law. Consumers, don't buy a pig in a poke. Check out business opportunities to make sure they're everything they claim to be."

Between July 1995 and August 1998, iMall marketed two Internet-related business opportunity programs using direct mail, radio ads, television infomercials, a promotional cassette, and telemarketing calls designed to induce investors to attend free seminars where they would hear about the business opportunities. The iMall Opportunity Program offered investors the opportunity to become "consultants" and make money selling Web pages on the iMall site. The Internet Yellow Pages (IYP) program offered investors the opportunity to make money selling advertising space on the IYP Web site contained within the iMall site.

Typically, the seminar presentations claimed that for a $2,995 fee and as little as five to ten hours investment a week, iMall consultants could make between $2,000 and $20,000 a month. Potential IYP investors were told that for a $2,000 investment and a five- to ten-hour commitment a month, they could earn between $2,000 and $5,000.

According to the FTC, the earnings claims were false and misleading in violation of federal laws. Most investors did not earn nearly what the seminar leaders claimed they could. In addition, the business opportunities qualified as franchises. The FTC's Franchise Rule requires a franchisor to provide prospective franchisees with a complete and accurate basic disclosure document containing twenty categories of information at least ten business days prior to the execution of a purchase agreement or the payment of money. The Rule also requires a franchisor to have a reasonable basis for any earnings representations, and to disclose the material bases and assumptions upon which those representations are made. Investors in IYP and the iMall Opportunity program were not properly supplied with the documents required by the Franchise Rule.

Settlement of the FTC charges will permanently bar Pickering and Comer from "advertising, marketing, promoting, offering for sale or selling any Internet-related business venture or business opportunity" or pay-per-call business. In addition, they would be required to obtain performance bonds in the amount of $500,000 before selling any business opportunity. The settlement also would bar them for ten years from selling franchises. They would be barred from future violations of the Franchise rule and from misrepresenting any fact material to a consumer's decision to purchase any service or product.

iMall and its agents and employees would be barred from violations of the Franchise Rule and from misrepresenting material facts about the income, profits or sales that can be or have been achieved through the use of any good or service or the length of time it will take to recoup the cost of a good or service. Finally, iMall will pay $750,000 and Pickering and Comer will pay a total of $3.25 million in consumer redress.

The Commission vote to accept the Stipulated Final Judgment and Order was 4–0.

NOTE: A Stipulated Final Judgment and Order for Permanent Injunction is for settlement purposes only and does not constitute an admission of a law violation. It was signed by the judge and entered by the court April 12, 1999.

Copies of the Stipulated Final Judgment and Order for Permanent Injunction are available from the FTC's web site at *www.ftc.gov* and also from the FTC's Consumer Response Center, Room 130, 600 Pennsylvania Avenue, N.W., Washington, D.C. 20580; 202-FTC-HELP (202-382-4357); TDD for the hearing impaired 202-326-2502. To find out the latest news as it is announced, call the FTC NewsPhone recording at 202-326-2710.

MEDIA CONTACT:
Claudia Bourne Farrell
Office of Public Affairs
202-326-2181

STAFF CONTACT:
Sara V. Greenberg or Andrew D. Caverly
Boston Regional Office
617-424-5960

(FTC File No. 972-3224)

◆ ◆ ◆

Aside from problems with the FTC, ads with suspect content may be all but unusable because they run afoul of the policies for acceptable advertising set by broadcasters and publishers of magazines or news-papers, who are justifiably wary of disseminating material that may get them named in a lawsuit, even if they have no role in creating it. The following is a comparatively short example of such a policy. It is a statement enumerating some of the sorts of ads that the *New York Times* will refuse. You may recognize that the restrictions echo FTC proscriptions. Also hiding in this short policy statement, which is a paragon of exclusion in about two hundred words, are refusals to print ads that are libelous, either to individuals or companies, ads that vio-late SEC or state securities laws, ads that would bilk naïve consumers, ads that violate federal or state fair housing and fair employment laws or discriminate on any unfair basis, and ads that are or may be obscene. Furthermore, the *Times* says, essentially, that it will refuse to run any *other* ad that it doesn't like or that could hurt its readers or their wallets, health, or "their confidence in reputable advertising and ethical business practices." That pretty well covers all the bases. Other venues for the broadcast or publication of ads have similar policies, sometimes much longer and more particular than this one. (For exam-ple, NBC's Broadcast Standards for Television are, literally, fifteen times longer than this statement of the *Times*'s policy.) Which tells us that even if a dubious ad makes it out of your shop, it may never be seen by its intended audience. Instead, it may fail to pass the stringent good-taste-and-good-faith standards of those who ultimately control what ads we all see—the media that promulgate them.

The following describes some of the kinds of advertising that the *New York Times* will not accept:

> *Generally*—Advertisements that contain fraudulent, deceptive, or misleading statements or illustrations. Attacks of a personal character. Advertisements that are overly competitive or that refer abusively to the goods or services of others.

Investments—Advertisements that do not comply with applicable federal, state and local laws and regulations.

Occult Pursuits—Advertisements for fortune telling, dream interpretations and individual horoscopes except when ordered for entertainment sections or guides and when the emphasis is on amusement rather than serious interpretation.

Foreign Languages—Advertisements in a foreign language (unless an English translation is included) except in special circumstances and when a summary advertisement in English is included.

Discrimination—Advertisements which fail to comply with the express requirements of federal and state laws against discrimination, including Title VII and the Fair Housing Act, or that otherwise discriminate on grounds of race, religion, national origin, sex, age, marital status or disability.

Offensive to Good Taste—Indecent, vulgar, suggestive or other advertising that, in the opinion of the *Times,* may be offensive to good taste.

This list is not intended to include all the types of advertisements unacceptable to the *Times.* Generally speaking, any other advertising that may cause financial loss to readers, injury to their health, or loss of their confidence in reputable advertising and ethical business practices is unacceptable.

For further acceptability information, please call 212-556-7171.

CHAPTER 4

Libel and How to Avoid It

EFAMATION IS THE NAME FOR THE HARM THAT RESULTS WHEN someone's reputation is damaged by an untrue statement. Defamation comes in two flavors, "libel" and "slander." Libel once referred only to printed defamation, slander only to spoken defamation. The advent of radio and television made the traditional libel/slander distinction outmoded. Now most jurisdictions in the United States regard defamatory statements made over the airwaves as libel. It is more logical to treat such statements like libelous articles in newspapers and magazines, because they are disseminated over wide areas and are therefore capable of causing great harm—rather than like slander, which historically has meant a defamatory statement spoken by one person to others, and thus is less likely to do as much harm.

The libel/slander distinction is important primarily because the penalties for libeling someone are more severe than those for speaking the same defamatory statement. Since any defamation that advertising creative people have to worry about is likely to result from a print, radio, or television ad, and that sort of defamation will be, legally, most likely libel, we will refer only to libel throughout this chapter. The advent of radio and television did more than complicate the definitions of defamation. The proliferation of other kinds of mass communications media, such as news magazines and tabloids (which have weekly press runs that would have dwarfed the yearly circulation of most of the popular magazines and newspapers of the early part of this century) has also greatly increased defamation case law. In other words, one zillion copies of the *National Enquirer* equals X angry celebrities equals Y libel suits.

Many of those libel suits result in court decisions that become part of the case law of the state where they were brought or, often, of federal case law. Advertising agencies and other people who create advertising haven't had a lot to do with creating this enlarged body of libel law, which has mostly resulted from disputes involving the legitimate (and, sometimes, illegitimate) press. However, advertising creative people, like any other citizens who create and disseminate any communications, need to know enough about the law to avoid libeling anyone.

Avoiding libel is, like virtue, its own reward. No one gives out medals, or Addys, for clean libel litigation records, but the truth is, if you *are* sued you may not be around long enough afterwards to win any medals. Libel lawsuits make even the plaintiffs unhappy and the defendants are usually left miserable, sometimes broke, and maybe unemployed.

Elements of Libel

Because of the variations between state laws, it is difficult to make any general statements about United States libel law that are not also somewhat misleading. However, boiled down to their common elements, U.S. statutes generally provide that libel is: (1) *a false statement* (2) *that is "of and concerning" the plaintiff,* (3) *that is published to a third party,* (4) *that is made as a statement of fact (i.e., is not just someone's opinion),* (5) *that causes harm to the plaintiff by injuring her or his reputation or subjecting her or him to shame and ridicule in the community, and* (6) *that is the result of some omission or fault of the defendant.*

We will look at each of the elements of libel in detail below.

False Statements

A "false statement" can be almost anything that can be broadcast, printed, or displayed and need not be a verbal statement. A photograph or drawing can libel someone just as surely as a printed verbal statement. True statements are never actionable for libel (although you may want to remember that even publishing the truth can get you in trouble for invasion of privacy, as we will see in the next chapter). However, you had better be able to prove the truth of any unflattering statements you make, because if you cannot, you may be found guilty of libeling someone in spite of the fact that you know you didn't.

"Of and Concerning" the Plaintiff

A statement "of and concerning" the plaintiff means a statement that can be reasonably understood to refer to the plaintiff. Obviously, this includes statements that name the plaintiff and photographs that include face shots of the plaintiff. It also means that even if the plaintiff is not named in the statement itself (or recognizably depicted in the photograph), if by either some outside facts known by some people who see the statement or some implication contained in the statement itself the plaintiff can be identified, then the plaintiff has been libeled.

For example, if a public service ad promoting racial harmony uses a photograph of a young black lynching victim under the headline "In 1955, the men of Greentown, Mississippi, murdered Hiram Edwards because he wanted to vote," any one of the thirty-four men who lived in that small town in that year who were not convicted of the lynching could be libeled by the imputation inherent in the ad. This is so even if there is no photograph of him or any mention of him by name. The implication of the headline is that all adult male citizens of the town are guilty of committing that heinous crime. It is obviously unlikely that every such man participated in the hanging, but the friends and acquaintances of each man will think only of that particular man when reading the ad, and his reputation would be damaged.

(This sort of example only works when the number of people to whom the defamatory statement applies is small. You might pause to consider if an acquaintance from the very small town of Greentown, Mississippi could be guilty of lynching. You probably would not stop to wonder if your friend from Chicago was one of the "Chicago gangsters" referred to in a political ad touting a candidate's illustrious record as a crime-busting D.A.)

The requirement that a libelous statement be "of and concerning" the plaintiff before it is actionable also includes mistaken identifications. For advertising creative people, supposedly fictitious names used in ads are a pitfall of this sort, since there may be a real Harrison P. Adams out there somewhere who objects to being named in an ad as a satisfied user of a certain brand of condoms.

However, name similarity is generally not enough to support a libel suit. There must be more than a simple coincidental use of someone's name to get you in real trouble. However, if Harrison P. Adams thinks hard enough he may be able to come up with some other similarities between your Harrison P. Adams and himself. (The man pictured in the ad has gray hair; Harrison P. Adams has gray hair. The man in the ad is dressed as a business executive; Harrison P. Adams is a business executive. And so on.) And your being innocent of libeling someone will not always prevent that person from filing a suit. Unfortunately, some people threaten to sue or do sue when they believe they can extort a settlement payment, regardless of the fact that they cannot win in court.

Communication to Another Person

The requirement that the libelous statement be communicated by the defendant to at least one other person besides the plaintiff is called the "publication" requirement. Here, "publication" does not necessarily mean publication in the ordinary sense of the word but rather, "dissemination by any means." If you think about it, it is obvious that no harm can result to the plaintiff's reputation (the heart of a libel claim) unless someone besides the defendant and the plaintiff sees the libelous statement or photograph. And you can't disclaim responsibility for disseminating a libelous statement just because someone else published it first unless you have acted responsibly to investigate and verify, independently, the truth of the statement.

For example, if you publish in a campaign ad a photograph of the other candidate accepting money from a furtive-looking man in a windbreaker and baseball cap who, it turns out, has a criminal record, and imply in the ad copy that the opponent candidate is accepting a bribe, you are not relieved from responsibility for your reckless charge just because the campaign manager for your client has already published the photograph and similar copy in a campaign flyer. If it turns out that the opposing candidate is innocent of accepting any bribe and that he was, in fact, simply giving cash to a parking lot attendant about whom he knew nothing, you (and the campaign manager and his candidate) could be in big trouble.

Statements of Fact

The general rule is that only a statement of fact can be libelous and that an expression of opinion cannot. This rule, like many legal standards, is simple in theory and confusing in practice, since courts often have a hard time distinguishing between statements that are in the nature of opinions and therefore not libelous and those that are presented as fact and therefore defamatory. The many rules and magic formulas that exist in various parts of the country for determining which statements are non-defamatory opinions and which are actionable statements of fact are too numerous for anyone but libel lawyers to really understand. In any event, they are too complicated to remember and apply in the real-life, daily circumstances in which most advertising creative people work. This really doesn't matter because most of these fine distinctions only come into play in litigation, and your whole aim should be to avoid lawsuits in the first place. This means that discretion is the better part of valor. You should simply stay away from any photograph or copy that may insult, anger, or embarrass anyone enough to result in a libel lawsuit, unless such a statement is one made in an area where only opinions are possible, such as matters of personal taste, literary criticism, religious beliefs, moral convictions, political views, and social theories.

If you make the statement in an ad (as someone did) that "The Wet Look Is Dead!" you are simply announcing a new trend in personal grooming. Makers of hair oil may not like what your ad implies, but they can't sue you (or your employer or your client). Try saying "Only Geeks Use Oilcan Hair Oil!", however, and you may be sued by the Oilcan Company. This distinction points out an important truth about advertising, one that relates to the opinion/statement distinction and also has broader application.

Generally, saying something positive about your client's products or services ("The French cuisine at Chez Richard is the finest on the Eastern seaboard") is much safer from a libel standpoint than any negative statement about your client's competitors ("The 'French' chef at Pierre's couldn't find France on a map").

Harm to the Plaintiff

To be libelous, a statement or photograph must cause harm to the plaintiff by injuring her or his reputation or subjecting her or him to shame or ridicule in the community. The more subtle applications of this standard can be hard to understand, but past court decisions give us a long list of the kinds of statements that, unless they are true, almost always result in judgments of libel. It is libelous to make an untrue statement that:

- SOMEONE ENGAGES IN CRIMINAL ACTIVITIES OR HAS A CRIMINAL RECORD ("Beauregard is a felon.")
- SOMEONE IS DISHONEST ("Carmen lied to her boss when she said she was ill last Tuesday.")
- SOMEONE IS UNETHICAL ("Angela has the ethics of a weasel; she taught her son how to cheat at cards.")
- SOMEONE IS INCOMPETENT OR UNSKILLED AT HIS OR HER TRADE, BUSINESS, OR PROFESSION ("Orville is a very bad accountant.")
- SOMEONE ENGAGES IN CONDUCT THAT RENDERS HIM OR HER UNFIT OR INCOMPETENT TO ENGAGE IN HIS OR HER PROFESSION OR OCCUPATION (This often depends on *what* conduct and *which* profession. Stating "Dr. Ortiz drinks on the job," if it is untrue, implies that Dr. Ortiz's behavior renders her unfit to practice medicine. Stating falsely that a bartender drinks on the job may not be libel, however, because of the differing professional requirements and standards for bartenders and doctors.)
- SOMEONE DRINKS TO DRUNKENNESS OR IS AN ALCOHOLIC OR USES ILLEGAL DRUGS OR ABUSES LEGAL DRUGS ("Geraldine drank like a fish at the museum benefit and passed out behind a statue.")
- SOMEONE ENGAGES IN IMMORAL BEHAVIOR OR, ESPECIALLY A WOMAN, IS "UNCHASTE" ("Hermione may be a brilliant scientist, but she sleeps with her best friend's husband whenever she has the opportunity." Stating that anyone, man or woman, is an adulterer or otherwise engages in any sexual conduct of which your grandmother would not approve is very dangerous but, because most men are less likely than women to challenge untrue statements about their sexual prowess and because defamation law has historically held that women are in a special category when it comes to their reputations for sexual chastity, libeling a woman is much more

dangerous than making the same libelous statement about a man. In light of the greater equality with which the law treats women and men today, this distinction may no longer be valid, but you'd rather find that out when the law changes than argue it in a libel lawsuit. Be wary of imputing anything less than Sunday school behavior to anyone, especially women, unless you know your statement is a true statement. Then, beware of a suit for invasion of privacy.)

- SOMEONE HAS A "LOATHSOME" DISEASE (Historically, this usually has meant leprosy or one of the "traditional" venereal diseases. Since, regrettably, we now know that there are many dangerous viruses circulating in singles bars, other sexually transmitted diseases may perhaps now be included in the list. Stating without foundation, "Lawrence caught herpes from that woman he met at Arnoldo's" is just as actionable as stating that he has syphilis.)

- SOMEONE IS MENTALLY DEFICIENT ("Xavier has Alzheimer's disease." This does not include statements of mental deficiency that are really in the nature of mere epithets, which are not, strangely, actionable, probably because the law presumes that people will not believe "Xavier is a peabrain" to be the literal truth, as they would believe a more particular statement.)

The categories of false statements listed above are all sure-fire ways to start libel lawsuits, but they are not by any means the only ones. Many successful (for the plaintiffs) libel lawsuits are brought because of statements that are much less obviously dangerous than, say, stating that someone is incompetent at his or her job or has a venereal disease. This very often happens because of statements that are, in themselves, relatively innocent but which are libelous when coupled with some extrinsic fact known to some of the people who see the false statement and know the plaintiff.

For instance, stating falsely that Edgar won $1,000 at the blackjack tables during a convention he attended in Las Vegas is not, in itself, defamatory. However, because Edgar's friends know that he is an official in a church that sternly prohibits gambling of any sort and that the convention was a church convention held in Las Vegas for the express purpose of converting gamblers into former gamblers, the statement libels him. Similarly, stating falsely that Anastasia married Harold last Saturday afternoon seems harmless enough unless you know that Anastasia is still Mrs. Ricardo Brown, since her divorce has not yet been granted, and that the reported marriage last Saturday would have made her a bigamist.

Omission or Fault of the Defendant

The requirement that a false statement must owe its falsity to some omission or fault of the defendant before the defendant can be held accountable offers defendants only some protection from the consequences of their blunders. The point is not whether you meant to libel someone but rather, whether the libel could have been avoided by your taking what would have been, in that particular situation, proper measures to ensure the accuracy of the statement you published. (In fact, in some circumstances, a "strict liability" standard may apply; that is, if you publish a false statement about someone that harms his or her reputation, the law provides that you will not be relieved of responsibility even if you were not at fault.)

Since the circumstances giving rise to libel lawsuits are never precisely the same from one suit to another, the best the law can do is to offer vague guidelines for the amount of care necessary to relieve you of any responsibility for making an otherwise libelous statement about someone. To make it even more complicated, there are different sets of vague guidelines for different plaintiffs and contexts. The two types of libel plaintiffs are: (1) the private citizen plaintiff, who has been libeled by a false statement which concerns some matter that has no bearing on public welfare; and (2) the public figure plaintiff who has been libeled by a false statement touching upon some matter of urgent public concern. In short, you can get away with saying a lot more untrue things about the president of the United States regarding his performance of his official duties (especially if you do not actually know that statements you published are false) than you can say about the sexual proclivities of Miss Turnipseed down the street, who keeps to herself and has never inserted herself into any public dialogue or run for public office.

Since even commercial speech (such as ads, annual reports, sales brochures, or billboards) is protected by the First Amendment, the fact that a false statement is made in an ad should not subject you to greater liability for libel than if it were made in a newspaper editorial. However, in the real world and with juries it just doesn't work that way. Whatever the law books say, juries and judges are more likely to find that a false statement made in an ad is libel than the same statement made in a newspaper column.

Which brings us to a very important point. The standard of care required to defeat a claim of libel—that is, how careful you have to be in order to wiggle out of responsibility for making a false statement that harms someone—is in the nature of a "defense" to libel. That is, it is one of the first areas that your lawyer will inquire into after you are sued. ("Did you know or have any reason to know that Miss Turnipseed had never been in a male strip club, Mr. Cellini, before you superimposed a photo of her over a photo of the entrance to The Playgirl Club? What reason did you have to believe that she was a model who posed for the photo you used rather than a private citizen whose photograph was taken as she stood in front of her dentist's office? Had you found the photographer who brought you the photo of Miss Turnipseed to be reliable and truthful in the past?") Your care or lack of it will be an important factor in any libel suit, but since defending even a libel suit in which the plaintiff does not win will still be very expensive and time-consuming for you, your client, and your employer, the very best thing to do, again, is to simply stay out of such suits.

It must be said that state laws govern libel and that libel law varies from state to state. But the somewhat confusing variations between state libel statutes really needn't concern you. Your job, really, is simply to know enough about U.S. libel law to avoid being sued in the first place. Since most of the materials an advertising agency or design studio create are disseminated beyond or outside the state in which the studio or agency is located, it is really a matter of luck, anyway, in which state a person who believes she has been libeled by your television spot lives. That state is where she will bring suit, and its laws will determine what law applies to that suit. It is far more productive to spend your time figuring out how to sidestep libel altogether than to worry about the differing consequences and standards of proof that apply in one state or another.

The best way to stay out of libel suits is to learn and use a few very simple rules. The following practices should be made a permanent part of your operating procedures and everyone who works for or with you should be made aware of the importance of these practices.

Rules for Avoiding Libel Charges

- Get releases for all photographs, including from any model who is paid for the use of his or her photo. Be careful never to "exceed" the permission given by any release. (For instance, if Miss Turnipseed posed as a fund-raising committee member for an ad soliciting donations to the local children's hospital, you cannot simply locate that photo in your files whenever you need a photo of a funny-looking little old lady. That would exceed the consent to the use of her photo that Miss Turnipseed gave when she posed for the ad for the children's hospital.) A sample release is included in the appendix of this book and releases in general are discussed in chapter 5.

- Be wary of making any statement or using any photo that would embarrass, anger, or humiliate the person who is the subject of the statement or photo, even if you don't think your ad actually libels that person. At least half of all the troublesome, expensive libel lawsuits ever brought were brought more because someone was mad and wanted revenge than because his or her reputation had actually been harmed. Angry people want immediate revenge; a libel lawsuit, especially if you or your client or employer have enough money to fund a fat damages award, may look like the best alternative to punching you in the nose.

- Consider the implications of your ad copy, photos, and illustrations. Even if no one is named or actually pictured, could someone feel that he or she is, by reference, included in a statement that is unflattering or embarassing?
- Never use first and last names, actual or fictitious, unless you are absolutely certain that you will not be offending the real, or another, "Minnie P. Gonzales."
- Don't hurry production of your materials so much that any important proofreading is slighted or releases are not secured. An ounce of prevention is worth a pound of depositions.
- Finally, get yourself a lawyer. Having a lawyer knowledgeable about libel law "on tap" for quick opinions doesn't cost much now (and, if your client agrees, the lawyer's fee can be passed along to your client as a cost of production), but hiring one to defend a libel lawsuit will cost lots later.

Bob and Carl and Actual Malice

One last cautionary comment about libel. Forget everything you learned about "freedom of the press" by watching movies about heroic investigative reporters. The standards for what they can say and get away with probably do not apply to you, partly because they are working journalists (maybe a court will feel that selling soap equates with revealing government corruption, but you don't want to find this out with yourself as the guinea pig), partly because the people they write about are public figures subject to greater scrutiny and given fewer rights to restrain what is said about them than private citizens, and partly because they are only movies, for goodness sake. In short, try to be like Caesar's wife (above reproach) rather than like Woodward and Bernstein. You won't win any Pulitzers, but you may stay out of trouble.

Is It Libel?

Q. *To illustrate an ad for a local alcoholism treatment center you use a photograph of the group portrait of the graduating class from a 1959 high school yearbook that you bought at a yard sale, under the headline "By the time they were forty, 20 percent of these seniors had drinking problems." One of the former seventeen-year-olds (in fact, the person who sold you the yearbook), now a psychologist in private practice in your town, sues you, saying that you have libeled him by implying that he is an alcoholic. Is it libel?*

A. Probably so. Although you did not name the man, you did publish his photograph, and even though he looks different from the way he looked when the graduation photo was taken, people who know him may recognize him. Since your ad says that 20 percent of "these seniors," a defined group of the forty-three people pictured, developed drinking problems, it is not unreasonable to assume that some-one will see your ad and believe the psychologist is an alcoholic, even though he has been a strict non-drinker all his life, and perhaps that he is unfit to practice his profession. Further, the likelihood that someone who knows the psychologist will believe that he is an alco-holic because of the ad is, ironically, enhanced by the fact that the ad is for and sponsored by a recognized medical treatment facility for alcoholism, since that circumstance adds credibility to statements made in the ad. You'll also be found guilty of invading the good doc-tor's privacy by making unauthorized use of his photo, but you'll be so upset by the court's ruling in his favor on the libel charge that you may not even notice.

Q. *In a sales brochure for your client's in-home water purifying system you state that it is "the only in-home water purification system marketed in the United States that is capable of removing the five most common dangerous contaminants from tap water." Sales soar. But your client is sued by a com-petitor corporation claiming that because its purifiers do remove from tap water the contaminants your brochure says only your client's products remove, and it makes specific representations to its customers to that effect, you have defamed it as a corporation by, in effect, accusing it of making false representations about its products. Is it libel?*

A. Yes. If your statement that your client's purifiers are the only ones marketed in the United States that remove the named substances from tap water is untrue, then the other companies that truthfully claim their products do so have been defamed. It makes no difference that you did not name the plaintiff company in your brochure. The fact that there are only four companies that market purifiers of the sort your sales brochure advertises, and the fact that the brochure states falsely that no other company's products can do what your client's products can do, are sufficient to damage the competitor cor-poration's reputation. A further damaging factor is the fact that the competitor corporation has been defamed before the very group whose good opinion it values, the consumers of in-home water puri-fying systems.

The competitor corporation will collect on the libel charge and, most likely, also on a false advertising charge. And your water purifier client will permanently remove your name from its Rolodex (unless the information you used in the libelous ad was furnished to you by your client, in which case he is the guilty party here and you are off the hook, since it was not your negligence that caused all this trouble).

Q. *For a promotion for your fast-food drive-in–restaurant client, you find an old photo of Bonnie Parker and Clyde Barrow and use it in a newspaper ad under the headline "Drive by Burger Biggie whenever you're on the run." The promotion, which features coupons printed with the slogan "A burger and fries or I'll shoot!" and take-out bags with the legend "Burger Biggie Bank" is a success. In fact, everybody loves Burger Biggie but the estate of one Eloise Fish, who was Clyde's sweetheart before he met Bonnie.*

Seems the photo you found was a snap of Clyde and Eloise, who lived a blameless life and never robbed even one bank, not of Clyde and the infamous Bonnie. Eloise's estate is threatening to sue unless it is paid a Burger Biggie bag of money. Is it libel?

A. No. Sorry, Eloise. You were wronged posthumously, but the law says that since you are dead you cannot be defamed, no matter how scurrilous the false statements made about you. If you were alive, your lawyer could win a lifetime supply of hamburgers for you. However, because you have gone to your reward, no one can sue to protect your good reputation, which you have presumably taken with you to trade for a halo.

Q. *You prepare a newspaper ad for your client, the local chapter of the League of Liberal Voters. The ad consists of a slate of candidates in an upcoming local election that the local League supports, urges readers to vote for the listed candidates, and concludes with a list of names of citizens who support the slate of recommended candidates. One name, "Carol Rose," appears as "Carroll Rose" because of a typesetter's error which your agency's proofreader failed to detect. Carol Rose is not too upset because her name is misspelled, but Carroll Rose calls the League in a very bad mood. It seems that he is upset because his friends may believe he is a League member when in fact he is a lifelong Republican and always votes for conservative candidates. He threatens to sue. Is it libel?*

A. Probably not. Even if Mr. Rose's friends and associates believe that he lent his name to the League ad there is nothing defamatory in even a false representation that someone is participating in an honorable way in the political process. Further, even though Mr. Rose is a Republican who would be unlikely to support liberal candidates, he could have good reasons for doing so. The implication that someone supports liberal candidates is not inherently defamatory or, in this situation, defamatory because of extrinsic facts known to the plaintiff's friends and acquaintances. Further, because half of the long list of people named in the ad are specifically identified as League members, there is little likelihood that anyone will believe that *every* name in

the ad is that of a League member. Finally, the degree of fault attributable to your agency in failing to detect the typo that turned "Carol"
into "Carroll" is not the sort of grievous negligence necessary for liability for libel in any context involving free speech and the political
process. You're probably off the hook, but have a talk with your proofreader. If this had been an ad for N.O.R.M.L. or a pro-choice abor-
tion rights group Mr. Rose could probably have won.

Libel by Photograph

Agatha and Lorenzo were, respectively, the creative director and head art
director for a television station in a mid-size city in the southwest. They
wanted very much to win an Addy, a goal that had eluded them for the past
two years. They were excited when their station manager gave them the
assignment of coming up with a full promotion—newspaper, TV spots, and
radio—for a four-part public service series on the problem of teen pregnancy, scheduled to air during the fall ratings period.

They came up with one newspaper ad that they liked so well they
decided to use it as the centerpiece for the whole campaign. They planned
to use a photograph of a diary, opened to a page on which the following
entry was written in a teenage girl's handwriting: "Dear Diary, today I
found out that I am pregnant. What will I do now?" Lying next to the diary
is a snapshot of Lorenzo's younger brother hugging his old girlfriend Susan.
The headline reads, "Guess what Mitzi found out today?" The elements of
the newspaper ad were used to create a similar television spot and the headline of the newspaper ad was used as the hook for their radio spots.

The station manager and marketing director loved the ad and the
television and radio spots that Agatha and Lorenzo developed, so much so
that the station increased its planned media schedule for the campaign. The
teen pregnancy series garnered a greater audience than had been anticipated, and Agatha and Lorenzo began filling out entry blanks for the local
Addy competition. Their bubble burst with the delivery of service of
process for a lawsuit filed by Lorenzo's brother's girlfriend, who sued the
station for libel and invasion of privacy. At trial, Susan's lawyer argued that
Susan had been libeled by the use of the snapshot in ads about a pregnant
teenage girl. She testified that she had never had sex, with Lorenzo's brother or anyone else, and had certainly never been pregnant. Susan's lawyer also
argued that the use of the snapshot of Susan in the newspaper and telcvi-
sion ads without permission from either Susan or her parents constituted
an invasion of Susan's privacy.

The station's lawyers argued that even though the station's ads had
used the snapshot of Susan, the ads had used the name "Mitzi" in referring
to the fictitious pregnant teenage girl who was the subject of the ad, and that
therefore the ad was not "of and concerning" Susan. Further, they argued

that the snapshot used in the ads was merely an inoffensive photo of two young people hugging innocently and was not at all defamatory to Susan.

Agatha and Lorenzo breathed easier when they heard the arguments of the station's lawyers; they felt they had been cleared, at least of the libel charge. Unfortunately for them, the court disagreed.

The court found for Susan on both the privacy and libel charges. It said that her privacy had been invaded by the use of the snapshot of her without her permission. And it dismissed out of hand the arguments of the station's lawyers that the ads had not libeled Susan. The judge said that the fact that Susan's name was not used in the ads was immaterial, since she could be easily identified by the snapshot and that a reasonable interpretation of the ads was that Susan was the pregnant teenager to whom they referred. The judge awarded Susan enough money to send her through college, all at the expense of the television station. Agatha and Lorenzo did win an Addy for their newspaper ad, but it didn't matter much because they were both out of advertising by then, having been fired by the station management shortly after the trial. Agatha framed her award but hides it in a drawer among her other keepsakes. Lorenzo uses his as a dartboard.

Business Libel

You should also know that corporations (as well as unincorporated businesses) can be defamed. Corporations don't have many of the rights to sue for libel that an individual has, since, for example, corporations don't have reputations of chastity or sobriety to protect. However, corporations can and do sue for libel on account of false and damaging statements made about their credit or property, corporate honesty, efficiency, and business performance. And since most corporations have more money tied up in their reputations in these areas than most individuals and, perhaps, more money to spend protecting their reputations, libelous statements about them can be very dangerous. In other words, if you step on the toes of a competitor company, make sure that it is only because the products you are selling out-perform the ones the company is marketing.

Libel lawsuits brought by corporations are just as tedious as those brought by individuals. Think of the recent suit brought against Oprah Winfrey by a Texas cattle raisers' association. She had said on the air that she thought it was unhealthy to eat beef. They sued, even though she is a journalist and was, arguably, expressing an opinion. Oprah won, but first she had to go through an expensive, time-consuming, and distressing lawsuit. If the queen of American talk shows can be sued for such a statement, isn't it incumbent upon you to be careful about the statements you make in print or on the air or the Internet? You don't have Oprah's fame or money, and you might have to settle the suit just to avoid paying your lawyers through trial. Be careful what you say.

A caveat. Lawyers and judges evaluate libel according to some standards that we aren't even going to peek at. That is, they make important distinctions between statements that are inherently libelous and those that are not, and between the kinds of harm that result from various types of defamation, and generally engage in a lot of hairsplitting that we will forego. All of these permutations are really of no concern to you. The metaphysics of libel vary widely from state to state. The only time you will ever encounter these finer points of libel law is when you are sued for making some defamatory statement, and at that point you (or rather, your lawyer) will be worried only about the law of the particular jurisdiction where the suit is brought.

CHAPTER 5

The Right of Privacy and How to Avoid Infringing It

THE RIGHT OF PRIVACY AND THE RIGHT OF PUBLICITY ARE RELATED rights by which, under U.S. law, individuals are allowed some control over the uses made in the media of their identities and of the facts concerning their lives, as well as the manner in which they are portrayed. Generally, private individuals possess and enforce the right of privacy and celebrities possess and enforce the right of publicity, although private citizens can also sue for infringement of their right of publicity and celebrities may sue for invasion of privacy. Although there are several important differences between the right of privacy and the right of publicity, the two rights are somewhat like fraternal twins, that is, they are not identical but they look a lot alike. We will consider these rights in this and the next chapter so you will learn to recognize each, learn to tell them apart, and never have to face down either evil twin in a courtroom.

Defining Privacy

The right of privacy is the right everyone in this country has to live free from four kinds of invasion of privacy:

1. FALSE LIGHT INVASION OF PRIVACY: invasion of privacy by being placed in a "false light" in the public eye
2. INTRUSION INVASION OF PRIVACY: invasion of privacy by intrusion into some private area of life
3. DISCLOSURE INVASION OF PRIVACY: invasion of privacy by public disclosure of private facts
4. MISAPPROPRIATION INVASION OF PRIVACY: invasion of privacy by the unpermitted commercial use of name or image

The best way to understand these four kinds of privacy invasion is to consider examples of each.

False Light Invasion of Privacy

False light invasion of privacy is very much like defamation. With false light invasion of privacy, however, the harm that the plaintiff claims is not that his or her reputation has been harmed, but that he or she has been portrayed falsely to the public and his or her dignity has been injured, with resulting mental suffering. Many statements that defame someone also constitute false light invasion of privacy, but defamation and false light invasion of privacy do not always accompany each other. The following examples illustrate false light invasion of privacy.

- You use, in a magazine ad for a singles bar, a photo from your files showing well-dressed young professional men and women gathered around a bar, laughing and talking, under the headline, "Where Topeka's Singles Swing." One of the men pictured sues for invasion of privacy, claiming that your use of his photo places him, a married man, in a false light and has embarrassed him among his friends, causing him to lose sleep and avoid answering his phone. Your lawyer advises you to settle the suit, since your use of the man's photo did place him in a false light, injured his dignity, and caused him mental distress. (Your lawyer also tells you that you are lucky that the plaintiff did not also sue you for defamation, since, arguably, you have also defamed him by implying that his adherence to his marriage vows, an area of his morality, is less than wholehearted.)

- To advertise the wares of your women's clothing boutique client, you come up with the idea of a weekly newspaper ad that masquerades as a fashion column. One week, you headline the column "Fashion Mistakes" and fill it with photos shot on the street of women whose fashion sense was on vacation the day their photos were taken. You obscure the eyes of the subjects with a black bar to conceal their identities in the manner of a fifties detective magazine and dissect, in print, the wardrobe of each, offering, of course, solutions available from the stock of your client.

   The woman shown wearing a sweatsuit with scuffed high heels sues, stating in her complaint that you have invaded her privacy by suggesting that she is a person who has bad judgment about her grooming and wardrobe, when in fact she was voted "Best Dressed" by her college sorority last year. Further, she says that your efforts to disguise her identity failed to do so, since she is six feet tall and has a mane of flaming red hair. Many of her sorority sisters have also called to taunt her about the photo, which has caused her great mental distress.

Your lawyer advises you to settle this one, but you are adamant that your efforts to obscure the identity of the plaintiff in the photo relieve you of any liability and refuse to make a settlement offer. You are sorry you were adamant when the judge makes his ruling. He says that your efforts to disguise the plaintiff's identity were insufficient and therefore of no effect, since several young women testified at trial that they easily recognized the photo as an image of their red-haired friend on a bad day. Because you exposed the plaintiff (who was impeccably dressed during the trial) to the public eye in a false light, resulting in her humiliation, the court awards her enough money to continue to dress stylishly right through her last year of college. (The good news is that she couldn't sue for libel, since the implications of your ad did not really amount to defamation.)

Intrusion Invasion of Privacy

Intrusion invasion of privacy involves some unreasonable intrusion upon the solitude and seclusion of someone or into her or his private affairs. In contexts other than advertising, intrusion invasion of privacy lawsuits often involve some physical invasion analogous to trespassing, such as a search by police without a warrant or entry into someone's home by journalists who employ false pretenses in order to get a story. Intrusion claims also quite often involve other sorts of unwelcome nosiness and pushiness, such as electronic eavesdropping, opening other people's mail, or photographs taken with a telephoto lens. Jacqueline Kennedy Onassis's well-known suit against the paparazzi photographer Ron Gallella was an intrusion invasion of privacy suit and was brought because he followed her and her children around constantly, leaping from behind bushes and chasing them in cars, in order to take photographs of them. Just as false light invasion of privacy is related to and expands upon defamation law, intrusion invasion of privacy is related to and fills in some gaps left by the law of trespass.

As we have seen, intrusion invasion of privacy often involves some unauthorized entry onto someone's premises, which is trespass. The difference between trespass and intrusion invasion of privacy is that the harm for which a plaintiff sues is not so much the physical trespass itself (which may be the subject of another part of the lawsuit) as the mental distress that results from the intrusion.

It is much less likely that a lawsuit for intrusion invasion of privacy will result from the activities of a graphic design firm or advertising agency than from those of, for instance, journalists (especially unscrupulous ones). How-

ever, the possibility, and danger, exists, and advertising creative people must be
aware of it in order to avoid it. The following examples illustrate some of the
sorts of intrusion invasion of privacy that are possible in an advertising context.

- You publish as the illustration for an ad for a new "retirement vil-
  lage" a photograph of an old man sitting inside the front window
  of a shabby little house. He stares sadly out the window. Your ad
  emphasizes the advantages of living, in old age, among others in a
  community environment, and implies that the old man is alone,
  lonely, and neglected. He sues, claiming that the photograph of him
  was taken without his knowledge by a photographer who must
  have been standing on the sidewalk in front of his house, shooting
  through the window. At trial, the photographer is forced to admit
  that those were precisely the circumstances surrounding the photograph. The court finds you (and the photographer and your client)
  guilty of intrusion invasion of privacy, and of false light invasion of
  privacy, since, despite appearances, the plaintiff is well-cared-for by
  his daughter, who lives with him. You saved a model's fee by using
  an existing photograph that you could get cheaply from the photographer, but you lost the war.
- You publish in an ad a photograph of a handwritten letter from a
  satisfied user of your client's product, a contraceptive jelly. The letter writer states in her letter that she has found the product to be
  superior to others on the market and has used it exclusively for
  three years. The ad runs in several mainstream women's magazines,
  but also in some sexually-oriented periodicals that you would not
  leave lying on your coffee table. The woman sues for intrusion invasion of privacy. It seems that you did not have her permission to
  publish her letter in an ad and that your use of the photograph of
  the actual letter, which included the woman's name and address, has
  led to a steady stream of unwelcome letters and anonymous
  obscene phone calls from men suggesting various activities involving contraceptive jelly. The trial judge is outraged by your (and your
  client's) carelessness and the frightening consequences of that carelessness. She awards a record amount in damages to the letter writer.
  You want your lawyer to appeal what you feel is the excessive
  amount of the award, but he tells you that you might as well pay
  up, because no appeals court is going to feel solicitous of your
  pocketbook after hearing the facts of the case.

Disclosure Invasion of Privacy

Disclosure invasion of privacy involves some public disclosure of embarrassing private facts about the plaintiff. It is the sort of invasion of privacy

that most people think of when they hear "invasion of privacy." The elements of this sort of invasion of privacy are that the information disclosed must be of such a sort that its disclosure would be embarrassing, objectionable, and offensive to a person of ordinary sensibilities, and the information must not have been public prior to the complained-of disclosure.

Disclosure invasion of privacy differs from defamation in one very important way. To constitute defamation, the information published about the plaintiff must be untrue. There is no such requirement that the information involved in a disclosure invasion of privacy suit be false; in fact, the heart of a disclosure invasion of privacy suit is that the information is true but private. In a way, disclosure invasion of privacy is the converse of defamation. In other words, if you publish untrue information about someone and that information damages his or her reputation or humiliates him or her, you may be sued for defamation. If you publish the same information about the person but it *is* true, and private, and he or she can reasonably object to its publication and is embarrassed by the disclosure of the information, you may be sued for disclosure invasion of privacy.

As with intrusion invasion of privacy, disclosure invasion of privacy suits result more from the activities of journalists than those of advertising creative people, but advertising creative people can get in big trouble with disclosure invasion of privacy claims just the same. A few examples of disclosure invasion of privacy will illustrate.

- To promote the annual state fair held each year in your city, you design a newspaper ad entitled "Fun at the Fair" and use an assortment of photographs of people who attended last year's fair. Among the photos you use is one of a young woman emerging from a midway funhouse. The woman is prevented by the stuffed animals she carries from holding down the skirt of her dress when jets of air in front of the funhouse raise it, à la the famous Marilyn Monroe photograph. Her entire derrière, clad only in cotton undies, is exposed to the view of the camera and several young male bystanders, who are obviously having "fun at the fair" at the expense of the exposed woman. She sues when your ad is published, claiming disclosure invasion of privacy.

  Your lawyer argues manfully at trial that since the photograph you used was taken in a public place, there were no "private facts" to disclose. The judge disagrees, stating that while the incident photographed did occur in a public place, you have increased exponentially the number of "bystanders" who witnessed the plaintiff's embarrassment and, indeed, would have never published the photograph if it did not depict her exposure. You lose, and so does your client the state fair board.

- In an ad promoting a new service of the largest hospital in your city, a clinic to treat impotence in men, you publish a list, furnished to you by the hospital, of the names and phone numbers of men who are peer counselors for the "Impotence Isn't Forever" support group that meets monthly at the hospital. The ad invites other impotent men to call one of these counselors to discuss becoming a part of the support group. Unbeknownst to you, one of the counselors whose name and phone number is published had not given his consent for his name and phone number to be included in the ad. He sues you and the hospital claiming disclosure invasion of privacy.

  The hospital's lawyer says that you really don't have to hire your own lawyer since you didn't do anything wrong, but then later seems to have forgotten his promise to "take care of" you. Finally, you haul in your own lawyer, at some expense, and he is successful in convincing the plaintiff's lawyers that you would not be found guilty at trial of violating the rights of the plaintiff since you had no reason to believe that the hospital had erred when it told you that the men listed in the ad had all consented to the publication of their names. The hospital settles with the plaintiff, and you don't have to pay anything toward the settlement, but the director of marketing at the hospital is fired and replaced by another marketing director, who hires his brother-in-law's agency to replace yours.

- A local plastic surgeon hires you to help him put together a slide show concerning his new technique for rhinoplasty for presentation at a medical convention in your city. Among the gory slides of nose surgery in progress, there are some "before" and "after" photos, which you feel are the only really interesting parts of the slide show. A local beauty queen agrees. She claims in the complaint she files for disclosure invasion of privacy that she had her nose "fixed" by the good doctor several years ago. She is happy with her new nose, but unhappy and embarrassed that the fact of the surgery has been made public by means of the slide show, especially since several of the plastic surgery residents in the audience are former college classmates of hers.

  The court finds for the plaintiff. Both you and your client are held liable. Your client is liable because even though he told you that he did not have permission to use some of the photos in his files, including the photos of the plaintiff, he is responsible for your actions as his agent. You are liable because you employed the art director because he put the plaintiff's photos in the slide show, who thought that they were the most persuasive examples of the surgeon's work and believed that the woman pictured in them would never find out anyway. You pay your lawyer's exorbitant fees and the fairly large damage award and then, for revenge, you fire your errant art director. However, not even that makes you feel much better and you vow to avoid plastic surgeons forevermore.

Misappropriation Invasion of Privacy

If this lengthy account of all the varieties of invasion of privacy is putting you to sleep, you should wake up now, because we are going to consider the variety of invasion of privacy that is most potentially dangerous to advertising creative people—misappropriation invasion of privacy. Misappropriation invasion of privacy involves the unauthorized use, for commercial purposes, of a person's name or likeness, with resulting damage to the plaintiff's dignity and peace of mind. In fact, any invasion of privacy suit involving any use of the plaintiff's identity in an advertisement or in any commercial context will be a misappropriation invasion of privacy suit, even if there are also other sorts of privacy claims involved. If you will look back at the examples of the other three sorts of invasion of privacy given above, you will realize that, in addition to illustrating those sorts of invasion of privacy, the examples also all illustrate misappropriation invasion of privacy. The following illustrations depict situations in which only a misappropriation invasion of privacy claim could properly be brought.

- Your client the furniture manufacturer names its new line of fancy baby furniture the "Susannah" line. You suggest that your client adopt a depiction of a pretty little girl as the portrait of the fictitious "Susannah." You survey all the photographs of pretty little girls you can get your hands on and choose one, of whose little girl you do not know, to give to your illustrator so he can transform it into a logo for the Susannah furniture line. The illustrator makes a nice line drawing from the photo, copying the photo faithfully. You are very happy with the drawing and your client loves his new logo. Unfortunately, the doting parents of "Susannah," whose real name is Cynthia Ann, recognize their daughter as the original of the Susannah logo and sue on behalf of their minor daughter for misappropriation invasion of privacy. They claim that they would never have permitted your client's use of their daughter's image and that they want to stop the commercial exploitation of their child because they believe it will damage her self-esteem. Cynthia Ann wins. Your self-esteem is also damaged, because you are in hot water with your client and out a lot of money.
- The winner of your city's annual marathon crosses the finish line wearing a pair of running shoes manufactured by your client. You

seize the opportunity and create a poster for distribution to all retail shoe stores that stock your client's running shoes. The poster uses a photo of the winner of the race, taken from a rear angle, which does not show the runner's face but prominently pictures the runner's shoes. The headline of the poster reads "Winners Wear Whizards" and the poster copy explains that the winner of the fifteenth annual Santa Fe marathon won wearing Whizard running shoes.

The winner, an accountant by profession, sues for misappropriation invasion of privacy. You are astounded when your lawyer tells you that the plaintiff can probably win his suit, because you believe that the fact that the plaintiff's face was not shown should eliminate the problem. It is news to you that, because the plaintiff can be identified as the runner in the photo by other information (he is the only person who won the fifteenth annual Santa Fe marathon), you have, as your lawyer says, "misappropriated his identity." Your lawyer recommends that you settle the case with a cash payment to the plaintiff. You know the rest of the story.

- A woman named Esmeralda Finnegan halts a bank robbery by using her karate skills on the two armed robbers who took her and seven other bank customers hostage. When interviewed after police arrived, she attributes her success in foiling the crime to the karate classes she took at Wong's Highway 96 Karate School. Wong's is your client. You reproduce the news story quoting Miss Finnegan in ads for Wong's. Even though neither Miss Finnegan's name nor her photograph appears in the ad other than the mention of her name in the reproduced news story, she sues for misappropriation invasion of privacy.

At trial your lawyer argues that you did not infringe the plaintiff's right of privacy because you merely reprinted a news story in your ad, did not say that the plaintiff recommended your client's school, and did not use any photograph of her. The court finds for the plaintiff, stating in its ruling that the use of the news story in an ad for Wong's constitutes an implication that Miss Finnegan endorses Wong's and is a misappropriation of her identity for commercial purposes. In other words, the plaintiff is right and you and Wong are wrong.

- During the first few weeks that your company's newest venture, a bar and restaurant called Smoothie's, is open for business, you hire a freelance photographer to take some pictures of the patrons. By offering cheap drinks during happy hour and specials for Friday and Saturday dinners, the flagship Smoothie's is a big hit in the college town where it opens. You are especially pleased with a series of shots your photographer took of an attractive local policewoman, who, with her drinking buddies, posed in uniform one night holding a mug of beer at the bar at Smoothie's. Because the policewoman is so attractive and because the Smoothie's sign over the bar is clearly visible in the photos in which she appears, you airbrush out her drinking companions and make the photo the centerpiece for the national ad campaign promoting the sixteen restaurants your employer is opening around the country.

Everything is going well until you receive a call from the general counsel for your employer, who tells you that the policewoman is suing for misappropriation invasion of privacy. You tell him you are sure that there has been some misunderstanding and tell him you'll call him back after you talk to the photographer.

You are relieved to hear the photographer say that he did, indeed, have permission to take the photos of the policewoman. He points out that the photos themselves obviously show that she was aware of the camera as she is smiling and looking directly at the lens. You are less happy to hear that he did not bother to get a signed release from the policewoman, but you figure you may be able to dodge the bullet anyway by relating to the general counsel what the photographer told you.

The general counsel doubts that what the photographer told you will get your employer off the hook for misappropriation invasion of privacy, but says he will do some investigating. The afternoon he takes the deposition of the policewoman he calls to chew you out. It seems that the policewoman admits that she posed for the photos and that they were taken with her permission. However, she says that the photographer represented that he was taking photographs of the opening night crowd at the restaurant for the local newspaper and for framing and hanging in the bar to commemorate the event. She states under oath that she would never have agreed to allow her picture to be used in advertising a bar. Furthermore, she has been called on the carpet by her superiors, who chastised her for violating the policy of the police department against any commercial endorsements. They told her that she could be fired for allowing a photograph of herself, in uniform, to be used in ads for an establishment that serves alcohol.

Your general counsel says that the photographer's representation that the policewoman agreed to have her picture taken is meaningless, since there is no proof at all that she agreed to allow it to be used in your ad campaign. He adds that, in any event, any verbal permission for photographs is nearly useless, since determining the extent of any consent to be photographed is nearly impossible without a written document to prove it.

Your wonderful ad campaign is pulled from the national publications in which it has been scheduled to appear. You are taken off
the Smoothie's project and your company ends up settling with the
policewoman for an amount larger than your annual media budget.
You vow never to use the incompetent photographer again, but you
recognize that this is perhaps a moot point, since you anticipate that
you will soon be fired for your role in the Smoothie's fiasco. And
every day on your way home, you take a much longer route than
usual in order to avoid driving past Smoothie's, which continues to
thrive, even without your assistance.

CHAPTER 6

The Right of Publicity and How to Avoid Infringing It

I F YOU ARE BEGINNING TO THINK THAT YOU CANNOT USE THE NAME OR likeness of any living person in an ad without his or her consent, you are right. In fact, in some states, and with regard to some people, you can't even use the name or likeness of someone who is deceased (without somebody's consent). The right of publicity is very similar to misappropriation invasion of privacy. These rights form a sort of progression, or chain, from defamation to false light invasion of privacy, to intrusion invasion of privacy, to disclosure invasion of privacy, to misappropriation invasion of privacy, to the right of publicity. Or maybe you would call it a vicious circle, because all of these terms name common rights that prevent you from doing a lot of things you might think are kosher, were you not now educated otherwise.

Defining the Right of Publicity

The last link in the chain, the right of publicity, differs from all of the other rights named above in one basic way. Any of the types of invasion of privacy discussed involves an assault upon someone's reputation, peace of mind, or dignity. In contrast, when you infringe someone's right of publicity you infringe a property right; that is, you may be sued because you have infringed someone's legal right to be the only one who profits from the commercial value of his or her identity.

Private individuals have privacy rights and so do celebrities (though perhaps to a lesser extent), but in most ordinary circumstances only celebrities have the right of publicity. That is because generally only movie stars, sports figures, famous authors, retired politicians, etc. have the sort of name recognition that makes someone's identity valuable to advertisers. When a private person's identity is used without permission for commercial purposes, that person sues for misappropriation invasion of privacy, not for infringement of the right of publicity. The right of publicity otherwise looks pretty much like misappropriation invasion of privacy. That is, an infringement of someone's right of publicity occurs when that person's name or likeness is used for commercial purposes without his or her consent. The following examples illustrate some of the characteristic features of right of publicity infringement disputes and suits.

Examples of Publicity Infringements

- You design packaging for a videocassette called "Golfing Tips of the Pros." You use photos on the cassette box of three famous golfers, Arnold Palmer, Jack Nicklaus, and Nancy Lopez. You neglect to ask anybody's permission to do so. You figure that all of the famous golfers whose photos you used are public figures and you remember hearing something about public figures having less ability to control press coverage of their activities than private individuals. When the videocassette hits the market, the representatives of Mr. Palmer, Mr. Nicklaus, and Ms. Lopez call up the video distributor, threatening to sue the distributor if the videos are not pulled from store shelves. They also want to know the address of your client, a video production company, in order to serve process in the lawsuits that are filed.

    At trial your client is forced to admit that the golfing tips embodied in the videocassette are actually tips from the pros at the Sunnydale Golf Club and that the three famous golfers had nothing to do with creating the video. The lawyers representing the golfers argue that your use of their clients' photos on the video box implies that those are the pros whose tips are included in the video and constitutes a violation of the right of publicity of the three golfers. Your client decides to cut his losses and settles. Your lawyer says you should be happy that the plaintiffs did not also claim a Section 43(a) violation, and that the video was pulled from store shelves before the Federal Trade Commission could find out that its packaging was materially misleading and commence a proceeding against your client for violation of its advertising regulations. You go home and think about what Shakespeare said about killing lawyers.

- In an ad for Glitter Gloves you use a photo of the back view of Michael Jackson onstage, dressed in characteristic stage attire with one gloved hand raised in the gesture he made famous. Well, actually, because you figured that Michael Jackson's fee for posing for your photo, if he would consent to do such a thing, would exceed by far your glove manufacturer client's entire advertising budget, the photo is of a model carefully dressed and posed to look like Michael Jackson circa 1985. Your client loves the ad. Michael Jackson doesn't.

Mr. Jackson's lawyers contact your client right after the ad appears in a national magazine, threatening to sue for what they say is your (and your client's) infringement of his right of publicity. They say that even though the photo is of a model dressed and posed to look like Michael Jackson at the height of his fame and is not Mr. Jackson himself, the intent and effect of the ad is to cause readers to believe that Michael Jackson is advertising Glitter Gloves.

You and your client consult an attorney, who tells you that Mr. Jackson's lawyers are correct in their assertions. Your lawyer says that your photo is so realistic that you have succeeded, regrettably, in appropriating Michael Jackson's "persona" without his participation or consent and that your use of the fake Michael Jackson photo is just as actionable as your use of an authentic photo of him without his permission. Your client pulls the ad, settles with Michael Jackson, and hires another agency. It also refuses to pay your last statement for your work on the "Michael Jackson" ad, leaving you holding the bag for all the production expenses and creative fees.

• You plan a "Fifties Days" promotion for all twelve locations of your restaurant client, the Jukebox Cafe. The centerpiece of your promotion will be a weekly Elvis look-alike contest. You will also produce souvenir Elvis coffee mugs and tee shirts for sale at the restaurants' gift shops both during and after the promotion. For the mugs and shirts you plan to use a vintage photo of a skinny Elvis Presley in performance with the slogan "I Saw Elvis at the Jukebox Cafe."

The restaurant company marketing director loves the Elvis contest idea and the mug and tee shirt tie-ins, but he says he is worried that you need permission from somebody to use Elvis Presley's photograph and name in the promotion. You assure him that you remember reading that no dead person can be defamed and that, therefore, it is unnecessary to get permission from anyone before launching the planned promotion. All the locations of the Jukebox Cafe sell record quantities of cheeseburgers during the Fifties Days promotion and you have to reprint the Elvis tees twice in order to meet the demand.

You bask in glory until the day you get a call from the corporate legal department of the company that owns all of the Jukebox Cafes. They say that they have been sued by the Elvis Presley estate for infringing Elvis Presley's right of publicity by producing and selling Elvis mugs and tee shirts. The suit asks for an injunction against further sales of the mugs and shirts, impoundment of all the unsold infringing mugs and shirts in your client's possession, your client's profits from sales of the items, and a substantial award of damages. You swallow your blue pencil and call a lawyer recommended to you by another graphic designer.

Your lawyer says that you are knee-deep in cheeseburgers because you have, indeed, run roughshod over the rights of the deceased Mr. Presley. You tell him that most people believe that Elvis Presley has been dead for years and ask him if he is one of those who think differently. He tells you that, for purposes of the lawsuit, it really doesn't make much difference—that under Tennessee law, the right of publicity, under some circumstances, survives the death of the celebrity and is owned and can be enforced by the celebrity's estate.

You tell him you did not know this. He says that it is obvious that you did not and that whether you knew what you were doing is immaterial. He advises you to do whatever you can to cooperate with the lawyers for your client and to settle the lawsuit. He also advises you that although only your restaurant client has been sued by the Presley estate, it is likely that you will, in turn, be sued by your client and thereby be brought into the same suit.

Your client settles the lawsuit quickly and agrees not to sue your company, but in return you have to agree to work for half your ordinary fees during the next year. You regret having to bite that bullet, but you feel as if you have escaped from a bad situation with as little harm to yourself and your pocketbook as possible under the circumstances. You are right.

Because right of publicity is a relatively new area of the law and has not been around long enough for all jurisdictions, courts, and legal scholars to agree completely on its shape, it varies widely from one jurisdiction to another. Most, but not all, of the states expressly recognize the right, either by court decision or statute. It is likely that the right of publicity will be recognized almost everywhere as soon as forward-thinking legislators pass right of publicity statutes in states where there are none at present.

Because right of publicity law varies widely from one state to another, and because you probably will not conduct an investigation prior to using a celebrity's identity to see just how much you can get away with under which statutes of which states, you are well-advised either to try to stay within the narrowest right of publicity restrictions that exist anywhere in the United States or to eliminate the guessing game and get the celebrity's permission to use her or his name or likeness. You may be able to get away with using without permission the identities of some celebrities who live (or lived) in certain states and never run afoul of the law. But the only way to know for sure is to go ahead and do it, and then wait to see if a lawsuit shows up in your client's mail—which is no way to run an airline.

Descendability of the Publicity Right

There are some other twists to right of publicity law that you may not expect. One of the more interesting ones is the fact that, in some states, the right of publicity is a "descendable" right. That is, if you are famous, in some states and under certain circumstances your heirs can continue to exclusively control and profit from the commercial exploitation of your identity after your death. This is unlike either the law of privacy or defamation. Your estate can't sue anyone for invasion of privacy or defamation if the alleged invasion or defamatory act occurred after your death; your rights in these areas die with you because you are presumed to be past caring what anyone says about you. But a celebrity's right of publicity is a property right more like trademark ownership than a personal right to protect feelings from assault. Property can be passed to heirs and so can the right to protect the right of publicity after the celebrity's death. Even if there is a limit on the time after a celebrity's death that the celebrity's estate can control the use of his or her name and likeness, it is probable that the estate will have used the celebrity's name and likeness widely enough during that period that the estate will have created trademark rights in the name and likeness that are protectable even after the time limit on the celebrity's right of publicity.

Identifiability

Another peculiarity of right of publicity law is the many ways by which a celebrity's right may be infringed. Generally speaking, the standard for identifiability is the same for right of publicity lawsuits as for invasion of privacy suits and libel suits. That is, if some people recognize the statement, photo, or even fictitious depiction as referring to the plaintiff, the defendant is in trouble. However, since a celebrity is, by definition, a person whose appearance, voice, and personal habits are so scrutinized and publicized that they become very well known, almost anything about a celebrity can identify him or her. This means that if you imitate any part of a celebrity's "persona," including his or her appearance, voice, singing voice, and nickname, sufficiently well that the ad embodying the imitation "works," you have infringed that celebrity's right of publicity. Think of it this way: If somebody is capitalizing on your hard-won fame by using your well-known nickname ("When you're 'The Greatest,' you fight in Slugger boxing shorts") or distinctive singing voice and style in an ad without your permission, you probably don't care whether it really is you in the ad or not, since what is being summoned up by the imitator, and stolen from you, is your reputation, not just your actual performance or image.

Non-News Media Defendants

The reason you need to know about the rights of privacy and publicity is, of course, so that you will be able to stay out of lawsuits. Many, and perhaps most, U.S. invasion of privacy lawsuits are filed because of transgressions by the news media, but that doesn't mean that non-news media defendants are safer from invasion of privacy suits than newspapers and magazines or the broadcast media. In fact, because the courts don't allow defendants accused of invading plaintiffs' privacy in commercial contexts to plead the various defenses related to freedom of the press that are available to media defendants, non-media defendants are found liable for invasion of privacy in a higher percentage of privacy suits than are media defendants.

Practically all suits for infringement of the right of publicity are filed against defendants who are in the chain of people who market a product, lots of them ad agencies. First Amendment defenses are also generally unavailable in those suits. This means that you, as someone who creates ads, must pay special attention to privacy issues and to possible publicity claims, since if you invade someone's privacy or infringe his or her right of publicity in an ad, you can't get off the hook by "pleading the First."

Sometimes copyright and trademark infringement suits result from what are essentially business disputes. That is, two parties who have differing ideas of who is entitled to ownership of a copyright or a trademark can't work out their dispute between themselves and so resort to the courts for a resolution of the dispute. Libel suits and suits for invasion of privacy or infringement of the publicity right are seldom as dispassionate as even a fiercely fought copyright or trademark suit because, by definition, all involve somebody's stepped-on feelings or reputation, or both.

Consider the fact that even lawyers, who usually speak in terms of "bringing an action" or "filing a complaint" have been heard to utter the phrase "slap those *'#@!*s with a lawsuit" in contexts involving clients who have (choose any two of the following) squashed feelings, a damaged or misappropriated reputation, or a fat wallet and fire in their eyes. For any non-media defendant, there is simply nothing to be won in any of the sorts of lawsuits we have discussed so far. Further, these types of suits are typically fought by plaintiffs as grudge matches long past the point when prudence would dictate that they let sleeping dogs lie. And despite the facts that there is now more legal protection available for celebrities than ever before and that marketers should now be well aware of the danger of using celebrities' identities without permission, there doesn't seem to be a decline in the number of right of publicity infringement suits. For example, Florence Henderson, who played the demure mom, Carol Brady, on the 1970s show *The Brady Bunch,* was recently forced to sue the manufacturer of tee shirts that used her picture above the caption "Porn Queen."

All this means that, with regard to privacy and publicity infringement suits (and, as we have seen, libel suits) an ounce of prevention beats a whole covey of lawyers for the defense. And prevention means releases.

Releases as a Solution

A release (also sometimes called a "consent" or "consent form") is simply a written document that evidences that someone has given his or her permission for his or her name, photograph, performance, or other element of his or her identity to be used for the purposes specified in the release. Releases don't have to be long or complicated to do the job. In fact, in many cases a verbal release would actually do the trick, but most people don't want to rely on the memory and honesty of someone else to prove that a use of that person's name or photo was a permitted use.

Written releases should be a part of your standard operating procedure, a routine part of your business that you *never* neglect. There are a few rules to remember in using releases:

- Have a lawyer prepare a release that is designed to work for you. Generally, the broader the release the better. That is, the less specific your release in stating the uses to which your subject agrees his or her photo can be put, the more leeway you have later. However, if the intended use for the photo is something that the model could object to if she or he is not made aware of it—such as the use of the photograph on packaging for condoms or in an ad for guns or cigarettes—include the specific purpose contemplated in a handwritten addition to the general release. This handwritten addition should be made on the same piece of paper as the general release, preferably in a space reserved for such additions, even if it must be made on the reverse of the page, and should be initialed by the person who signs the release at the same time he or she signs. Your release should give you permission to alter the photo, since only having permission to use it "as is" may make it unusable for your purposes. (The release reproduced in the appendix of this book may do the trick, but it also may need modification to work for you. Talk to your lawyer if you are in doubt about whether it will work in your situation.)

Have your release printed on your business letterhead and carry a supply of blank release forms with you so that you will have them whenever you need them. Make sure your employees and any freelancers you hire know that you expect them to secure signed releases on your behalf.

- Get a signed release from everyone who appears in any photo you may use in an ad or publication or in any other way. Make *no* exceptions. Get releases even from people in the background of street, party, or other group shots, unless their faces are not visible and their own mothers wouldn't recognize the set of their shoulders and the color of their hair. Get releases even from paid models. And be especially sure to get releases from private individuals who are not paid for their services. Make sure that you get mom or dad or a legal guardian, not just Aunt Linda or the child's agent or chaperone, to sign a release for anyone under twenty-one, the upper-limit age of majority (in some states), since the signature of a minor may invalidate the release.

- Never obtain a release by trickery or in any circumstances that could lead to a later challenge that the subject of the photograph or ad copy was misled as to the use of it. If you don't tell the whole truth about the uses that will be made of a photograph or copy depicting or mentioning the person who signs a release, how can he or she validly agree to allow that use?

- Keep a central file of all releases you obtain, arranged alphabetically by the names of the people who sign the releases and by year. Or, even better, keep one copy of each release with the negatives for the photos of the person to whom the release applies and one in a central file to ensure against loss. It is also best to give a copy of the release to the person signing it, but that person probably won't keep his or her copy and, anyway, you are the one who needs proof that the release was signed, not the model or subject.

Make sure that you indicate on the back of contact sheets, on negative envelopes, or in some other reliable way the name of each subject of each group of photos. Ditto for letters from consumers or copy that mentions Mrs. Jones of Toledo as one of the many satisfied users of LawnJockey lawnmowers. Otherwise, things may get mixed up and Jim may sue you for using his photo because the only permission you had to use it was, in reality, a signed release from Chris.

- Never vary your firm policy of obtaining releases from everyone whose photo you take or hire to be taken, and from anyone you "mention" by name or by identifying information in any ad, brochure, or other commercial publicity product (such as a corporation annual report). And never use a photo or copy from a freelancer without seeing and keeping a copy of the release from the subject of the photo or copy. Never. Behead any employees who are lax with regard to obtaining releases. They can get you in a lot of trouble.

CHAPTER 7

Copyright Infringement and How to Avoid It

THE ONLY THING WORSE THAN HAVING TO SUE SOMEONE FOR COPYRIGHT infringement is being sued yourself. If you create advertising—and especially if you license or assign your creations to a client or prepare them for an employer—you must know not only how to protect your own rights but also how to avoid trampling those of others. If you are not careful to avoid using the work of others without their permission, you and your client or employer may end up in court defending against a copyright infringement suit. Even if you are never sued for your infringing actions, the rules of fair play dictate that you avoid transgressing the rights of other creative people. And if you suspect that your own work has been used or copied without your knowledge, you need to know how to evaluate the suspected infringement in order to determine whether you have a valid complaint. To determine whether your rights have been infringed or your work infringes someone else's work, you must first have a good understanding of what rights copyright gives to copyright owners. Basically, only the person who created the copyrighted work (or someone to whom he or she has given permission to use the work) is legally permitted to reproduce, perform or display it, distribute copies of it, or create variations of it.

Defining Infringement

The federal copyright statute defines copyright infringement with a simple statement: "Anyone who violates any of the exclusive rights of [a] copyright owner . . . is an infringer of . . . copyright." Copyright infringement is actionable in federal court because it is a violation of rights granted under federal law; that is, any copyright infringement lawsuit must be filed in one of the federal district courts distributed throughout the country.

The question of just *what* actions are sufficient to constitute a violation of the rights of a copyright owner is left for courts to answer as they evaluate the circumstances in each case of claimed infringement. The body of law made up of court decisions in copyright infringement cases is called copyright "case law." Copyright infringement suits can arise from the unauthorized exercise of any of the exclusive rights of copyright. However, as a practical matter, copyright infringement suits most commonly claim that the defendant copied the plaintiff's work without permission or that the defendant has used the plaintiff's work without permission. In the context of advertising, unauthorized use of a work is as likely to occur as unauthorized copying. We will consider both sorts of infringement; first, the sin of infringement due to unauthorized copying of a copyrighted work.

Copyright case law is the source for the test for copyright infringement where unauthorized copying is claimed and the standard for applying the test to the facts in particular copyright infringement cases. Sometimes an infringer *has* intentionally copied the copyright owner's work in an effort to steal its successful features and profit from them. However, many copyright infringement lawsuits are brought because the plaintiff wrongly believes that someone who has created a *somewhat* similar work has infringed the plaintiff's copyright by copying the plaintiff's work. It is a common mistake. Many highly publicized copyright infringement lawsuits (quite often brought against the producers of successful movies or records) are brought on grounds too slender to support a finding by the court of infringement. Understanding copyright infringement means understanding the standard courts use in evaluating whether accusations of copyright infringement are true.

The Test for Infringement by Unauthorized Copying

In suits claiming unauthorized copying, assuming the copyright in the work that is said to have been infringed is valid and that work was created *before* the work that is accused of infringing it, and in the absence of any admission by the defendant that he or she *did* copy the plaintiff's work, courts ordinarily judge copyright infringement by a circumstantial evidence test.

The circumstantial evidence test for copyright infringement by unauthorized copying has three parts:

1. Did the accused infringer have *access* to the work that is said to have been infringed so that copying was possible?
2. Is the defendant actually guilty of *copying* part of the plaintiff's protectable expression from the plaintiff's work?
3. Is the accused work *substantially similar* to the work the plaintiff says was copied?

If you can remember and understand these three parts of the test for copyright infringement—"access," "copying," and "substantial similarity"—you should always be able to decide correctly for yourself whether a work of yours infringes someone else's work or whether someone else has infringed your copyright.

Access to the "Infringed" Work

"Access" simply means what it says. Did the accused infringer have access to the "infringed" work before creating the "infringing" work? It's very important to remember that the action for which the copyright statute prescribes penalties is *copying,* not the mere *coincidental creation* of a work that is similar or even nearly identical to a pre-existing work. In most cases, access is not presumed but must be proved before the questions of copying and substantial similarity even enter the equation.

This means that if you write an ad for a client auto dealer about the safety features of the minivans it sells and another copywriter creates a similar ad about the same models of minivans for a competing auto dealer, each of you owns a valid copyright in your own ad. This is so even if both ads employ line drawings of the vans with arrows pointing to safety features, both run under the headline "Safety First for the Family," and both quote U.S. Department of Transportation statistics regarding the low number of deaths and serious injuries in accidents involving the advertised vans. If neither you nor the other writer copied the other's work, both ads are protected by copyright law, even if their content and presentation are nearly identical.

This is easier to understand if you remember that our copyright statute rewards the act of creation. You own the copyright in a product of your own imagination, so long as your imagination—and not that of another creator—really is the source of your work. This is true regardless of what anybody else in the world comes up with before, at the same time as, or after you create your work.

If you are a freelancer, the obvious implication of the access requirement in proving copyright infringement is that good documentation of your attempts to sell your works to those who are in a position to exploit them can be critically important in the event someone decides your work is good enough to steal. If you know where your proposal or demo tape or script has been, you may be able to prove that an infringer had "reasonable opportunity" (which is usually sufficient proof of access) to copy your work.

Copying of Protected Expression

The circumstantial evidence test for copyright infringement is like a three-legged stool. All three legs of the test are necessary to support a claim of copyright infringement, and the absence of proof of one of the three parts of the test means an infringement suit will fail. Proving the second element of copyright infringement—copying of protected subject matter—is just as important as proving access and substantial similarity, but would-be plaintiffs often gloss over this requirement in the mistaken assumption that *any* copying is sufficient to support an infringement suit.

To understand what constitutes copying of protected expression, you must consider what elements of your work are not protected. The copyright statute specifically excludes from protection "any idea, procedure, process, system, method of operation, concept, principle or discovery." And there are several categories of elements of copyrightable works, some of them important to the overall quality of a work, that are not protected by copyright.

If you review the list of *exceptions* to the general rule that copyright protects what you create, you can better apply the second part of the test for copyright infringement. This is: *Does the material suspected to have been copied from the "infringed" work include protectable expression?* If your answer is "yes" and it can be proved that the accused infringer had access to the work that is said to have been infringed, you must then evaluate whether the theft was substantial.

Substantial Similarity

The third part of the test for copyright infringement is determining whether the "infringing" work is "substantially similar" to the "infringed" work. Substantial similarity is hard to define. Even the courts have never been able to come up with a hard-and-fast test for determining substantial similarity. This may be because no such test is possible—each copyright infringement case must be decided entirely on the facts of *that* case, and what happened in a similar suit has no real bearing on the question whether *this* defendant did, indeed, create a work that is substantially similar to that of *this* plaintiff. The test for copyright infringement is like the system one Supreme Court justice once said he used for determining whether a work was obscene. "I can't define it," he said, "but I know it if I see it."

Although it's not possible to pinpoint the border between infringing and non-infringing similarity, a map of the danger zone between the two exists in the form of copyright case law. Courts do not require plaintiffs to demonstrate that the defendants' works are nearly identical to their own works to prove substantial similarity. However, courts will not interpret even several small, unimportant similarities between the works in question as substantial similarity. In short, "substantial similarity" is just that: substantial. The *sort* of similarity between two works is just as important as the *degree* of similarity—the judgment of substantial similarity is both *qualitative* and *quantitative*.

Further, although plaintiffs in copyright infringement suits routinely hire expert witnesses—usually people who are very familiar with the sort of work that is the subject of litigation—to testify as to what similarities exist between the works at issue, courts judge whether those similarities are substantial by the "ordinary observer" test, which is a sort of "man on the street" view of the effect of those similarities. Courts try to decide whether an ordinary observer, reading or hearing or seeing two similar works for the first time, would believe that the "infringing" work and the "infringed" work were the same. If so, substantial similarity exists. This means that you already have the equipment you need—your own eyes and ears—to decide for yourself whether someone's work infringes yours.

Examples of Substantial Similiarity

Some examples of actions that will always result in infringement if the work copied is not a public domain work will help you to grasp the difficult concept of substantial similarity.

Outright duplication of significant portions of a work obviously results in substantial similarity. This sort of substantial similarity has been characterized as taking the fundamental substance of another's work and is the sort of copying that is often called simply "plagiarism."

Another sort of substantial similarity has been called "comprehensive literal similarity." This occurs when, as a whole, the accused work tracks the pattern of expression of the work said to have been infringed and uses the same theme or format. Close paraphrasing of an entire protected work or significant portions of it would produce this variety of substantial similarity.

A third variety of substantial similarity is the taking of portions of a work that are important to the impact and character of the work but that do not amount to a large portion of the infringing work. This sort of infringing substantial similarity points out the fact that what is significant is the importance of the material taken from the infringed work rather than simply the quantity of the infringing work that the stolen material constitutes. In other words, an infringer cannot escape responsibility for his or her actions by pointing out how much of the infringing work was *not* stolen.

Striking Similarity

There is one situation in which one part of the three-part test for copyright infringement need not be proved. That is the situation in which there is "striking similarity" between two works. Essentially, this is just a specialized application of the three-part infringement test. In cases where the similarity between the two works at issue is so striking that there is no explanation for such overwhelming similarity other than that one work was copied from the other, courts say that access may be assumed and the circumstances that made the infringement possible need not be reconstructed by the plaintiff. The "striking similarity" approach to proving infringement is rarely allowed by courts, which prefer to see plaintiffs prove every element of their cases.

Creator Beware

Copyright infringement is an area of real danger for creative people. Consequently, anyone who aspires to earn a living by exploiting the products of his or her imagination needs to know enough about copyright infringement to stay out of danger. People think that creating advertising copy, photography, or jingles are nice, safe jobs that can't get anyone in trouble. In reality, what you do with your typewriter, camera, or keyboard in your own little workspace can land you in federal court, where you will be asked to explain just *what* you did and *why* and *when* you did it.

If You Want to Be a Plaintiff

If you think someone has infringed your copyright, see a lawyer who's well versed in copyright law. Most lawyers will not charge you for an initial consultation about a possible copyright infringement case. You'll need the objective evaluation an experienced lawyer can give you, since creative people are notoriously poor judges of whether their works have actually been infringed. Your lawyer should be willing to tell you whether there has been an infringement and, if so, whether you're likely to prevail in court. If you don't like what the first lawyer you consult says, make an appointment with another for a second evaluation.

But don't wait too long before you take your suspicions of infringement to a lawyer because the "statute of limitations" (the period within which you must file suit) for copyright infringement is only three years from the date the infringer commits the infringing acts. (In the case of a continuing infringement, such as manufacturing a large number of copies of a pirated CD over a period of time, the statute runs from the date of the defendant's last infringing act.) After three years, your infringement suit may be barred. That is, the court will throw it out because you did not file it within the prescribed three-year period. You snooze, you lose.

If you win your copyright infringement suit, the court may issue a permanent injunction that prohibits any further use of the work that violates your copyright. It may order the seizure and destruction of any copies of the infringing work and award you "actual damages" (the profits the infringer made from the infringing work and the money you lost because of the infringement). As a practical matter, people who create advertising are paid more for their creative services than for the physical products that result from those services. This means that filing a copyright infringement suit against someone who steals your ad campaign may not net you much money—it may be that the harm that occurred is that your client or employer was indignant to find a carbon copy of the campaign you created for him in the morning paper advertising a competitor's products, rather than that the sale of thousands of unauthorized copies of your work unjustly enriched the defendant. The copyright statute deals with this common situation by providing that the court may award "statutory damages" (a range of money damages the court is allowed to award you in lieu of actual damages), plus the expenses of the suit that you've had to pay and attorneys' fees. Statutory damages are often awarded to punish the infringer without requiring the plaintiff to prove that the defendant made *what* profit on each of the *how many* unauthorized copies that were sold.

Use of a Work without Permission

An accusation of copyright infringement due to an unpermitted use of a copyrighted work is at least as dangerous for advertising creative and production people as a claim that they have infringed a copyright by unauthorized copying. As we have seen, use of a copyrighted work, and the right to control any such use, is one of the rights given to copyright owners by federal law. Unless you have acquired from the owner of a copyright the right to use the copyrighted work, either by license, assignment, or transfer (more later about these three ways of acquiring rights in a copyright), your use of it violates, or infringes, the rights of the owner. Since few advertising creative and production people create every element of every ad they produce for their clients or employers, a recurring situation in their professional lives is the necessity to acquire from someone else, either a creator or a copyright owner, the rights to use a photo or piece of music or written composition.

Most advertising and marketing people are accustomed to this process. They call up their favorite illustrator to produce a nice sketch of their client's new bank building to use on Christmas cards to be sent to the bank's customers. The illustrator produces the sketch, the cards are produced and sent, and everyone is happy. But what happens when the client bank wants to use the sketch on the calendars it hands out to its customers as promotional items, as well as on its new letterhead stationery and on its statement envelopes?

What should happen, and sometimes does not, is that the illustrator is paid for each additional use of his or her sketch. Because the illustrator is a freelancer working for the ad agency, he or she owns the sketch from its creation and continues to own it unless he or she signs some document transferring rights in the sketch to the agency or the bank. All that can be reliably assumed from the creation of the illustration is that the illustrator has given a nonexclusive license to use the sketch for the original project— the Christmas cards. Any additional use should produce an additional fee for the illustrator.

This rule is widely ignored. Agencies and clients almost routinely re-use elements of ads and whole campaigns without paying the actual owners of copyright in elements of those ads for the right to do so. In fact, most assume that because they commissioned the elements that are re-used, they own the copyright in them. This is never the case with a freelancer, unless the freelancer signs a work-for-hire agreement. It is, however, the situation with employees who create such materials as part of their jobs; their employers own the products of their labor on the job from the creation of those products. If you are a copywriter, graphic artist, or photographer employed full-time by an ad agency or advertising production company, you already know that your employer owns what you produce. If you are no one's employee, you may want to take a firmer stand against the sort of unthinking assumptions common among those who hire you that they own the copyrights in the materials you produce for them.

Acquiring Rights

Anyone who employs freelancers should adapt and routinely use one or all of the form agreements that are included in the appendix of this book. These agreements should be presented whenever any work produced by a freelancer is commissioned and should be delivered with the finished work; no check in payment for such work should be issued unless a signed agreement has been received. But play fair. Talk frankly with your freelancer about what use you expect to make of his or her creation and negotiate a fair price for the labor involved in the production of the copyrighted work *and* for the use that will be made of it. And if you or your client want to use a freelancer's work again, pay again for the right. Anything else is copyright infringement. If you acquire the right to use a work and then exceed the rights granted to you, you have violated the retained rights of the freelancer. Unless you acquire ownership of an entire copyright for the whole term of copyright, you are like a tenant who occupies a rented house past the expiration of the lease, or a farmer who rents one farm and proceeds to also cultivate fields he has not rented.

Often freelancers object to transferring ownership of their copyrights to those who will use them. This is because many commissioning parties routinely ask for an assignment of *all* the exclusive rights of copyright for the full term of copyright. This leaves the author of the work with no further control over use of the work for the period of time the transfer is effective. In cases like this, the best solution is a license of copyright tailored to the client's needs. Unfortunately, the people who commission work from freelancers often do not distinguish between payment for the services of a freelancer and payment for the right to use the copyrighted work the freelancer's services produce. Their attitude can be, *What do you mean I've only paid for your work writing this article? For* that *amount of money, I want to* own *it*. The best solution to this dilemma is to work it out in advance, when the work is commissioned. A forthright negotiation at that time can save disagreements later. And a written agreement documenting the deal that is struck eliminates later doubt.

The form agreements in the appendix can be easily modified for use in most situations where advertising producers employ freelancers or want to acquire rights in the works of freelancers. Make them part of your routine office procedure and file the signed agreements you negotiate in a safe place, since they may document rights that will endure for some years in the future. You may be able to forget them, but it is just as likely that you won't. If you need them, you'll be glad to find them in your file cabinet, waiting to eliminate whatever doubt you have about what you can do with a freelancer's work. For a more detailed discussion of copyright rights, ownership, and duration, see *The Copyright Guide* by Lee Wilson, from Allworth Press.

And never use any photo, music, or copy without having acquired the right to do so. Unless the material you use is in the public domain, such as an etching from a book published in 1830, you will be violating somebody's copyright rights. Ad people, who are accustomed to fast lives and instant gratification, sometimes don't feel like going to the trouble of investigating the copyright status of a work that they want to use. It can be hard to track down information on the owner of a photograph and harder still to get permission to use it. But it's necessary. Think how dumb you'd feel testifying in a copyright infringement suit that you didn't get permission to use the photograph because it looked like it would take about ten phone calls and all afternoon and you had a golf game that day. If you can't find the copyright owner or if the copyright owner withholds permission to use the work you want, that's that. Under ordinary circumstances, there is nothing in the law that compels a copyright owner to allow use of a work if he or she doesn't feel like it, no matter how much money you offer and no matter how badly you want it. There is, of course, one avenue left open to you in such a situation—take your own photo or write your own copy or compose your own music. Life's tough, but that's why they pay you the big bucks.

Defenses to Infringement

But there's a loophole, sort of. As in any civil or criminal litigation, the defendant in a copyright infringement suit may offer various arguments to demonstrate either that his or her actions did not infringe the plaintiff's rights or, if they did, that there are good reasons why the court should not punish the defendant. These arguments that a defendant makes in self-defense are called "defenses." Many defenses to charges of copyright infringement are technical in nature. Others are rarely used. By far, the most important and the most commonly used of such defenses is the defense of "fair use." It's important to know something about fair use, both to know when you've strayed past its boundaries and to understand that sometimes your own works may be used without your permission without giving rise to a copyright infringement lawsuit.

Fair Use

There are situations in which you may use parts of another person's copyrighted work without that person's permission and without infringing that person's copyright. This sort of use is called "fair use." The fair use defense can render otherwise infringing actions non-infringing.

Fair use is a kind of public policy exception to the usual standard for determining copyright infringement; that is, there is an infringing use of a copyrighted work but because of a countervailing public interest, that use is permitted and is not called infringement. Any use that is deemed by the law to be "fair" typically creates some social, cultural, or political benefit which outweighs any resulting harm to the copyright owner.

Courts consider a long list of factors in determining whether a use is "fair." The copyright statute identifies six purposes that will qualify a use as a possible fair use. They are uses made for the purpose of "criticism, comment, news reporting, teaching (including multiple copies for classroom use), scholarship, or research." Once any use of a copyrighted work has met this threshold test, that is, has been proved to have been made for one of these six purposes permitted in the statute, the use must be examined to determine whether it is indeed fair.

The copyright statute lists four factors that courts must weigh in determining fair use. They are:

1. THE PURPOSE AND CHARACTER OF THE USE, including whether such use is of a commercial nature or is for nonprofit educational purposes. (Educational, research, criticism, and news reporting uses are almost always fair; commercial uses, such as uses in advertising, are seldom fair uses.)

2. THE NATURE OF THE COPYRIGHTED WORK. (The permissible uses that may be made of informational works are considerably broader than permissible uses of creative works. However, courts have yet to permit the fair use defense to infringement in a case involving an *unpublished* work, where the private nature of the work is ordinarily protected.)

3. THE AMOUNT AND SUBSTANTIALITY OF THE PORTION USED IN RELATION TO THE COPYRIGHTED WORK AS A WHOLE. (This is the "substantial similarity" question again. It is quantitative and qualitative; that is, did you quote the twelve-page climactic scene of a

mystery novel, thereby disclosing the identity of the killer, or did you quote only a three-paragraph section that describes the city where the detective works?)

4. THE EFFECT OF THE USE UPON THE POTENTIAL MARKET FOR OR VALUE OF THE COPYRIGHTED WORK. (This evaluation is often determinative in a court's decision whether the use constitutes infringement. It is undoubtedly the most important of the four factors to be weighed in determining fair use. If the market for the copyrighted work is significantly diminished because of the purported fair use, then it is not a fair use. Fewer readers will want to buy a book if its most sensational and newsworthy sections have been previously excerpted in a magazine. A related factor that is considered is the effect of the purported fair use on any of the rights in the copyright of the work said to be infringed. If, without permission, one person writes and sells a screenplay based on another person's copyrighted novel, the right to prepare and sell a screen adaptation of the novel may have been lost to the author of that novel.)

The House Report that accompanied the 1976 Copyright Act is informative because it illustrates the scope of the fair use section of the statute with several examples of fair use:

> . . . quotation of excerpts in a review or criticism for purposes of illustration or comment; quotation of short passages in a scholarly or technical work, for illustration or clarification of the author's observations; use in a parody of some of the content of the work parodied; summary of an address or article, with brief quotations, in a news report; reproduction by a library of a portion of a work to replace part of a damaged copy; reproduction by a teacher or student of a small part of a work to illustrate a lesson; reproduction of a work in legislative or judicial proceedings or reports; incidental and fortuitous reproduction, in a newsreel or broadcast, of a work located in the scene of an event being reported.

Careful Fair Use

Care should be taken that any use of another person's copyrighted work without permission falls into one of the fair use exceptions to infringement. After all, no one wants to be a defendant in a copyright infringement lawsuit, even if the court eventually holds that the acts the plaintiff objects to are, in reality, permissible under the fair use doctrine. Keep the following rules in mind when you consider using someone else's work.

1. Quotations of short passages of copyrighted works, such as the sort of quoting found in book reviews or news stories, is generally safe in any context where the First Amendment protection of free speech can be reasonably invoked, even if the piece in which the quotation is used has a partially commercial purpose.

2. Parody of copyrighted works is not a permissible fair use unless the parody uses only so much of the parodied work as is necessary to "call to mind" the parodied work and is dangerous to attempt without very careful attention to the question of infringement. Anyone who must use more than a small segment or feature of a copyrighted work to make a parody of that work effective should consider approaching the owner of the copyright in the work for permission to use whatever portion of the work is necessary.

3. Direct quotations should always be attributed, as should closely paraphrased statements. It is very important to understand, however, that you cannot escape responsibility for copyright infringement simply by attributing the lifted portion of any work to its author; if the "borrowed" segment amounts to a substantial portion of the copyrighted work, attribution does not eradicate your sin. As indicated earlier, you should also avoid any use of even two- or three-paragraph direct quotations or close paraphrases if they embody the "meat" of the work from which they were taken or if use of them would diminish the salability of that work.

4. Working journalists and people affiliated with nonprofit institutions such as schools and churches have more latitude in using other people's copyrighted works than the average painter or writer or composer. A professor who duplicates a poem to use as a handout in an English class is probably not going to run afoul of the copyright owner of the poem. However, Kinko's encountered big trouble in the form of a lawsuit for copyright infringement when it disregarded this principle of the law of fair use. Without permission from the copyright holders, Kinko's was assembling from many sources "anthologies" consisting of writings taught in university courses and selling them to students. These makeshift anthologies hurt the market for the books that legitimately contained the copied writings. Kinko's lost the suit, and it has been remarkably attentive to the interests of copyright holders ever since.

5. Using unpublished works without permission is dangerous, even if the use is minimal. A tension exists between the owners of such materials and historians and other scholars who may want to quote from them. It is understandable that anyone who needs to reproduce in a biography or journal article long passages from the unpublished letters or manuscripts of his or her subject would dis-

like this restriction. However, the law protects the privacy of those who do not wish to make their writings public and does not require the owners of those copyrights to pay any attention at all to even the most valid requests for permission to reproduce and publish such works. Presently, only the most narrow uses may be made of unpublished works without the consent of the owner of copyright in them and disregarding restrictions placed on the use of unpublished materials is dangerous. Even close paraphrasing of such materials may be actionable.

In addition to these general rules, remember that people who create advertising are laboring under an even greater disability than most other people who want to make use of someone else's copyrighted work. Any such would-be "fair use" by an advertising creative professional is likely to be inherently a *commercial* use and it may be that there is no possibility that the use can be made without infringing the rights of the owner of the work so used. Whether this is always so depends greatly on the quantity and quality of the borrowed material. If in doubt whether you are about to infringe someone's rights, get a lawyer to review your proposed ad before you proceed with production. If you already have a lawyer "on tap," this can usually be accomplished by phone, fax, or even e-mail.

In any event, don't just assume that you can get away with it and no one will notice. We are, as a society, much more aware of our rights in intellectual property such as copyrights and trademarks than we once were. This goes double for people whose livelihood depends on their being able to profit from the creations of their imaginations. And our burgeoning communications media practically ensure that nothing published or broadcast is simply local anymore. Even if you publish your infringing ad only in Denver and the photographer whose photograph you used without permission works in Maine, his buddy in Colorado may fax it to him by the afternoon with the message "Isn't this photo a part of your 'America the Beautiful' series? Congratulations on selling it to the Giganto Corporation for their new ad campaign. I hope you were paid well." Get the picture? In determining whether your work infringes someone else's copyright, let your conscience be your guide; if you think that you have taken more than inspiration from another copyrighted work, you could very well have stepped over the meandering boundary between permissible use of another's work and "substantial similarity."

If You Become a Defendant

If someone sues you for copyright infringement and is able to prove to the court that an infringement took place, that copyright owner may obtain an injunction to halt further sales, distribution, or dissemination of the infringing work and you could be forced to pay a substantial judgment, including any profits you have made from the infringement and, possibly, the attorneys' fees and costs of the successful plaintiff. The lawyers' fees incurred in defending a copyright infringement suit through trial can be, in themselves, enormous, even if the judgment is not. And even if the case is settled before it goes to trial, you still may have to pay a cash settlement to the plaintiff, as well as your lawyer's fees for handling the case to the point of settlement. Finding yourself on the receiving end of these remedies for infringement will make you regret that you were ever so foolish as to trifle with the copyright of the plaintiff.

Is It Infringement?

Q. *Your boss puts you in charge of writing the sales training manual that will be sent out to all the branch offices of your company. You are a fan of Mark McCormack's book* What They Don't Teach You at Harvard Business School *and decide to "paraphrase" two chapters of this bestseller as sections of your training manual. You proudly present the finished manual to your boss, who takes it home to read over the weekend. You are chagrined and surprised when he demands to see you first thing Monday morning. It seems that your boss is also a fan of Mr. McCormack and has recognized the source material for the two "paraphrased" sections of the manual. He says that you and your company could be sued by McCormack and his publisher. You are almost sure that paraphrasing McCormack's material is all it takes to eliminate the threat of any lawsuit. Is it infringement?*

A. Yes, of the most blatant sort. While it is permissible to quote authorities in any field ("McCormack believes that . . .") or even to cite their theories without attribution ("Many business theorists hold that . . ."), use of whole chunks of their writings is a violation of their rights and the rights of their publishers, to whom they have assigned the exclusive right to reproduce and disseminate their works. When you "paraphrased" Mr. McCormack's chapters, you followed them line by line and simply changed the way his ideas were expressed. While no one's *ideas* are protected by copyright, their expressions are protected. Your paraphrasing was a bodily theft of Mr. McCormack's expressions of his ideas. The fact that you changed Mr. McCormack's words makes little difference, since the sections of your training manual based on his chapters are simply reworded duplications of his statements. That's copying of protected expression. *And* substantial similarity. Your boss is also right that both you *and* your employer can be sued for copyright infringement. As a full-time employee, you are an agent of your company. Any action that you take during the course of performing your duties as an employee is attributable to your company. Your boss is one smart guy. Maybe that's why he's the boss. Next time, if you can't come up with your own material, either hire someone to write your manual (on a work-for-hire basis) or copy *The Prince* by Niccolo Machiavelli, written in 1513, or *The Art of War by Sun Tzu,* written more than 2,500 years ago. But stay strictly away from the work of anyone who ever saw an electric lightbulb.

Q. *You reprint the entire text of Martin Luther King, Jr.'s famous "I Have a Dream" speech on "parchment" paper in a form suitable for framing for your employer, a small and struggling but well-regarded liberal arts college, which sells the printed speeches for ten dollars each to raise money for a new library. Is it infringement?*

A. Almost certainly. Any use of the full text for Dr. King's 1963 speech without the permission of his estate constitutes infringement, especially if that use is made for commercial gain, as in this situation. It is possible that you could successfully argue that your otherwise infringing use of the speech is actually a "fair use" because it was made on behalf of and for the benefit of a nonprofit educational institution, but it is more likely that a court would, at the very least, require your college to pay a royalty on each copy of the King speech sold. The King estate could also ask the court to stop the sale of the speech, to compel the destruction of all unsold copies of it, and to make the college, your employer, pay it the profits from all sales made. Even national heroes have copyright rights.

Q. *You want to use Grant Wood's famous painting* American Gothic *in a magazine ad for your travel agency ("Bored at Home?"), so you shoot a copy of it from an Art Institute of Chicago guidebook, blow it up a little, add copy, and run the ad in the travel section of the Sunday paper. Is it infringement?*

A. Yes. You are in double trouble with this ad. Grant Wood painted *American Gothic* in 1930. Although he died in 1942, the copyright in the painting, which will endure through the end of 2025 if it was renewed after the first twenty-eight-year term of copyright protection, is owned by his estate. Not only did you not have the right to use Wood's painting without permission, you also did not have the right to copy the photograph of the painting. The Art Institute of Chicago owns the copyright in that photograph and your copying the photo without permission may constitute a second infringement of copyright. You'd better bone up on the duration of U.S. copyrights so you will know, in the future, that U.S. copyrights generally last until seventy years after the death of the author of the copyrighted work, which means that the copyrights in many famous works will not expire until well after you do.

Q. *You use, on the cover of your corporation's annual report, a photo of a small segment of a* Wall Street Journal *article that contains a twenty-five-word quotation naming your corporation as an innovator in its field. Is it infringement?*

A. No. Your use of the *Wall Street Journal* quotation is a fair use of that publication's copyrighted story in two ways: it is a properly attributed short quote used in a First Amendment context, since the annual report is the corporation's way of informing its stockholders about the corporation, and you used only a small portion of the *Journal* story, not enough to constitute "substantial similarity" between the text of the annual report and the *Journal* story. Reprinting the whole story without permission for distribution to stockholders would be a different matter.

Q. *You own an auto dealership and advertise yourself as "The Super-Dealer." In your newest ads, which you dreamed up yourself, you use a photo of yourself dressed in blue long johns, a red cape, and a wide gold belt, standing shoulder-to-shoulder with those other super-heroes, Batman and Superman, who appear as their original cartoon-figure, comic-book selves. Is it infringement?*

A. Yes, two kinds. You infringed the copyright rights of the publishers from whose comic books you copied the cartoon figures you used and you infringed their trademark rights by using the well-known super-heroes to attract attention to your ads. You are in more trouble for your trademark transgression than for your copyright infringement. Duck into a phone booth and disguise yourself as a smarter person.

Q. *Armed with a brand-new diploma in hotel/restaurant management, you go to work for your Uncle Vito, helping him run his restaurant, Vito's. Driving to the restaurant on your second day of work, you hear on your favorite oldies station the Billy Joel standard "My Italian Restaurant." You get the great idea to use the song as the background for the new radio and television spots you talked your uncle into the day before. You buy a copy of the Billy Joel album that includes "My Italian Restaurant," get your uncle to narrate the spots, and rush to get them on the air. Your uncle loves the spots and you begin to think about asking for a raise.*

Then one morning your uncle receives by certified mail a "cease and desist" letter from a New York law firm representing Billy Joel's record company and music publishing company. The letter informs your uncle that his use of the Billy Joel recording of the song "My Italian Restaurant" in ads for Vito's is an infringement of the copyright rights of both the record company, which owns the copyright in the recording of the song, and the music publishing company, which owns the copyright in the song itself. Your uncle calls you and wakes you up to ask "Is it infringement?"

A. Yes. The New York lawyers are right. They demand that your Uncle Vito immediately "cease" use of the recording or song and "desist" from any additional use of either and offer to forego filing suit if your uncle pays a settlement of $10,000 within thirty days, in lieu of the licensing fees they would have charged had he contacted them before using the song and recording. The lawyer you and your uncle consult brushes aside your arguments that, since no more than sixty seconds of the recording were used in any spot, your use of the song and recording does not constitute infringement and that, in any event, your uncle shouldn't be sued, since neither you nor he *intended* to trespass on anyone's rights. Your lawyer says that any broadcast of any recording of a copyrighted song in a *commercial* context is infringement if it is made without the permission of the owners of the copyrights in the recording and in the song because it is a violation of the copyright owners' exclusive right to control performances of their copyrighted recording and song. He says that using sixty seconds or thirty seconds or even ten seconds of a three-minute recording is more than sufficient to eliminate any argument that Vito's use of "My Italian Restaurant" was merely an incidental, "fair" use of the song and recording. He tells you that it is immaterial that you did not realize that your actions amounted to infringement, since copyright infringement is judged by evaluating the quantity, quality, and context of the use of the copyrighted work, *not* by gauging the wrongful intent of the accused infringer.

When you make your brilliant argument that you know for a fact (because you once had a summer job as a deejay) that radio stations do not call up record companies and music publishing companies to ask permission before playing each recording they broadcast, your lawyer reminds you that radio stations (and other users of copyrighted recordings) pay license fees each year to the performing rights organizations that collect such fees on behalf of songwriters and publishers. Uncle Vito settles. You are out of bright ideas. And out of a job.

CHAPTER 8

Choosing Protectable Trademarks

I N ADDITION TO COMING UP WITH A NEW TRADEMARK THAT WILL GRAB the attention of consumers and determining that it will not infringe an established trademark, it is important to consider whether the name or symbol you choose will be eligible for federal trademark registration. This is, or should be, an area of concern for anyone who participates in the process of proposing and creating new trademarks, since many of the potential problems that the trademark owner may eventually encounter with the new trademark can be completely eliminated when the trademark is first conceived.

There are two types of trademark registration: 1) state trademark registration, which is cheap and easy to obtain and confers some benefits, and 2) federal trademark registration, which is not easy to obtain, but which confers much greater benefits. Since most trademark owners want to be able to register their marks federally, that is, with the U.S. Patent and Trademark Office, we will discuss restrictions on federal trademark registration.

The federal trademark statute, which governs trademark registration, imposes certain restrictions on which marks can be granted federal registration. The inherent characteristics of the mark determine whether these restrictions will prevent the eventual registration of the trademark. Problems posed by these restrictions can be largely eliminated by carefully avoiding a few varieties of marks that can cause the Trademark Office to deny a registration application.

The Ten Deadly Sins of Trademark Selection

There are ten reasons the Trademark Office will deny federal registration to a trademark (other than defects in the form of the application or some other procedural problem). They are the following:

1. THE MARK IS CONFUSINGLY SIMILAR TO A TRADEMARK THAT IS ALREADY FEDERALLY REGISTERED. The test the Trademark Office uses to determine whether your mark is "confusingly similar" to a registered mark is the same "sight, sound, and meaning" test used by judges in trademark infringement suits to decide whether the plaintiff does indeed have grounds to complain about the defendant's use of its name. However, the only thing the Trademark Office will do to you if you adopt a name that's too close to a registered trademark is deny your application to register your name. Any liability that may be incurred by the infringing use of the previously registered mark is beyond the purview of the Trademark Office; it remains the job of the owner of the registered mark to sue you (or your client, which might be just as big a misfortune).

2. THE WORD OR, MORE TYPICALLY, THE SYMBOL FOR WHICH REGISTRATION IS SOUGHT DOES NOT FUNCTION AS A TRADEMARK, THAT IS, DOES NOT ACT IN THE MARKETPLACE TO IDENTIFY THE SOURCE OF THE GOODS OR SERVICES TO WHICH IT IS APPLIED. This basis for refusing federal registration is most often cited in applications for design marks that the Trademark Office believes are being used on goods merely for purposes of ornamentation rather than in any way that indicates the source of the products. In other words, the famous JORDACHE® jeans hip pocket embroidery designs may not have achieved federal trademark registration if they had not become "distinctive of the goods," that is, if they had not begun to function to indicate to consumers that the jeans that bore them were manufactured by Jordache. The same could be said of the NIKE® "swoop" design that has become almost as well-known as the Nike name.

3. THE MARK IS "IMMORAL, DECEPTIVE, OR SCANDALOUS." To be rejected for registration on this ground, a name has to be blatant. Some marks that are slightly risqué make it to registration, but none that are really off-color or offensive will be granted registration. Usually mild double entendres, obscure sexual slang, and all but the most shockingly vicious phrases or symbols will pass muster with the trademark examiner who reviews your registra-

tion application, even though it is the examiner's job to try diligently to figure out why it should not be granted. Before you cry "First Amendment" and "government censorship," bear in mind that the Trademark Office will not, no matter how much it hates a trademark, forbid its use; the government just draws the line at registering any immoral, deceptive, or scandalous name. In any case, you should avoid proposing any really offensive name for your or your client's product or service because consumers may object to it and may have an aversion to requesting it from retailers. Moreover, some advertising media may refuse to air or publish ads that include the offending name.

The "deceptive" part of this restriction is usually not much of a problem unless your proposed mark is going to get you or your client in hot water anyway. For instance, if you get the bright idea to call a line of cubic zirconia jewelry BUDGET TIFFANY because your client intends to copy the famous jewelry retailer's designs and you intend to imitate its famous robin's-egg-blue packaging, the Trademark Office will deny any application to register the name on the ground that, because your client has no connection whatsoever with the famous jeweler, the name is deceptive. But by the time your client receives the Trademark Office's rejection of its application, the mark will already be in litigation initiated by the lawyers for Tiffany's, for the offenses of trademark infringement and trade dress infringement.

(Trademark infringement is a civil offense, which means that infringers are sued in civil courts, not brought up on criminal charges by the district attorney. Infringers pay for their transgressions in dollars, not days in jail. Which is funny, if you think about it, because if someone breaks into your apartment and steals your stereo, he can be imprisoned, but if he infringes your hard-won trademark, which is like stealing your reputation, he won't go to jail, even though his infringement of your trademark may have cost you a lot more than your stereo was worth.)

4. THE MARK DISPARAGES OR FALSELY SUGGESTS A CONNECTION WITH PERSONS, INSTITUTIONS, BELIEFS, OR NATIONAL SYMBOLS, OR BRINGS THEM INTO CONTEMPT OR DISREPUTE. This restriction is similar to the "immoral, deceptive, or scandalous" restriction. For example, if you want to call your rock band TRICKY DICK in honor of the only U.S. president ever to resign from office, that's your business, but the Trademark Office may deny your application to register that name on the ground that it dis-

parages Richard Nixon. It doesn't matter that TRICKY DICK is merely a nickname for Richard Nixon. It doesn't even matter that he is now deceased. And your arguments that Mr. Nixon's reputation would be hard to hurt aren't going to make the slightest difference to the Trademark Office.

Applications that imply nonexistent connections with particular well-known institutions will also be denied. For instance, the Trademark Office would not grant a registration to a home-security company called F.B.I. SECURITY; call your company LAW ENFORCEMENT ALARMS, though, and you may be able to register the name. Ditto for a restaurant named SEARS AND ROEBUCK, or HARVARD for scholastic aptitude tests.

And no matter how clever you think it is, the Trademark Office will refuse to register any name or logo that disparages any belief or national symbol. If you're a group of Jewish cantors who sing traditional Jewish songs at wedding receptions you may be able to call yourselves STARS OF DAVID and convince the Trademark Office to register the name, since your use of it would not be disparaging. However, you wouldn't be able to register that name for any rock band without running into some trouble from the Trademark Office, which could reasonably interpret your use of the name or symbol as disparaging.

The same goes for crucifixes. If you manufacture and sell white chocolate crucifixes under the name IMMACULATE CONFECTIONS, don't expect the Trademark Office to allow you to register that mark. In fact, the same obstacle will be encountered by anyone who attempts to register any name or symbol dear to the adherents of any religion, including Eastern religions as well as more familiar Western belief systems.

All this is also true for "national symbols." If you design as the trademark for a nightclub a logo depicting Uncle Sam wearing red lipstick and rouge, white theatrical makeup, and blue eyeshadow, the Trademark Office will turn down any application to register the logo, even if your only goal in depicting Uncle Sam in such a manner is to make him look like the female impersonators who appear at the club. Your manner of using the famous American symbol will be interpreted by the Trademark Office as bringing it into contempt or disrepute.

5. THE MARK CONSISTS OF OR SIMULATES THE FLAG OR COAT OF ARMS OR OTHER INSIGNIA OF THE UNITED STATES OR OF A STATE OR MUNICIPALITY OR A FOREIGN NATION. The American flag, for

instance, belongs equally to every American citizen. Since trademark registration gives the registrant the exclusive right to use the registered mark, the trademark statute prohibits the registration of any mark that consists of the American flag. This doesn't mean you can't use the American flag as a part of a logo design; you just can't register that flag logo as a trademark. (If your logo includes the American flag only as a small part of a larger design, you may be able to register the entire design by disclaiming any exclusive right in the flag portion of it.)

The same holds true for other official symbols from just about everywhere. The manufacturer of a line of women's dresses named LA FRANCE cannot register the French flag as its trademark. Nor can a restaurant called THE LONE STAR CAFÉ register the state flag of Texas as its logo.

6. THE MARK IS THE NAME, PORTRAIT, OR SIGNATURE OF A PARTIC-
   ULAR LIVING INDIVIDUAL WHO HAS NOT GIVEN HIS OR HER CON-
   SENT FOR USE OF THE MARK, OR IS THE NAME, SIGNATURE, OR
   PORTRAIT OF A DECEASED PRESIDENT OF THE UNITED STATES
   DURING THE LIFE OF HIS OR HER SURVIVING SPOUSE, UNLESS THAT
   SPOUSE HAS GIVEN CONSENT TO USE OF THE MARK. The Trademark Office cannot grant exclusive rights in the name or likeness
   of a living person without the consent of that person. This is an
   easy restriction to understand. How would you feel if you woke
   up one morning and found that the Trademark Office had given
   somebody else the exclusive right to use your name for a product or service without your permission? You'd be upset, right?
   Well, everybody feels the same way, which is why you have to
   prove to the Trademark Office that any living person whose
   name you use as a trademark consents to that use before you can
   register the name.

   However, you can call your outdoor-equipment shop DR.
   LIVINGSTONE, I PRESUME, after the famous Englishman who
   explored Africa, or name your line of women's cosmetics CLEO-
   PATRA'S SECRET or bottled olive oil DA VINCI. David Livingstone, Cleopatra, and Leonardo Da Vinci were all real people, but
   "were" is the operative verb. They are no longer living and are,
   therefore, no longer in a position to object to your use, without
   permission, of their names or to profit themselves from such
   uses. (Consider, for example, SHAKESPEARE fishing rods; no one
   had to ask the famous bard for his permission to use his name as
   a trademark.)

A caveat, however. Recall that famous people acquire with their fame the "right of publicity," and that sometimes this right can be inherited by descendants. Basically, the right of publicity is a celebrity's right to be the only person who profits from the use of her or his famous name. (See chapter 6 for a more detailed explanation of this right and how it works.) This means that you should not only avoid choosing as a trademark the name of any living person but should also be very careful about adopting the name or even the nickname of any famous figure who died after, say, 1900.

Remember that this restriction applies even if your client owns the company that will own the proposed trademark. Honest. Paul Newman had to give his written consent before the trademark used to market his salad dressings and spaghetti sauces, NEWMAN'S OWN®, could be registered. Ditto for Dolly Parton and the DOLLYWOOD® amusement park, and Oprah Winfrey and the popular OPRAH® television show.

So much for living people. The dead presidents restriction is sort of a leftover from when companies were likely to name their products after popular politicians in an effort to appeal to the people who made the politicians popular—you know, "TEDDY ROOSEVELT MOUSTACHE WAX." This restriction is of less concern to marketers than many of the others in the Trademark Office's long list of types of unregistrable marks, but it could play a role in your choice of a name for a new product. For example, during the lifetime of Jacqueline Kennedy Onassis you could not have registered the name JFK for rocking chairs similiar to the one used by the late president without her permission. The trademark statute doesn't say what happens if the dead president is female; presumably, her widower would have to consent to any use of her name. (Apparently the men—they were men—who wrote our trademark statute back in the forties thought that the possibility of a woman being elected president was so slender as to be nonexistent, so they specifically worded the statute in terms of deceased male presidents.)

7. THE MARK IS "MERELY DESCRIPTIVE" OF THE GOODS OR SERVICES IT NAMES. Many marketing people hate this restriction and make rude noises when their lawyers remind them of it, since they believe that the more a new product name describes the product or service it names, the better a trademark it is. If you think about it, you will realize that this is not the case.

In actuality, the best trademarks are fanciful, that is, they don't mean anything much, they just capture the imagination and come to signify the particular product they name rather than being equally applicable to any product of the same kind, which is the case with marks that are descriptive. Think of KLEENEX® or EXXON® or WISK®; none of those marks mean anything as ordinary English words, but they each immediately bring to mind the specific products marketed under them.

Besides this important consideration, there is the fact that the Trademark Office almost always disallows an application to register a descriptive mark. It will not allow, by virtue of a federal trademark registration, one company to bar all others from using what are simply ordinary words to describe a product or service. If you ask yourself whether a proposed mark would tell consumers what a product or service is, or in the case of names for publications, by whom the publication is intended to be read, you can ferret out descriptive marks before they are adopted and later turned down for federal registration.

Now, it must be said that there are many trademarks that are very descriptive that are currently registered in the U.S. Patent and Trademark Office. These marks, for the most part, started out as unqualified for registration because of their descriptiveness but later, because of the fame they acquired as the products or services they named became well known, came to signify to consumers the products or services of their particular companies. In short, after a while the Trademark Office will reconsider allowing registration of descriptive marks that have achieved some fame. But at the trademark selection stage in the history of a product, this exception to the descriptiveness restriction should not make any difference to anyone who wants to come up with a mark that won't have to work at becoming eligible for federal registration.

8. THE MARK IS "DECEPTIVELY MISDESCRIPTIVE" OF THE GOODS OR SERVICES IT NAMES. This restriction on registration is akin to some of those mentioned above, designed to deter the adoption of misleading or distasteful trademarks. "Deceptively misdescriptive" means a mark that falsely suggests that a product or service has some characteristic that it does not indeed possess—in other words, the mark describes what it names, but falsely.

For example, LAPIS for a line of blue glass-bead jewelry would not be granted registration, since the Trademark Office would hold that the word "lapis," when used for blue jewelry not made of the semiprecious stone lapis lazuli, was a "deceptively misdescriptive" name that could mislead consumers. The same argument would apply to, say, TOP GRAIN for vinyl luggage, SILK-SHIRT for women's polyester blouses, or PURE GOLD for jewelry that is merely gold-plated.

This restriction against registering deceptively misdescriptive marks is intended primarily to discourage actual attempts to mislead consumers, but it should not be disregarded if your intent is to use an ironic name as a trademark. You may get the joke in your new mark, but the Trademark Office will not be persuaded to register it by the mere fact that the name is funny if it transgresses one of the trademark statute's restrictions on registrability. For example, DR. FEELGOOD'S HEALTH TONIC used for bottled beer may not be registrable, no matter how much you or consumers like the name for its wackiness.

9. THE MARK IS "PRIMARILY GEOGRAPHICALLY DESCRIPTIVE OR DECEPTIVELY MISDESCRIPTIVE" OF THE GOODS OR SERVICES IT NAMES. When the name of a product or service includes a geographic term or place name, such as the name of a river or mountain, that either tells where the product or service comes from or suggests falsely that it comes from a place that it does not, that name will run afoul of this restriction when its owner seeks to register the mark federally. The general rule has long been that if the Trademark Office can find a geographic term in any atlas or gazetteer, registration will be denied to the mark that contains it.

The reasoning behind the first part of this restriction is that if a product comes from a geographic region named in its mark, the registration of the mark would unfairly deny other manufacturers from the same region the right to use the geographic term to describe their products. For example, CARRARA STONE for marble from Italy would be unregistrable because more than one company markets marble building materials quarried from the famous deposits at Carrara and the phrase "Carrara stone" applies equally to all such products.

The reason for the second part of the restriction, that registration will be denied to any mark that suggests a nonexistent geographic origin, is similar. If the marble was not quarried in Italy at Carrara, the name CARRARA STONE would be geographically deceptively misdescriptive because it would lead consumers to a false conclusion about the origins of the stone. This restriction has more application to manufacturers of cheese, wine, bottled water, and other products tied to certain regions than it does to the marketers of most other products, but it can have an unexpected effect on the uninitiated.

The restriction on registration of geographic marks also applies to graphic representations of a state or country. If your entire logo is the map of a state or some other recognizable representation of a piece of the world, the Trademark Office will deny it registration.

Now bear in mind that you can make up fictitious place names all day long and your clients can register them as trademarks; EMERALD CITY for mobile homes or BIG ROCK CANDY MOUNTAIN for sugar cubes would be registrable. And you can use actual place names in purely fanciful ways because no one will be likely to believe that they are used to indicate the origin of a product or service. KENYA for safari-style sport clothing would be registrable and BLUE DANUBE® has long been used for a china pattern.

And remember that, as is the case with some other restrictions on registration, famous marks enjoy different rules. (Consider the country music stars, the group ALABAMA®, for example.) When a geographically descriptive name that the Trademark Office considers unregistrable comes to signify only the product or service it names, it becomes registrable because, in effect, its fame enables it to escape the anonymity inherent in a geographic name and to function as a trademark. But trademark fame is not always easy to achieve and it is a much better idea, when adopting a new mark, to choose one that won't have to outshine competing marks before achieving registrability.

10. THE MARK IS PRIMARILY A SURNAME. Personal names have long been considered not to be inherently distinctive when used as trademarks, which is another way of saying that they are descriptive or generic and can't, in and of themselves, point to a particular source for a product.

Think of this example: There are four zillion people in the United States named Smith, so the source of SMITH'S SOCKS for children could be anyone in the country whose name is Smith. Moreover, until one SMITH'S SOCKS became well-known enough to transcend the anonymity of most surname marks, all the Smiths in the United States could market socks using their mutual surname without infringing each other's trademark rights,

because none of them would *have* any protectable legal right in
that name. In other words, surname marks do not work as trademarks until they have achieved something called "secondary
meaning," which is a term trademark lawyers use to mean
"Everybody knows that trademark because it's so famous."

Now, obviously, there are many famous surname trademarks
that have been granted federal trademark registration by the
Trademark Office. That is because WATERMAN® for fountain
pens, SMITH BROTHERS® for cough drops, CAMPBELL'S® for soups,
LIPTON® for tea, WILSON® for sporting goods, HOOVER® for vac-
uum cleaners, and CRANE® for stationery are all trademarks that
have risen above anonymity by virtue of having achieved strong
reputations in the marketplace. Since a trademark represents the
reputation of a product or service in the market, this is just a way
of saying that over the years these surname marks have achieved
trademark status sufficient to persuade the Trademark Office to
allow their registration.

Design Elements of Marks

It is important to remember that all the restrictions on registration listed
above can also apply to design trademarks or trademarks that combine
graphic elements and words. You may be able to get away with proposing,
and your client may be able to register, BON VIVANT for a "parfum" that is
actually manufactured in New Jersey without running into the geographically misdescriptive restriction on registration. But use a map of France as
the background for the words BON VIVANT on the perfume bottle labels
and the Trademark Office will reject the application to register the mark.

Similarly, although ASTRONAUT for children's pajamas would, alone, be
registrable, the use of the word "astronaut" in conjunction with sketches of
Alan Shepard and Sally Ride without their permission would cause the registration application to be rejected. (In addition, this use would probably
result in a suit for infringement of the astronauts' right of publicity.)

A caveat. Despite having a whole book of written-down rules to
operate by, the Trademark Office, like God, often moves in mysterious
ways. This means that all of the above statements about what are and are
not registrable trademarks are subject to some Trademark Office exceptions, whims, and inconsistencies. However, it is important to choose a
trademark that can be registered, because many unregistrable marks are also
all but unprotectable. That is, it may be next to impossible to prevent someone else from using an unregistrable mark, depending on the characteristics of the mark. Marketers invest millions every year in promoting and

publicizing their trademarks and want to be able to be the only ones who benefit from these expenditures. This may be impossible if the marks they choose are unregistrable.

That's where advertising creative people, in agencies and in-house, can earn their paychecks. Propose only marks that you believe can be registered federally by using the "Ten Deadly Sins of Trademark Selection" list as a guideline in selecting proposed marks. Leave the final opinion as to the registrability of any proposed mark to someone who pays for malpractice insurance—your trademark lawyer. You don't have to function as a trademark lawyer in order to do your job, but you can forestall a great many problems if you know a little about what you are doing when you create a new trademark.

CHAPTER 9

Clearing New Trademarks for Use

T
RADEMARK INFRINGEMENT IS A REAL DANGER FOR ANY AGENCY, STU-
dio, marketing department, or business that creates a new trademark,
which can be any symbol, word, name, or combination of elements
that is used to represent a company and its products or services in
commerce. Both international and domestic trade are burgeoning in
the United States. This means that trademarks are proliferating and that it
is much more difficult than it once was to come up with a trademark that
is not too similar to an older, more established mark. This chapter is
designed to tell you how to do your best to avoid being accused of or sued
for trademark infringement, which can be very big trouble indeed for those
who don't recognize the pitfalls that are possible in the process of naming
a new product. Doing your best to keep your client and yourself out of
trademark infringement lawsuits is called "trademark clearance." It is a
process that is critically important to everyone involved in the creation of
new trademarks.

Avoiding Established Marks

The first step in avoiding infringing an established trademark is to con-
sciously avoid choosing for any product or service a name or design that is
identical or closely similar to another trademark that is already in use for a
similar or related product or service.

This seems too obvious to mention, but it needs to be said. More than
a few trademark infringement lawsuits have been filed because someone
mistakenly thought that because a name or design worked once it could
work again. This means that in developing ideas for a new trademark, you

should ask anybody who proposes one where the idea came from. Ignorance of trademark law will not save you from a trademark infringement lawsuit if you step on the toes of a trademark owner determined to protect its established mark.

And it doesn't matter that you came up with the proposed new trademark without the knowledge of the established mark that it infringes; if it infringes the older mark, the source of your proposed mark is irrelevant. Nor will changing a few letters or design elements in an existing mark, or spelling it differently, or even combining it with other words or symbols save you from a charge of infringement, unless the changes you make are so significant that they eradicate the confusing similarity between the old and new marks.

Trademark Searches

The second important way to avoid trademark disputes is the trademark search, which is a search made by a professional trademark search firm to locate any established trademarks that are similar enough to your proposed mark to be confused with it. The trademark search firm will examine federal and state trademark registration records and data on unregistered but currently used marks and will compile data on marks similar to the proposed mark in a trademark search report.

Because this data needs interpretation, which is not furnished by the trademark search firm, you really need a lawyer for a trademark search, contrary to what you will hear occasionally from even reputable trademark search firms. A lawyer will properly instruct the search firm as to the direction and scope of the search when commissioning it, evaluate the raw data in the search report, and give a legal opinion assessing the degree of risk, if any, involved if the proposed mark is adopted. And not just any lawyer will do. You need a *trademark lawyer* to conduct a trademark search after you have narrowed your proposed marks to two or three possibilities.

Be prepared to find out that your favorite proposed mark is already being used by someone else; it happens every day to some designer or advertising creative person who spent weeks developing what she or he believed to be a unique new mark. The good news is that it is much easier and much less expensive to discard a proposed mark before any money is spent advertising it than to abandon a new trademark six months into your first big promotion of it.

Advising the Trademark Owner

Of course, if you own or work for an ad agency or graphic design studio and are given the task of creating a mark for a client, you can't compel your client to hire a trademark search firm. However, you can make sure that you formally recommend, in writing, that your client conduct a search to "clear" the mark you suggest. Your job is to help choose a mark that works for the new product or service and, above all, doesn't cause problems. At the very least, you want to avoid being blamed for any problems that may result from the new mark. If you routinely recommend trademark searches, you won't lose the confidence of your clients because of what they perceive to be your negligence. Although it is not your *legal* responsibility to determine that any mark you propose to a client will not infringe someone else's mark, a client who has been hit with a trademark infringement suit may fail to make that distinction. Clients will always be fickle, but trademark searches give them one less basis for deciding that you should be replaced.

All this is also true for in-house creative and marketing people, except that for them the stakes are higher. If you work for a company and are asked to name a new product or service, failing to recommend a trademark search could cost you your job. Unless you know that your company's legal department, if there is one, or an outside law firm is handling a search, recommend one at the very beginning of the trademark selection process. The least that will happen is that you will look like you are doing your job; the best result of your recommendation may be that you save your employer a great deal of money by averting an avoidable problem.

Most experienced marketing people view trademark searches as a necessary part of the process of launching new products or services. It's your obligation to point out the pitfalls inherent in ignoring the fact that adopting a trademark without investigating its availability can result in real trouble. Any professional learns that part of success in business is "encouraging" clients and employers, in a loud voice if necessary, to do what is best. This is your line: "Mr. Jones, I'm sure a man of your experience understands the necessity for a search to clear this proposed mark for use before you invest a zillion dollars in it. When may I expect to see a copy of the search report?" Nobody is happy with anybody else after any business dispute, and trademark infringement lawsuits are likely to have everyone involved in the creation of the offending trademark pointing an accusing finger at everyone else. Luckily, you can help eliminate much of the risk in adopting a new trademark simply by remembering that the risk exists and advising your client or boss to take steps to avoid it.

Preliminary Searching

Even though you need a lawyer to interpret the raw data in a trademark search report, it is possible for you, by yourself, to conduct a preliminary search to eliminate some unavailable marks early in the trademark selection process. This is possible by using a trademark directory or an online or CD-ROM trademark database.

By consulting a trademark database—in either print or electronic form—at the point in the trademark selection process when you have narrowed your choices for the new mark to three or four names, you can eliminate any marks that are already registered or are the subject of pending registration applications. This saves the expense of conducting a full trademark search for every possible name and speeds up the selection process by halting your further consideration of marks that are already registered or are soon to be registered for products or services similar to the one for which you are selecting a mark.

Trademark directories or databases list trademarks that are registered and therefore already in use by someone else. Marks are listed alphabetically, according to the category of product or service they name or designate. Using a trademark directory or database correctly takes a little practice and requires a basic knowledge of what constitutes trademark infringement, but anybody who can use a dictionary can learn to use either as effectively as a lawyer. There is one print directory of word marks. It is *The Trademark Register,* which includes trademarks currently registered in the U.S. Patent and Trademark Office as well as applications that are published and pending in the Trademark Office. Marks are listed by the class of goods or services they name and are searchable by the first word of the mark only. No information is given on owners of the marks listed. At more than two thousand pages, the 2000 edition of *The Trademark Register* is priced at $495. It offers information current through the end of the year preceding publication. *The Trademark Register* is available from The Trademark Register, Suite 2100, National Press Building, Washington, DC 20045 or by calling (202) 347-2138.

Such directories can be very useful in eliminating from consideration any mark that is unavailable because of a current or pending registration in the U.S. Patent and Trademark Office, but they are not updated as frequently as online and CD-ROM databases, they do not contain as much information about the marks they list, and they make searching for internal verbal elements of marks difficult. Fortunately, there is a good and inexpensive online search resource. The leading U.S. trademark search service, Thomson and Thomson, offers the Saegis online trademark database. You must become a Saegis subscriber to use this database, but there is no initial fee and the use charges, which are based on the number of records you view and their format, are reasonable. For information on Saegis call Thomson and Thomson Online Services at (888) 477-3447 or write the company at Thomson and Thomson, 500 Victory Road, North Quincy, MA 02171-3145.

Both Thomson and Thomson and The Trademark Register also maintain Web sites that offer information about their products and services. Thomson and Thomson's Web site address is *www.thomson-thomson.com.* The Trademark Register maintains a Web site at *www.trademarkregister.com.*

It is very important to realize that looking up a proposed trademark in a trademark directory or database and failing to find it listed as an already registered mark does not necessarily mean that the mark is available. The absence of a mark *only means that you should proceed to the next step in the trademark clearance process,* which is the full trademark search commissioned and interpreted by a lawyer. Trademark directories and databases only short-circuit further pursuit of unavailable marks; they cannot finally clear a mark for use.

Trademark Clearance Checklist

If you carefully follow each instruction listed below, your chances of adopting a trademark that leads to a dispute or lawsuit is very small. Think of the whole clearance process as insurance against trouble that no one needs.

1. FIND OUT WHERE PROPOSED MARKS COME FROM. Ask everyone on the task force you create to propose one or more names for your new product or service. And ask them to briefly describe the sources of the names they propose. For example, for a fashion doll, "MIRANDA (after the heroine of Shakespeare's play *The Tempest*)," or, for a stuffed toy dog, "PUPSY (my best friend's dog's name in 1965)." Reject any proposed name that derives from the name of *any* commercial product or service, previously or currently in use, or the name of any person alive during this century. (Further, because one of your primary goals in selecting a new trademark should be to select one that is capable of being protected and registered with the U.S. Patent and Trademark Office, eliminate any proposed name that transgresses one of the statutory bars to federal trademark registration discussed at some length in the previous chapter.)

2. NARROW YOUR LIST OF PROPOSED MARKS TO FIVE OR FEWER MARKS. Pick your favorite marks for further consideration. You can do this by polling your creative team or asking the opinion of the management of the company whose product or service the new mark will name. This is also the time for focus groups or consumer surveys regarding your proposed marks. This step allows you to put your efforts into marks that are likely to succeed from a marketing standpoint. However, don't undertake any test-marketing of the new product or service under any proposed name at this point, since such marketing on even a small scale may lead to liability for the infringement of an established mark.

3. CONDUCT A "STOP-AND-GO SEARCH" FOR EACH MARK. A "stop-and-go search" is a stage of preliminary trademark searching during which you look up each mark on your short list of proposed

marks in a trademark directory, stop considering any mark that would likely infringe an established mark, and go on to the next proposed mark on your list, repeating the process. Eliminate any proposed mark that is similar to 1) any mark registered in the same class as that in which your new mark would be registered, even if the established mark is used for goods or services that are dissimilar to yours, or 2) any mark used for goods and services that are related or similar to yours, even if the established mark is registered in a different class.

Further, abandon any proposed mark that is at all similar to any famous mark, since it is possible that such a proposed mark could lead to liability under the Trademark Dilution Act, even if it is used for vastly dissimilar products or services than those named by the famous mark. At this stage of clearing a mark, "famous" can be described as any mark that is immediately recognized by 30 percent or more of your creative team. (See the next chapter for more information about the Trademark Dilution Act.)

4. FIND A TRADEMARK LAWYER. Unless an attorney in your company's legal department or your regular lawyer is well versed in trademark law, find a trademark lawyer. Trademark law is a narrow specialty and most lawyers who do not regularly practice trademark law find it confusing and even infuriating. Just by reading this book you will have learned more than many lawyers know about trademark law. You wouldn't ask an auto mechanic, however competent he is, to fix your stereo—so hire the right kind of lawyer to help clear your new mark. If you don't have a trademark lawyer at the start of the clearance process, move this step in the process to the top of the list and begin there.

5. COMMISSION A TRADEMARK SEARCH. Have your lawyer hire a trademark search firm to conduct what is called a "full" trademark search for the most promising proposed mark on your short list. A full search is a search of the trademark records in the U.S. Patent and Trademark Office and in all the state trademark offices, and of phone directories and trade directories and other databases, which offer information on unregistered but valid marks. If you are in a real hurry, commission searches for two or three of your proposed marks at the same time so as to get the news about the availability of these marks all at once rather than searching one mark and then searching another on your short list of proposed marks if the first proves to be unavailable.

So that your lawyer may instruct the search firm correctly as to the scope of the search, make sure that you give him or her the following information:

a) *A copy of the proposed mark, spelled as you intend to use it.* The actual verbal content of the proposed mark is very important. A word spelled one way may be available while the same word spelled in another way may not be.

b) *An accurate and full description of each product or service that the proposed mark will name.* That is, if you intend to market action figures, comic books, a board game, and children's videos under the mark JUSTICE CRUSADERS, your memo to your lawyer on the subject would describe these products as "toy action figures, named collectively 'Justice Crusaders,' based on the characters of the 'Justice Crusaders' series of comic books, and a board game and videotapes featuring these characters." Because a trademark naming these products would have to be searched in four classes to compare it to established trademarks for goods similar to the JUSTICE CRUSADERS products, the search will be much more extensive and complicated, and somewhat more expensive.

c) *A list specifying the anticipated territories where the products to be named by the proposed mark would be marketed.* Most trademark searches are of U.S. records only. This is fine, as far as it goes. However, many marketers, especially those who market easily exportable services or goods, want, at least eventually, to expand their market to other countries. If you have any plans at all for such expansion, let your lawyer know, since clearing a mark for international use involves searches of records in the other countries where it will be used. Failure to clear a mark in another country where marketing is planned can result in a suit for trademark infringement in that country, which is as much of a problem, or more, as a U.S. suit.

6. FOLLOW YOUR LAWYER'S ADVICE. Lawyers' fees buy not only legal services, but also the informed judgment that good lawyers develop over the years of their practice. Your lawyer's evaluation of the likelihood that your proposed mark will conflict with an established mark is the heart of the opinion letter that he or she will write after carefully reviewing your search report. In formulating this evaluation, your lawyer will weigh many factors, large and small, gleaned from the information in the search report. Your lawyer should try to accurately assess the chances of conflict, but most lawyers will be conservative in this assessment. If you feel that your lawyer is being overcautious in recommending that you

abandon your plans to use a proposed mark, get another trademark lawyer to evaluate your search report, which is yours, since you pay for it.

Whatever you do, however, don't just ignore your lawyer's reservations and cautions about a mark. This is reportedly what the marketing department at Nike did when it named a new women's running shoe INCUBUS®. The Nike legal department had apparently advised the marketing department that the word "incubus" means "an evil spirit believed to seize or harm sleeping persons" and had recommended that another mark be chosen. Marketing ignored the advice. After the INCUBUS shoe was introduced, somebody noticed that Nike had chosen a bad name for the shoe and stories started appearing in the press. The shoes were recalled at some expense. Nike was embarrassed. It's a safe bet that the folks in Nike's marketing department wish that they had not ignored the advice of the company's trademark lawyers.

7. REGISTER YOUR PROPOSED MARK(S). After you have cleared one or more of your proposed marks for use, file an intent-to-use application to register any mark that you think you may use, or recommend that your client do so. This serves several purposes:

   a) *Filing an intent-to-use application, in effect, "reserves" any mark for which such an application is filed.* As soon as the application is filed, it becomes a part of Trademark Office records and will begin to turn up in other people's trademark searches, resulting in their avoidance of the proposed mark it names.

   b) *Filing an intent-to-use application extends your rights or those of your client in the new trademark.* Once the proposed mark is in use and the registration application is granted, the date of first use of the mark is presumed to be the date the registration application was filed, even if that is months or even years before the actual date of first use of the mark. And because the deadline for filing proof of the actual use of the mark can be postponed to up to thirty-six months after the filing date of the registration application, you or your client can take plenty of time to develop the new product or service the mark will name, as well as the marketing campaign for it, secure in the knowledge that no one else can register the mark beforehand. If you or your client file to register several marks and end up using only one, the extra applications to register the marks that will not be used can simply be abandoned. When an application to register a mark is abandoned, nothing is lost but the filing fee and the fee the trademark lawyer charges to prepare the application.

c) *Filing an intent-to-use application negates the biggest unavoidable drawback of trademark searches.* Because trademark searches report the status of the trademarks they include as of the date the search was conducted, they become outdated quickly. This cannot be helped. Like a weather report, a trademark search that is accurate today may be inaccurate tomorrow. However, if an intent-to-use registration application is filed as soon as the trademark lawyer lets you or your client know that a proposed mark appears to be available for use, the danger that the report will soon be "stale" is negated. Filing to register a proposed mark gets your name or that of your client in the hat as the owner of that mark ahead of anyone else who may decide to adopt it. This is because when the application is eventually granted, you or your client will be able to use as your date of first use of the mark the date the application to register it was filed. Priority of use is usually determinative in questions of trademark ownership, so filing an intent-to-use application can effectively eliminate any competition for ownership of the mark.

Design Trademark Clearance

A trademark can be a symbol or a name or word. The best trademarks are visually memorable, even if they are primarily verbal. Think of the familiar, distinctive-typeface trademarks for COCA-COLA®, KLEENEX®, and L'EGGS®. As famous as these marks are, even more effective are the symbols that immediately communicate, without words, that the products to which they are applied originated with their manufacturers. A good example of this is Apple Computer's striped apple-with-a-bite-missing logotype. Computer consumers in any part of the world are likely to recognize the Apple logo and to know that it guarantees high-quality products. In an era when many marketers aspire to market their products internationally, symbol trademarks are more important than ever before. Unfortunately, the continuing proliferation of trademarks has made it difficult to create a trademark that is safe to use.

In order to avoid creating trademarks that infringe existing marks, you must know something about the standard used to judge trademark infringement. Trademark infringement is evaluated by applying the "sight, sound, and meaning test." That is, the proposed mark is compared to estab-

lished marks for similarities of appearance, sound when spoken, and meaning. If there are enough similarities between the proposed mark and an
established mark that consumers are likely to confuse the two marks if they
are used for similar goods or services, the proposed mark is said to be "confusingly similar" to the established mark and cannot be used without the
risk of a lawsuit for trademark infringement. While it is easier to compare
verbal marks for confusing similarity, it is equally important that the evaluation of similarities be made for trademarks whose impact is primarily visual. This group of marks includes marks that consist of a name or word that
is rendered in a distinctive typeface and marks that include or consist of
logotypes.

Obviously, when comparing design marks for similarities, the "sound
when spoken" part of the three-part infringement test does not apply.
However, the absence of this part of the infringement evaluation test makes
the other two-thirds of the test proportionately more important. With
design marks, whether your company or your client will face a federal lawsuit for trademark infringement (just after spending most of the advertising
budget for the year to introduce the new logo you designed) depends
equally on what the logo looks like and what it "means."

The evaluation of a proposed logo starts with a consideration of the
broadest possible group of established marks that are similarly configured.
For instance, if Texaco were only now considering adopting its familiar
five-pointed-star-in-a-circle logo, all established star and star-in-circle
marks would be examined to determine if the "new" Texaco logo infringed
any of them. All marks that included other prominent visual elements
besides star designs could be eliminated from the universe of marks examined for confusing similarity because such additional elements would eliminate any real probability that consumers would confuse the Texaco mark
with them.

Similarly, all star marks that consisted of realistic drawings of stars
could be dropped from the ongoing comparison; all such logos would be
dissimilar enough to the highly stylized Texaco star design to eliminate any
real chance of consumer confusion. Any remaining star marks would be
scrutinized carefully to judge whether it is likely that the "proposed"
Texaco logo would be confused with them. If such marks were used to
market products or services that were remote from petroleum products or
gas station services, any similarities that existed would be of less concern.
However, the closer the products or services named by an established mark
were to Texaco's, the more serious an impediment to the adoption of the
Texaco mark the established mark would be. Even if the proposed Texaco
mark were nearly identical to an established mark used to market sophisti-

cated medical apparatus to hospitals and physicians, the hospital-equipment star trademark could be of very little concern to the petroleum company. This would depend largely on whether there was any overlap in the marketplace between the two marks; if not, they could coexist comfortably in American commerce without bumping into each other.

Images and Words

These same evaluations would be made in clearing for adoption and use a mark that consisted of a name or word rendered in a distinctive typeface. The difference, of course, is that there would be an additional important element in the search—the verbal content of the mark. The verbal content of a mark is usually considered to be its dominant element for purposes of comparing it to existing marks to determine confusing similarity. However, the visual impact of such a proposed mark is by no means immaterial, especially in a situation where the verbal content of the mark is not so different from that of other marks used for similar products. For example, if a shoe manufacturer adopted for its new line of ladies' shoes the name SWEET FEET and printed the mark in a script typeface in navy blue ink on the insoles of its products, it might encounter some opposition in the form of a cease and desist letter from the marketer of the SUGAR FOOT line of women's footwear, especially if the SUGAR FOOT mark were applied to SUGAR FOOT products in the same location and with the same color ink in a similar typeface. The verbal elements of these two marks do not sound alike when spoken and do not have identical meanings. However, the products they name are identical. The choice of a script typeface for the new SWEET FEET mark is all that is necessary to push SWEET FEET into "confusing similarity" territory, where the SUGAR FOOT manufacturer will have no choice but to challenge it.

The good news for the SWEET FEET graphic designer is that, although the designer may not have been consulted about the name of the new shoe line—which, of course, contributed to the problem with the SUGAR FOOT people—the designer is not helpless when it comes to protecting the Sweet Shoes Company from a trademark infringement suit. The designer can insist on seeing the report for the trademark search that the Sweet Shoes marketing department had performed before it chose the name SWEET FEET. (And the SWEET FEET designer wants the *report,* which consists of fifty to one hundred pages of data, including reproductions of design marks, produced by a trademark search firm on similar marks already in use, rather than the opinion letter, which is based on the search report and written by the trademark lawyer who interpreted the report data but only in terms of the verbal elements of established marks versus those of the proposed mark.) And the designer can, using what can be learned by looking at the existing established design trademarks in that report, steer clear of any design for the SWEET FEET name that is at all similar to any established mark with any similar meaning.

SWEET FEET, rendered in a block, serif typeface with each letter in a different bright color, may be dissimilar enough to the SUGAR FOOT mark to avoid any potential problem with the SUGAR FOOT folks, who may ignore it and never even think of calling their lawyer. This depends in part on factors that no one connected with the new mark can really predict. One such factor is the plans its owners have for the SUGAR FOOT mark. Do they plan to expand their use of it or is it an old mark for an unprofitable line of shoes that they intend to phase out? Another is the vigilance of the SUGAR FOOT lawyers, who may be in the habit of suing any competitor who adopts any mark that is at all similar to the SUGAR FOOT mark or may, instead, take a more laissez-faire approach to the inevitable elbowing between competitors that occurs in a free market economy.

The same clearance process is possible for design trademarks that include no verbal elements, but the evaluation of similarities is a little more difficult because confusing similarity may result from more subtle similarities between proposed marks and established marks. The time to perform a trademark search for a design-only mark is after you have narrowed the field of proposed designs to three or fewer logotypes. Then, unless the possible choices are all simply variations on one basic design, commission a trademark search for the first-choice design. A search of all registered and unregistered U.S. design trademarks will cost a little more than $500. The lawyer's fee for interpreting the raw data in the search report will be $400 to $500. Either way, ask to see a copy of the search report and the trademark opinion letter, but don't attempt on your own to decide whether your proposed logo gets the green light. By seeing the search report, you will gain valuable information about other existing marks already in use for similar goods or services, but no matter how good a marketer you are, you don't have the specialized training to also function as a trademark lawyer. If your lawyer deems the design you created unavailable for use, move on to the next proposed mark on the short list of those under consideration.

Happy Endings

A cease and desist letter—a nasty document that demands, under threat of being sued, that you "cease" from doing something that is claimed to violate the rights of the person or company sending the letter and thereafter "desist" from ever doing it again—is only the start of the troubles that can befall you or your client if you make a wrong choice in choosing the design for a new trademark or fail to jump through all the hoops in the process of clearing a proposed mark for use. The next step after a cease and desist let-ter is a lawsuit requesting that the court order the products bearing the new mark pulled from distribution in order to avoid confusing consumers and damaging the reputation of the plaintiff company. ("Edna, were those pumps you liked so well SWEET FEET shoes or SUGAR FOOT shoes?") Such suits are often settled out of court, but a settlement would involve the aban-donment of the new mark and probably the payment of a sizable amount in lieu of damages the court could award. Neither scenario is likely to make your employer or your client happy about having adopted a new mark.

CHAPTER 10

Using Other People's Trademarks—Safely

LMOST EVERYONE KNOWS THAT SELLING TOOTHPASTE OR SNEAKERS or brokerage services by using a trademark that belongs to someone else is a quick ticket to a federal lawsuit for trademark infringement. The law allows marketers to protect themselves from interlopers who want a free ride on their established reputations in the marketplace. They do this by means of lawsuits to preserve the integrity of their trademarks, which represent them to the public. The penumbra of protection granted an established trademark extends to identical marks and to marks that, although not identical, are similar enough to confuse consumers. Usually, the comparison to determine trademark infringement is made between marks used to market similar products or services. However, the more famous and unusual the trademark, the wider the scope of protection trademark law grants it; no one can use KLEENEX or COCA-COLA or EXXON for *any* product without encountering serious opposition from platoons of trademark lawyers for those companies, especially since the Trademark Dilution Act became effective in early 1996. (See the discussion below of the Trademark Dilution Act.)

There are other ways to infringe a trademark besides adopting a name for a product or service that is confusingly similar to an established mark for a similar product or service. Because trademark owners are vigilant in protecting their trademarks, wariness in the matter of other people's trademarks is a very good idea. However, such wariness can lead to an exaggerated fear of trademarks that belong to others and unnecessary maneuvering to avoid any mention or depiction of them. Surprisingly enough, there are some circumstances when using someone else's trademark *is* safe.

Broadly speaking, the law gives a trademark owner protection against any action that creates confusion about that trademark in the minds of consumers. This means that the dividing line between safe and unsafe uses of a trademark is where consumer confusion begins. Determining whether a given use of someone else's trademark will lead to a lawsuit is simply a matter of determining, under all the circumstances, whether that use will confuse anyone.

There are two common varieties of use of someone else's trademark that are usually safe and one that is, by definition, almost never safe. An examination of each of these situations will demonstrate the considerations involved in using other people's trademarks.

Incidental Use of Trademarks

More than one creative director has called in a lawyer to evaluate whether the presence of a COKE® can sitting on a table in a photograph is enough to disqualify the photo for use in an ad that isn't supposed to advertise COKE products. Before the lawyer can answer the question, he or she will have to see the photograph in question and read the ad copy, because the two important factors in evaluating whether the Coca-Cola Company is likely to sue are the emphasis of the photograph and the context of the use of the COKE logo.

Trademarks are a part of our world; they pervade every environment of modern life so thoroughly that it is next to impossible to walk down a street or visit a public place or sit in a room without being surrounded by trademarks of every sort. This means that any realistic depiction of a street scene, restaurant setting, or home or office situation will include representations of the trademarks found in that environment. Even though the trademarks that appear in such depictions are the valuable property of the companies that own them, in a way they also belong to the rest of us because they are a part of our lives. The First Amendment protects commercial speech such as advertising as well as other sorts of speech. This means that, as a matter of free speech, we have a right to "mention" the trademarks around us, either verbally or visually.

Which brings us back to the COKE can in that photograph. Although free speech gives us the right to talk about or depict the world we live in, including trademarks, trademark law limits that right to some extent by discouraging certain sorts of uses of trademarks. The law would allow the Coca-Cola Company to sue the ad agency and the agency's client for trademark infringement if anything about the photo that included the COKE can implied that there was some connection between COCA-COLA and the product advertised in the ad for which the photo was used. The same would be true if consumers could infer from the ad that the Coca-Cola Company somehow sponsored the ad or the product it advertised. As a practical matter, it is not likely that either of these grounds for suit would exist unless the COKE logo was legible and the can on which it appeared was a prominent element of the photograph; a background depiction of the can wouldn't create a problem, especially if the can wasn't an emphasis of the photograph.

Similarly, the context of the appearance in an ad of a "borrowed" trademark is important. If the COKE can photograph depicted the scene around the pool at an upscale resort hotel in an ad for that hotel, implying, however obliquely, that COKE is a favorite drink of carefree, wealthy people who look good in stylish bathing suits, the Coca-Cola Company probably would not object to the incidental appearance of its name and logo in the ad. If, however, the COKE can appeared in an objectionable photograph or if that photograph were used in any unsavory context, the Coca-Cola Company would be inclined to take whatever action was necessary to halt further use of the photo, especially if the COKE can was prominent in the photograph. The Coca-Cola Company, along with everybody else in the world, knows that villains and heroes and every other variety of human being drink COCA-COLA soft drinks. However, it is understandable that no one in Atlanta, except the lawyers who earn their living by guarding the various valuable COCA-COLA trademarks, would like to see an ad photo prominently depicting a COKE can lying on a heap of rancid garbage or a broken COKE bottle being wielded as a weapon in a bar fight. Similarly, an identifiable depiction of a COCA-COLA product used in an ad for a topless bar, or cigarettes, or a personal hygiene product could earn the animosity of the Coca-Cola Company. Any use of a trademark in an unsavory context can lead to a claim of product disparagement, which is comparable to a defamation suit brought on behalf of a trademark. (Again, this is how Oprah Winfrey became a defendant in Texas.)

Comparative Advertising

Strangely enough, there is one variety of calculated, obvious use of other people's trademarks that will seldom cause trouble if carried out carefully. This is the use of trademarks belonging to competitor companies in comparative advertising. Trademark law does not prohibit *non*trademark or informational uses of the trademarks of others but, rather, punishes uses that confuse consumers. Comparative advertising informs consumers by explicitly comparing the merits of one product with those of another. The competitor's product, which always suffers from the comparison, is mentioned specifically in the ad copy and its package is usually pictured beside the advertiser's product in a head-on shot. Such ads require by their very nature that the products compared be carefully identified before the distinctions between them are drawn; only a very clumsy ad would fail to make entirely clear whether JOY® detergent or IVORY® detergent cuts grease faster in laboratory tests. The test for trademark infringement is whether the public will be confused by the use of the mark. Since the possibility of consumer confusion is eliminated in comparative advertising, so is the likelihood of any charge of trademark infringement.

However, only claims that are truthful and that can be substantiated are safe. Because exaggerated claims or claims that can't be documented can lead to false advertising suits or unfair competition claims, every statement in a comparative advertising campaign should be carefully documented and every element of the campaign should be carefully designed.

Comparative advertisements can safely make use of competitors' trademarks if they are carefully constructed. Using a photo of another company's product or mentioning the product by name in an ad that compares it to your company's product is not an infringement of the trademark rights of the other company if the ad truthfully compares the products named by the trademarks, and if the character and arrangement of the visual elements and the content of the ad copy do not create any likelihood that consumers will somehow mistakenly believe that your company's product has some relation to the product of the other company.

Although properly designed comparative advertising does not usually lead to trademark infringement suits, there is one caveat. Whenever you use a trademark belonging to someone else in an ad, it is only prudent to state who owns that trademark in order to emphasize that the mark has no connection with the advertiser's product. This is easily accomplished by means of a "footnote" ownership statement. That is, a short statement should be included somewhere along the bottom margin or up the side margin of print ads and at the bottom of the screen in television commercials to the effect that "DOVE® is a registered trademark of the Lever Brothers Company."

The competitor's trademark should be used in exactly the form it appears on the competitor's product; that is, if it is a federally registered trademark and bears the ® symbol, that symbol should be used in the ownership statement. If the mark is not registered, no such symbol will appear, or the ™ symbol will be used in conjunction with the mark. In this event, the usage as it appears on the product should be duplicated and the ownership statement should read something like this: "CRUNCHIES™ is a trademark of the Toasted Oats Company and is not owned or licensed by the makers of SWEETIES™ brand cereal." A statement that your client's competitor owns its mark should completely eliminate any valid claim that the comparative ad creates confusion regarding the ownership of the mark or the manufacturer of the product it names. However, because not just any such disclaimer will suffice, any such ad and proposed disclaimer should be reviewed, before the ad is published, by a lawyer who can evaluate the possibility that the ad will result in an infringement lawsuit.

It is important to remember that the laws regarding comparative advertising in other countries may vary considerably from those in the United States. Be especially sure that any ad you prepare that mentions another company's trademark and will be published or circulated outside the United States will not furnish the owner of the other trademark with grounds for suit. Marketers use comparative advertising because it is effective. A comparative ad can lure consumers away from a familiar product by convincing claims of the benefits of a "new and improved" rival product or of a product that has been shown to be "75 percent more effective in laboratory tests." This is enough to make the owners of the product that fares badly in such comparisons want to do whatever they can to stop the further publication of the ad. A lawsuit can do this.

If a competitor finds your comparative advertising objectionable and the law in one or more of the countries where the ad appears supports that viewpoint, you will be vulnerable in any country where your competitor can file a suit with a straight face. Maybe U.S. law, with its predisposition to allow free speech in all possible contexts, can't be used as a club to stop your trumpeting the better performance of your product, but the laws of other markets may, and every segment of international commerce counts. Japanese, Swedish, or German money can fatten the bottom line for marketers just as well as American dollars, and perhaps somebody who works for your competitor wouldn't mind a long trip abroad at company expense to hire and supervise the lawyers who will be suing you under laws that you never heard of. Since you can't keep a tame trademark lawyer in your desk drawer to consult whenever you need advice, put his or her phone number on your speed dial.

Trademark Parody

When a company decides to market a product under a name that is a parody of another mark, it is engaging in trademark parody. Trademark parody is almost always a bad idea, for two reasons. The first reason is that one of the kinds of confusion that trademark owners can legitimately complain about in court is "dilution," which is a claim that someone's use of an established mark is eroding the mark's strength even though the complained-of use is made in connection with a product that is unrelated to the product named by the established mark. If this fact alone isn't enough to convince you that trademark parody is almost invariably a dumb idea, consider this: only very famous trademarks are parodied. A parody of an obscure mark just wouldn't work. This means that the parodist is picking on a company rich enough to finance a trademark infringement lawsuit out of its petty cash. And since the passage of the Trademark Dilution Act, suits for dilution are easier for owners of famous marks to file and win.

Another factor in trademark parody that often contributes to the problems that parodists face is that the parodied mark is often the butt of a joke that may be off-color. Nobody likes a wise guy. The owners of the parodied mark may be so enraged by the parody of their mark that they will rush to file a trademark infringement suit and ask for an injunction against the parodist. Courts are usually sympathetic to the interests of the owners of famous trademarks; as a result, trademark parodists are routinely enjoined from pursuing their bad jokes at the expense of the well-known marks they parody.

You can understand trademark parody better by considering a few trademark parody cases in which the parodists were ordered by the court to give up making jokes at the expense of the plaintiff trademark owners. The pairs of marks that were the subjects of these suits tell the story in themselves; if reading the list makes you wince, you're getting the right idea about trademark parody. Not surprisingly, all these defendants lost in court.

PLAINTIFF COMPANY:	DEFENDANT TRADEMARK:
Coca-Cola Company	"Enjoy Cocaine" (used, on a poster, in a script and color identical to those used for the COCA-COLA® logo)
Anheuser-Busch, Inc.	"Where There's Life . . . There's Bugs" (for a combination floor wax–insecticide, in a parody of the Anheuser-Busch slogan "Where There's Life . . . There's Bud")®
General Electric Company	"Genital Electric" (used, on men's underwear, in a script monogram similar to the GENERAL ELECTRIC® script logo)
Johnny Carson	"Here's Johnny" (used, as the name of a line of portable toilets, in a parody of the phrase associated with the famous comedian; no trademark infringement was found, but the court found that Mr. Carson's right of publicity had been violated)

Not every trademark parody is ruled a trademark infringement. For example, the use in a florist's ad campaign of the slogan "This bud's for you" was held not to infringe the trademark rights of Anheuser-Busch, Inc. In its ruling, the court specifically mentioned the innocuous and pleasant nature of the florist's slogan. As a practical matter, all this tells us is that *sometimes* parodists win in court. Since paying to defend a lawsuit is almost as much a misfortune as losing it, this is really no encouragement to would-be parodists. The best thing to do with famous trademarks is to steer clear of them, especially if your parody is smutty or would associate a famous mark with an unsavory product.

More than one trademark infringement lawsuit has been brought simply because the trademark owner was angry and felt like doing something about it. If this doesn't scare you, consider the fact that owners of famous trademarks have whole platoons of trademark lawyers who have to justify their existence by periodically going after evildoers. If they are short of true bad guys this month, you and your ad may look like very good targets. When it comes to using someone else's famous trademark in an ad without permission, discretion really is the better part of valor.

The Trademark Dilution Act

Owners of famous trademarks gained substantial new protection from the federal Trademark Dilution Act of 1995, which became effective in January of 1996. The act formalizes and makes a part of the federal trademark statute a principle of trademark law that had been available as a ground for suit in only about half the states. It allows the owners of an existing "famous" trademark to ask the court to enjoin the use of the same mark by another company—even if there is no likelihood of confusion between the marks—on the ground that the defendant's use of the mark, even for non-competing goods or services, "dilutes" the distinctive quality of the famous mark. This allows the owners of truly famous marks to stop the use of their marks by the marketers of noncompeting goods and services as well as by competitors. One of the first lawsuits brought under the new act was initiated by Hasbro, Inc., which owns the trademark CANDY LAND® for the famous children's board game, against a company that had adopted the domain name candyland.com for a sexually explicit Web site. Hasbro was successful in having the domain name enjoined on the basis that its use would dilute the strength of the CANDY LAND mark. Other, similar cases have followed. A recent example is the suit brought by Federal Express to halt the use of FEDERAL ESPRESSO as the name of a Syracuse coffeehouse.

The new act defines "dilution" as "the lessening of the capacity of a famous mark to identify and distinguish goods or services, regardless of the presence or absence of 1) competition between the owner of the famous mark and other parties, or 2) likelihood of confusion, mistake, or deception." Although most really famous marks are registered in the U.S. Patent and Trademark Office, federal registration is not a prerequisite for protection of a mark under the act, which protects registered and unregistered marks equally, given an equal degree of fame.

The Trademark Dilution Act enumerates several factors to be considered in evaluating whether the mark owned by a plaintiff in a suit under the act really is distinctive and famous enough to be protected under its provisions. These include the following:

- The degree of inherent or acquired distinctiveness of the "famous" mark
- The duration and extent of use of the "famous" mark
- The duration and extent of advertising and publicity for the "famous" mark
- The geographical extent of the trading area in which the "famous" mark is used
- The channels of trade through which the product or service named by the "famous" mark is sold
- The degree of recognition of the "famous" mark in the trading areas and channels of trade used by both the owner of the "famous" mark and the defendant against whom the injunction is sought
- The nature and extent of any use by third parties of marks that are the same as or similar to the "famous" mark
- Whether the owner of the "famous" mark has a valid federal registration

These factors are not exclusive; that is, they are specifically not the only factors that may be considered.

For most trademark owners, the Trademark Dilution Act will not offer any more protection than the federal trademark statute offered before the new act was passed. This is understandable; very few marks can hope to reach the level of fame required to trigger protection from trademark dilution under the new law. For an understanding of the sort of fame that courts are likely to require before invoking the penalties of the new law, we have only to look to the LEXIS® case, decided not long before the new act was passed.

The manufacturer of the automobile LEXUS® was sued by the owners of the online legal research service LEXIS® on the ground of dilution. LEXIS lost. The court held that LEXIS was not well-known enough outside the legal community to have suffered dilution at the hands of the automobile manufacturer. In other words, the sort of fame necessary to support a claim of trademark dilution is what used to be known as becoming "a household word." When the great majority of consumers are aware of a mark and the products or services it names, it is "famous" in the sense meant by the Trademark Dilution Act. If only some people are aware of the mark, or if almost everyone in a certain profession or industry is aware of it but practically no one outside that group is, the mark has not (yet) achieved the degree of fame necessary to command this very broad protection under the law.

Most marketers need only remember that a long-standing guideline for trademark selection is even more important since the passage of the Trademark Dilution Act. "Stay away from famous marks" is better advice than ever. Now owners of famous marks have a more direct and powerful way to stop you from naming your motor oil COORS® or your line of kids' clothing CHEERIOS®.

The new statute specifies several legitimate uses of famous trademarks that will not create any liability under the law. These exclusions from the proscriptions of the act are a response to legitimate First Amendment concerns. The new act expressly exempts:

1. Fair use of a mark in comparative advertising.
2. Parody, satire, editorial commentary, and other noncommercial uses of a mark.
3. Any form of news reporting or commentary that mentions a mark.

The Etiquette of Trademark Usage

The only thing left to say about using other people's trademarks is that you should do so carefully. This boils down to the following four rules:

1. Trademarks are proper adjectives; remember to use them as such. It is a "KLEENEX tissue," not just a "kleenex," and you wear "LEVI'S jeans," not just "levis."
2. Trademarks should never be used as nouns or verbs; you do not "XEROX" a document, you make a photocopy of it, and it *is* a "photocopy," not simply a "xerox."
3. Spell it right. Most importantly, capitalize trademarks; it is "COKE," not "coke," and "CUISINART," not "cuisinart."
4. Give a mark its due. If it is a registered mark, use the ® symbol in conjunction with the mark in at least the two or three most prominent uses of the mark in a text or an ad. If it is not registered, use informal trademark notice, i.e., the ™ superscript or subscript, if the owner of the mark does so on its products. (If the mark names a service, the trademark owner may use SM to indicate this.)

If you are confused about the proper spelling of a trademark or whether it is federally registered and therefore entitled to be escorted by the ® symbol whenever it appears in print, you can research the mark on the International Trademark Association (INTA) Trademark Checklist Web site at *www.inta.org/tmchklst.htm*. This Web site lists nearly four thousand trademarks and the generic terms for the products and services they name and indicates proper spelling, capitalization, and punctuation. If you can't find the mark you are investigating or don't have access to the Internet, call the INTA Trademark Hotline at (212) 768-9886. The hotline operates weekdays from 2:00 P.M. to 5:00 P.M. eastern standard time.

Your rights won't be affected if you fail to follow these rules in using other people's trademarks, but theirs may be diminished. A trademark that is used incorrectly can become "generic"; that is, the mark loses its ability to refer to a particular product or service and comes to indicate a whole class of products. If this happens, the original owner of the mark loses the exclusive right to use it. In determining whether a mark has lost its significance as an indicator of *one* company's products or services, courts often consider whether a trademark owner has acted against infringers. You may have no legal *duty* to use the marks of others carefully, but they may have a very good legal reason—the preservation of their rights—to challenge any misuse of those marks.

Because a trademark represents the reputation in the marketplace of the products or services of the company that owns it, it may be that company's most valuable asset. It is understandable that trademark owners pay close attention when their marks are used by people they never met in ways they don't necessarily approve of. That's why they spend time writing letters to people who misuse them and money to publish ads to explain proper trademark usage. The way to avoid trouble when using other people's trademarks is to handle them like you would handle other people's money—carefully.

CHAPTER 11

Trademarks in Cyberspace

L IKE ALL FRONTIERS, CYBERSPACE IS LARGELY POPULATED BY MAVERICKS
and rebels who like the cyber-atmosphere of "If you can imagine it,
you can do it." Unfortunately, the very dearth of rules that makes
cyberspace so intriguing to everyone who has something to say or
sell electronically is also causing problems. Americans often complain
about overregulation by local, state, and federal governmental agencies and
authorities. But many who are familiar with the problems that have arisen,
as everybody and his brother scramble for their piece of turf in cyberspace,
would agree that some corners of cyberspace have needed *more* rules.

The one aspect of cyber-commerce that has consistently produced
the largest number of disputes is the ownership of domain names. (A
domain name is the heart of an e-mail address. In the e-mail address *john-
jones@jonesventures.com,* "jonesventures.com" is the domain name.) Domain
names tell Internet users where to find companies and individuals in cyberspace. They function like ZIP codes do for "snail mail"; they direct e-mail
and other communications to the right cyberspace neighborhood to find
the person or entity named in the first part of the e-mail address. They
allow Internet users to visit World Wide Web pages.

The system of categorizing Internet user addresses according to type
is familiar to most Internet surfers. The five major nonmilitary domains are
".com" for commercial entities, ".gov" for governmental bodies, ".edu" for
educational institutions, ".org" for organizations, and ".net" for networks.
Because innovative marketers have found ways to sell everything from coffee to books online, and because the revenues available to smart Internet
marketers seem limitless, the most crowded part of cyberspace is the commercial district, where all the .com addresses are located.

Internet addresses are actually a series of numbers. However, because people who want to locate an Internet merchant are much more likely to remember a verbal address than a series of numbers, domain names are alpha and/or numeric names that a computer can convert to numeric addresses. There is presently no complete directory of domain names. This means that the best domain names look like the names of the companies that own them; this sort of domain name creates an expectation as to who can be found at the Internet address it names. If you are familiar with a company and its domain name resembles the name of the company, you know what you will find at its address on the Internet. Such Internet addresses are easy to guess and easy to remember. For example, because "ibm.com" is one of the elements of the Internet address for IBM, anyone can guess that that address belongs to that company.

Obstacles on the Superhighway

So far, trademark disputes have been one of the biggest legal impediments facing Internet marketers. The gist of trademark law is that every marketer is entitled to his or her own reputation in the marketplace. Any interference with this—any act that causes consumers to confuse the products or services of one marketer with those of another—is trademark infringement. Until recently, the legal status of domain names was not a settled area of the law, but anyone who understands trademark law knows that domain names are more than just virtual street addresses. One variety of trademark infringement is confusion as to sponsorship or affiliation. If, on account of unintended similarities between a domain name and the name of an unrelated company, consumers are likely to believe that there is some relationship between the owner of the domain name and the unrelated company, the company's trademark rights have been infringed. While this remains one of the many sets of circumstances that can give rise to trademark infringement, it has not been the biggest problem for U.S. businesses. Infringers who inadvertently adopt a domain name that implies they are connected with an established, well-known company are rarer than a more common sort of cyberspace trademark infringer: the cybersquatter, whose actions are anything but inadvertent.

In recent years, trademark disputes have resulted when competitors, pranksters, and opportunists have registered domain names that are related to the names of established companies. Apparently, many such domain-name registrations have been made for the sole purpose of selling the registered domain names at a profit to the people who are logically affiliated with the names. These domain name speculators have often been called "cybersquatters" or "cyberpirates." The predations of cybersquatters have often been bold, daring, and even arrogant. A journalist registered the domain name mcdonalds.com as a part of his research for an article for

Wired magazine. Needless to say, McDonald's was chagrined to find that the most obvious domain name it could choose had already been registered. Some overeager capitalist at Sprint Communications registered mci.com; not surprisingly, MCI Telecommunications objected. The Princeton Review, a leading test-preparation company, registered kaplan.com, a domain name based on the name of its competitor, Stanley Kaplan Review, and planned to set up a Web site that compared the two companies' products, presumably showing the alleged inferiority of the Kaplan products. The domain name mtv.com was registered and used by a former MTV employee. The domain names windows95.com and nyt.com were registered by people who were not connected with, respectively, Microsoft and the *New York Times.* Although several of these early "land grabs" resulted in lawsuits, no reported court decisions resulted because all four disputes were settled out of court. Most of the terms of the settlements in these disputes, including any amounts paid the domain-name hijackers, were not disclosed, but it is telling that all the companies that complained because someone else had registered versions of their names now own those domain names.

The short but lively life of the Internet has been strewn with incidents like these. And the varieties of hijacking have proliferated as the sophistication of Web sites—and the number of those who want to exploit the burgeoning commerce on the Internet—have increased. In a recent study of Web identity infringements conducted by Cyveillance, a domain monitoring company, the following infringements were found to be the most common, in order of prevalence:

- Unauthorized use of logos and images
- Use of both visible and hidden text
- Unauthorized use of a company's name or product in metatags
- Software, music, and video piracy
- Unauthorized distribution or sale of consumer goods
- Framing (displaying someone else's proprietary content in a window within another site without permission, thus implying a relationship or affiliation)
- Use of a company name on a competitor's site
- Use of logos or images in a pornographic context
- Gripe sites and negative newsgroup postings

You don't have to be a trademark lawyer to realize that most of these infringements—and maybe all of them, if the circumstances were correct—involve trademark infringement.

Until recently, cyberpirates have been able to register numerous domain names they had no intention of using with relative impunity. A lawyer for the plaintiff in one recent lawsuit brought against a cybersquatter said that the defendant had registered "more than 1,000 domain names, many containing the identities of celebrities, names of sports teams, and other protected trademarks." After registering names similar or identical to established trademarks, cybersquatters have offered to sell the registered names for extortionate prices (from $10,000 to $3 million or more, by one estimate), have diverted Internet traffic to their own Web sites, and have offered pornographic material at the sites designated by the fake, hijacked names. Some courts have sided with the owners of the established trademarks, but the legal remedies available to stop cyberpirates have been uncertain and expensive, mainly because there was no federal statute that directly addressed the problem. The Lanham Act, the federal trademark statute, wasn't an exact fit and didn't provide easy solutions to those victimized by cybersquatters. And protection under the Trademark Dilution Act is expressly limited to "famous" marks, a category that does not include most of the trademarks, even fairly well-known ones, in use in U.S. commerce.

Anti-Cybersquatting Consumer Protection Act

But the heyday of cyberpirates is over, perhaps, ironically, because one of these name hijackers picked on the wrong person. Senator Orrin Hatch was offered the domain name senatororrinhatch.com for $45,000. Senator Hatch didn't get mad; he got even. Stating that cybersquatting results in consumer fraud and public confusion and impairs electronic commerce while depriving legitimate trademark owners of substantial revenues and consumer goodwill, Senator Hatch was the Senate sponsor of the Anti-Cybersquatting Consumer Protection Act. This federal statute, signed into law on November 29, 1999, prohibits certain tactics commonly employed by cybersquatters that were not clearly defined as prohibited under previously existing federal law. Under the provisions of the new Act, a trademark owner may now file a civil suit against anyone who, with the bad-faith intent to profit from the use of the trademark, "registers, traffics in, or uses a domain name" that is "identical or confusingly similar to" the plaintiff's trademark or is "dilutive" of the plaintiff's famous trademark. Among other predatory activities, the Act makes actionable the practice of registering domain names similar to the names of established businesses with the intent to sell the names, at a profit, to those businesses.

A business that has been victimized by a cybersquatter must prove in any lawsuit brought under the new Act that the accused cyberpirate acted in "bad faith." If the defendant in a suit of this sort can show some reasonable basis for its belief that it was entitled to register and use the domain name at issue, then the court will not find that cybersquatting has occurred. For instance, if the Great American Produce Company sued Great American Bus Tours under the new Act for registering greatamerican.com, the Great American Produce Company would lose its suit because the court would hold that Great American Bus Tours had demonstrated no bad faith in registering a domain name that could equally as well relate to the produce company. (The problem of more than one company with equal rights to the same domain name may be alleviated by the fact that it is now possible to register domain names as long as two hundred characters. Previously, there was a twenty-three-character limit. Now, Great American Produce Company can register greatamericanproducecompany.com and Great American Bus Tours can register greatamericanbustours.com and neither will have to fight the other over a shorter domain name.

The Act also indicates that certain acts on the part of the defendant in a suit brought under the new law may be considered probative of the bad faith of the accused cybersquatter. The (nonexclusive) list of acts includes: diverting consumers from the plaintiff's Web site to that of the defendant, so that confusion is likely to result; offering to sell the domain name to the plaintiff; providing false or misleading contact information to the domain name registry or failing to keep this information up to date; registering multiple domain names that are similar or identical to established trademarks; and registering a domain name that is the same or similar to the plaintiff's trademark, which is famous.

The Act provides an innovative solution to the problem of finding cybersquatters, who often provide misleading or incomplete information when they register domain names in bad faith. Plaintiffs can sue the problematic domain name itself if the cybersquatter who owns the registration for the domain name cannot be found. The relief that can be granted by a court in a case of this sort is limited to the cancellation or forfeiture of the domain name or transfer of the domain name to the plaintiff.

A court can order a cybersquatter defendant to transfer ownership of the questioned domain name to the plaintiff whether the registration of the hijacked name took place before or after the new Act became law. However, money damages can only be awarded to victorious plaintiffs for prohibited activities of defendants that occurred after the effective date of the new Act (November 29, 1999). If the registration of the pirated domain name occurred before that date, no damages may be awarded for the bad-faith registration; however, the use of the pirated domain name after that date can be the basis of an award of money damages, even if the domain name was registered earlier.

The Act allows plaintiffs who prevail in court to recover three times their losses due to the prohibited activities of the cybersquatter, the profits of the cybersquatter attributable to those activities, court costs, and, sometimes, attorneys' fees. The Act also allows the court to award statutory damages from $1,000 to $100,000 instead of actual damages. This allows a plaintiff to recover monetary damages without having to prove either its own losses or the profits of the cybersquatter, a process that can be extremely time-consuming and difficult and may net less than the cost of determining these sums.

Already, aggrieved trademark owners have filed a number of suits under the Anti-Cybersquatting Consumer Protection Act. Most of the early suits involved famous or globally significant trademarks, often sports trademarks such as americascup.com, worldwrestlingfederation.com, and teamnewzealand.com.

ICANN Dispute Resolution Policy

Originally, the U.S. government's National Science Foundation assigned all Internet domain names, both military and nonmilitary. As the Internet grew, this job became a big one. The National Science Foundation created the InterNIC (the Internet Network Information Center) project to provide Internet management services. The National Science Foundation entered into a contract with a Herndon, Virginia, company called Network Solutions, Inc. (NSI) and delegated to NSI the tasks of allocating and managing the registration of nonmilitary domain names. NSI remains a leading registrar of domain names.

In late 1998, the U.S. government gave the Internet Corporation for Assigned Names and Numbers (ICANN) authority to oversee the Internet's domain name system. Since then, ICANN has been tangled in what has been, essentially, a turf war with Network Solutions. The two Internet administrators have now settled their dispute.

Now ICANN offers a domain name dispute resolution policy. ICANN's policy governs all domain name disputes after January 3, 2000 and is an alternate course available to those who think that they have been victimized by cyberpirates. Under the ICANN policy, a trademark owner must show that the domain name is identical or confusingly similar to the owner's mark, that the domain name registrant has no legitimate interest in the domain name, and that the domain name "has been registered and is being used in bad faith."

Aggrieved trademark owners began using the ICANN dispute resolution policy almost immediately. In almost all of these early disputes, the disputed domain name has been awarded to the trademark owner. You can read about the ICANN policy, and other matters relating to ICANN's activities and goals, at *www.icann.org/general/faq1.htm#udrp*. NSI has also posted very good information about the ICANN policy at *www.domain-magistrate.com*.

Internet Population Explosion

In 1993, there were only 8,700 registered domain names. In 1999, NSI registered more than five million new domain names. Dot coms comprise 79 percent of these new registrations and the United States accounted for the most registrations. Companies eager to stake their claims to cyberspace territory routinely register every conceivable version of their corporate names and trademarks, as well as domain names related to their products, such as Procter and Gamble's dandruff.com, badbreath.com, and underarm.com.

Although cybersquatting appears to be on the decline in the United States, it is increasing elsewhere. According to one estimate, in at least eighty-four countries anyone can register a pirated domain name without challenge. This means that the best protection against cyberpirates is preemptive registration of domain names based on valuable trademarks. But American businesses have been dilatory in registering versions of their corporate names as domain names. Incredibly, it seems that the American business community is still comparatively unaware of the potential problems of Internet marketing. In the first quarter of 2000, NameEngine.com, a company that registers Web domain names and researches their ownership, reported that more than half of the Fortune 500 companies own fewer of the worldwide domain names logically related to their corporate and product names than other companies and individuals. But this will change as more and more American marketers become aware of the danger cybersquatters pose to their hard-earned trademarks.

Signing Up and Signing On

Applications to register new domain names in the United States may be submitted electronically to Network Solutions, Inc. (Other entities are responsible for registering domain names in other world jurisdictions.) You can call Network Solutions at (703) 742-4777 for information concerning registering a domain name or access this information at *www.networksolutions.com*. The NSI Web site allows you to search available names, e-mail NSI, and register a domain name.

Making and Managing Contracts

M AYBE NOBODY MENTIONED IT WHEN YOU WERE STUDYING THE Romantic poets, or Napoleon's Russian campaign, or Cubism, but anyone who works in advertising needs to know a lot more about contracts than most other former liberal arts majors. Perhaps nobody mentioned this fact because your professors didn't realize you'd be working as a cog in the great machine of American capitalism. But it's a fact of life in the advertising business, where many of the relationships you will be a part of during your career will be governed by contracts. This means that it is important to understand what contracts are and how they work. Even if you work for someone else. Especially if you are a freelancer or own your own agency or studio. You, bunky, need to understand contracts: how they arise, what constitutes a contract, the effect of the provisions in contracts you are likely to encounter, what you can do if you want out of a contract, and what someone else can do to you if you fail to live up to your part of the bargain. Even though you should hire a lawyer to draft complex agreements and should consult a lawyer before signing the contracts that are offered to you, *you* will be the person signing on the dotted line and *you* need to have an understanding of what a contract is and does. But it's not so bad. In fact, if you read and understand this chapter, you'll be at least as well-versed in contracts as most of your peers.

Defining Contracts

A contract is a set of legal rights and responsibilities created by the mutual agreement of two or more people or companies; it is the body of rules, so to speak, by which a particular business relationship is to be run. A contract is the agreement itself, not the paper document that commemorates the agreement. In fact, some contracts don't even have to be in writing to be valid, although written contracts are almost always a good idea.

Except in old movies, written contracts do not depend on complicated legal language for their legal effect. The goal of the lawyer who "drafts," or writes, a contract is to set out in completely unambiguous language the agreement reached between the parties to it. This generally means that the more clearly a contract is written the more effective it is as a contract; but eliminating ambiguity may also require more detailed language than most people are accustomed to using and may result in a much longer written agreement than the lawyer's client thinks is really necessary. However, in a skillfully drafted agreement *every* provision is necessary. Even in the case of an apparently simple agreement, a good contract lawyer will write an agreement that not only provides what happens when the agreement is working but also what happens when it *stops* working.

Sections of a Contract

No particular "architecture" is required to make a written document a contract. What determines whether a document is a binding agreement is the content of the language, not the form in which the language is arranged in the document. However, formal written agreements are customarily divided into certain standard sections:

- INTRODUCTION. The introductory section of a formal written agreement gives the exact legal names, and sometimes the addresses, of the parties to the agreement, and indicates their legal status (an individual doing business under a trade name, a partnership, or a corporation). It also gives the shortened forms of the contracting parties' names by which they will be referred to in the agreement ("Reginald Jones, hereinafter referred to as the 'Writer' . . ."). The introductory section may also specify the date the agreement is made or becomes effective, which may be a date either before or after the date the agreement is signed.
- PREMISES. The "premises" section of a formal written agreement sets out, sometimes after the word "Whereas," the set of circumstances on which the agreement is founded, or "premised." This section makes certain representations about the facts that have influenced the parties' decision to enter into the agreement. Although it may look like excess language to non-lawyers, in reality the premises section sets out information that could be important if, in a lawsuit based on the agreement, a court had to "construe," or interpret, the written document in order to rule on the intent of the parties

when they entered into their agreement and the representations that may have induced it.

- BODY. In the body of most contracts the various points of agreement between the parties are enumerated in a series of headlined or numbered paragraphs. Each such paragraph sets out one facet of the agreement and all probably use the word "shall" to indicate the mandatory nature of the action expected from each party. These provisions are the heart of the contract, since they reflect the terms of the agreement that have been reached between the parties. They also comprise the section of a contract that is most subject to negotiation, since the parties to the contract, or their lawyers, may feel that some haggling over "how long" or "how much" or "who pays" is necessary to reach the optimum agreement.

  These paragraphs are where, among many other possible provisions, the services to be rendered by one or both parties are described in detail; the copyrights and trademarks or right to use a celebrity's name are licensed for a period or vested in one party; the fee that will be due one party or the split of revenues is specified, as well as any periodic or recurring payments, such as re-use fees or royalties; the duty of one party to pay certain specified expenses is set out; the role of one party as agent for the other and the limits of that agency are specified; and the term of the agreement is specified, including any "holdover" periods during which responsibilities of the parties continue for a time.

- MISCELLANEOUS. Besides all the major points of the agreement, a formal contract will contain what are sometimes entitled "miscellaneous provisions" and what lawyers often call "boilerplate." These provisions look unnecessary to most non-lawyers, since, among other things, they set out methods for handling various events that may never occur, but they can be crucially important. For example, one standard miscellaneous provision is the "venue clause." A venue clause states that any lawsuit based on the agreement will be brought in the courts of a specified state or city and that any dispute will be decided according to the laws of that state. This sort of provision can determine whether you sue to enforce your agreement in your home city and state or, at increased expense, in a distant city.

  Another very common miscellaneous provision is called the "merger clause." Merger clauses occur in various forms, but they all provide essentially the same thing: *Whatever verbal representations or discussions preceded the signing of this contract are deemed to have been "merged" into this written agreement and if there was some verbal representation that has not been included in this written document, it was left out on purpose.* Which means that, no matter what they said they'd pay you when you were being courted for the project, they only have to pay you whatever amount is specified in the written agreement. In other words, get it in writing.

Another provision that can become incredibly important in the right circumstances is the "indemnity clause," which is a provision that says that one party will bear all the responsibility for its actions relating to the agreement and will "hold" the other party "harmless" for any results of those actions that create legal liability to any third person.

- SIGNATURES. The signatures of the parties ordinarily appear at the end of the agreement, after a sentence something like this: "In witness whereof, the parties to this Agreement have executed this document in two (2) counterpart originals as of the fifth day of September, 2000." This language means: *We, the people who have signed below, have signed in order to show our acceptance of the terms and conditions of our agreement that are expressed in this document and our intent to abide by those terms and conditions.* This language is followed by spaces for signatures and addresses, if those addresses were not included in the introductory section of the agreement or elsewhere. In the case of a representative of a business who is signing for that business, a space is provided to specify the title of that person. When an individual signs, there may be a space for his or her Social Security number.

  The spaces for such information accompanying the signatures on a contract are often considered to be merely formalities of no great import. This is not so. The space for specifying the title of a person who signs on behalf of a partnership or corporation is a good example. If the person who signs is not a general partner of the partnership or an officer or agent of the corporation who has the actual authority to bind the business in an agreement, the signed, written document may be ineffective to create an actual agreement between the purported parties to it. It's like this: If your crazy cousin Melvin signs a sales contract to buy a cabin cruiser on behalf of his father's office supply store, the contract will be invalid and unenforceable unless Melvin is an officer of his father's corporation or his father's general partner. In the lives of advertising people, this facet of the law generally will come into play only if somebody is trying to get out of a contract. They may be able to wiggle out of the agreement Melvin made if they can say: *Melvin never had the authority to hire your agency to produce a PR film featuring him as the star and you should have known so, since he plainly indicated that he was only the Third Assistant Warehouse Manager when he signed that agreement.* Seasoned businesspeople learn early to deal only with actual decision makers instead of minions whenever this is possible. Watch who signs your contracts, too.

And remember, especially in the case of releases, which are often really short agreements, that under state laws a minor cannot make a binding agreement in most situations. Always insist that the parent of any minor sign for the child, and make sure you know the age of majority for the state in which the release or other contract is entered, since it varies. Don't base any big project on the participation and services of a minor without a lawyer's advice, because you may be left without your talent and without recourse to enforce the minor's agreement.

Informal Agreements

The basic parts of an agreement named above are the sections you'll see in agreements drafted by lawyers. You also need to know about less formal agreements, mostly so that you can recognize them and avoid them. There are three kinds of informal agreements to watch out for: "deal memo" agreements, an exchange of letters, and verbal agreements.

Deal Memos

A short "deal memo" used to set down the terms of an agreement on the spot can be a binding agreement. These are properly used, mostly only by lawyers, to agree preliminarily on the basic terms of complicated agreements and typically are used to get negotiations started, pending the day the basic agreement terms are expanded to full, formal written documents. However, people who don't really know what they're doing also use the term "deal memo" for sketchy documents they jot down or type up during the course of negotiations. Sometimes, improperly, they call the headache they write for themselves a "letter of intent," which sounds harmless and too preliminary to be binding but isn't, because what controls the legality of any written document is *not* the title of that document but what it says. What they mean to do is write down the agreed terms of a proposed agreement that they have not yet firmly decided to enter. They don't think that they are writing a real contract, but they may be, depending on *what* they write. If the basic terms of the agreement are included and the document is signed, a court may find that it embodies enough of the essential ingredients of a contract to be binding, whether both parties knew and wanted this and regardless of what it is called.

The thing about this kind of deal memo is that it can be like a gun that nobody thought was loaded. Lawyers know how to include a "sunset clause" in any document that is not a final expression of the agreed arrangement; that is, they will include a provision in a deal memo to the effect that if a formal agreement is not signed by a certain date, the agreement is off and the partial agreement, the deal memo, will have no further effect after that date. This is necessary because of the possibility of becoming legally bound by any written document that sets out the basic terms of an agreement, even if you do not intend it to be the final expression of your complete agreement. But amateur lawyers and sometimes businesspeople who are otherwise savvy will instead create documents that don't expire under their own terms and omit many important provisions.

For instance: Let's say I am willing to take photographs of your client's new ergonomic computer keyboard at your client's Seattle factory for my regular day rate. This much we agree on. But we haven't agreed on several other points that are important, such as: *Who pays my travel expenses to Seattle—you or me? And do you put the airfare on your corporate card or do I bill you for the ticket? And what do I get paid for travel days? What about the extra days I will have to stay in Seattle if the outdoor shoot is rained out? And how long do you anticipate using the photos, and where? If this is going to be a worldwide campaign to introduce the keyboard or if you want the right to use my photos for more than a year, I'll want to be paid extra, depending on the scope of the use. Or maybe you want to own the copyright in the photos. That's OK with me, but ownership, and unlimited use, will cost you more and the law says that unless I sign a written document specifically transferring ownership to you, the copyrights are mine. Will I be paid according to my usual schedule—one-half of my fee up front and one half on delivery of the photos? And one more thing. I refuse to do this shoot if I have to work for that art director I don't like—can we put you in the agreement as a "key man"?*

Even a simple business agreement can get complicated. Simply agreeing on *what* and *how much* and *when* is not enough. Especially if the agreement is verbal.

Verbal Agreements

Writing down and signing agreements that aren't really hatched yet is dangerous, but what you *say* can be just as dangerous. This is because it is possible to be legally bound by a merely verbal agreement, despite what most people think. If you reply "Sure, OK" when someone asks you to work for a reduced rate putting together a publicity campaign to raise money for a local non-profit and you fail to show up for the publicity committee meeting because you've had second thoughts about spending the time necessary to produce a competent campaign for so little money, you could find yourself being sued for "non-performance"—and for money damages—by the non-profit. And you could lose in court. This is because oral short-term agreements that do not involve large sums of money can be just as valid as written agreements. Verbal agreements are harder to "prove"—that is, it is harder to determine just *who* promised *what* if the agreement is not in writing, but they can be just as valid.

If you think that a verbal agreement you enter into to perform services isn't binding and can't cause you trouble, ask Kim Basinger, who tried to back out on a verbal agreement to appear in a movie she later decided was objectionable. The movie producers sued, and won, and she was forced to declare bankruptcy. It could happen to you, so be careful what you say and never say "yes" before you can see what you are agreeing to in writing.

Exchange of Letters

An exchange of letters (or almost any other written documents, including e-mail messages and faxes) can also constitute a contract between the people who write them if they contain the basic terms of the deal and contain language that can be construed to show that there was agreement between the letter writers. If you send a letter or an e-mail message that states "I'd give a million dollars to have you endorse our golf carts," it may be interpreted as an actual offer for employment by the pro you met at the golf tournament. This is so even though you actually meant your statement only as flattering hyperbole to accompany your request for an autographed photo. If the pro writes back and says yes or shows up in your office to say the same, you may have just become party to an endorsement contract.

Be careful what you write in your letters. It's wise to couch your negotiations, whether written or verbal, in clearly contingent language such as "I *would consider* your proposal to illustrate your children's book *if you offered to pay me* half the royalties earned by the book." Never say "I *will illustrate* your children's book *if you pay me* half the royalties earned by the book" unless you really mean it and, even then, add a hedging sentence like "Of course, before I commit to any such arrangement, I would have to have my lawyer review your formal, written agreement." More than one innocent has been surprised that somebody thought something had been firmly promised when all that was meant was "I might."

Offer and Acceptance

It is important to understand that the basis of all contract law is the offer-and-acceptance sequence. When someone offers you work or a business arrangement, it is just that, an offer. That offer is just a proposal until you accept the terms of an offer. Then the offer and your acceptance become a contract which, in almost every instance, needs to be reduced to writing. If you turn down someone's offer, you have "rejected" the offer and cannot later compel that person to give you what was offered if they don't want to then enter the agreement they formerly proposed. Similarly, once you have accepted someone's offer, a contract exists, sometimes even if it is not yet documented in writing, and that person cannot simply decide to call the deal off because they think they can do better elsewhere, or they offered you too much money, or someone more desirable has become available for the project. And making a new offer, or "counteroffer" in response to an offer has the same effect as simply turning down the offer—it nullifies it. If the person with whom you are negotiating accepts your counteroffer, an agreement is formed. If that person responds to your counteroffer with another counteroffer, the process continues until one of you accepts the other's last counteroffer, at which time an agreement is reached and, probably, the agreement should be memorialized in writing.

This brief account is only a flyby of an area of the law that has filled whole lawbooks, both with the basic offer-and-acceptance sequence and with the numerous rules that have arisen over the years to govern more exotic variations of the basic sequence, such as the now quaint "mailbox rule," which has to do with whether a mailed acceptance of an offer is effective when it is deposited in the mail or when it is received by the person who made the offer. (Usually when it is mailed.) All you need to remember is that you had better be sure you really mean to offer what you say you do, because your offer can magically become a binding contract without any other action by you.

Words, both spoken and written, have power. And because the law assumes that adults will say what they mean and live up to what they say—or agree to do so in writing—any businessperson must understand the importance of careful language. In any setting where somebody's services may be hired—either yours or theirs—and somebody—either you or they—will be expected to pay for those services, watch what you say and watch what you write. Or, as Emily Dickinson said, "A word is dead when it is said, some say. I say it just begins to live that day." Emily was right.

The Roles of Lawyers

Sometimes businesspeople think that if they can write an ad or a business letter or the text for an annual report, writing a contract can't be too hard. They will write, and sign, a homemade agreement in the mistaken belief that if both parties to the agreement are honest, they don't need to hire a lawyer to draft the agreement. A contract of this sort is like an airplane you build in your basement—you may not know whether you omitted some important step in building it until it crashes and burns.

The main problem is that these agreements are usually not only binding but also probably ambiguous. If you sign one of these you can end up being bound by the terms of an agreement that no one can figure out without a lawsuit. Owning a typewriter and a dictionary is not qualification enough to practice law, even if you're only writing an agreement for yourself. In fact, who is more important to protect from half-baked, amateurishly drafted contracts than *you?* If you intend to enter an agreement, get a lawyer to negotiate the best terms or draft the agreement for you.

The easiest and most economical way to use the services of a lawyer when you are contemplating a contract is to conduct preliminary discussions with the person who will be the other party to the agreement and settle on the basic terms to the agreement. Then, write a file memo for your lawyer, briefing him or her about the proposed agreement and your goals in entering it. Your memo to your lawyer isn't a contract or other legal document and doesn't have to be written with any particular care, past informing your lawyer what it is you plan to do and what terms you have reached with the other person who will sign the final agreement. Your memo is, rather, an informational document and so long as it is organized well enough that your lawyer can figure out what you mean, you should include in it as much information as you think might be useful, including some background information. *This* is where smart businesspeople exercise their writing skills—in communicating with their lawyers. Such a memo will enable your lawyer to begin writing the agreement. When the draft agreement satisfies you, submit it to the other party as a formal offer. The other party may then ask for various provisions to be modified or for some to be added to reflect his or her interests. After a little more negotiation, you will—or won't—be able to create the final draft of the contract, the one that you and the other party to the agreement will be happy to sign because it embodies the terms that you have previously discussed.

Lawyers handle this sort of negotiation for their clients all the time, but there is no rule that *requires* your lawyer to negotiate for you. You can review the other party's requests for changes in the agreement, discuss your feelings about them with your lawyer, and get back to the other party yourself. When you and the other party to the agreement have settled on mutually satisfactory terms, you can sign the agreement. This both preserves your relationship with your client and gives you the benefit of legal advice. Although this exercise may seem like a lot of work that could be bypassed, in the case of most agreements of any duration or import it is not. The more important an agreement is to you or your business, the more important it is to document it accurately.

The short form agreements given in the appendix section of this book, the Form Copyright License, Form Copyright Exclusive License, Form Copyright Assignment, Form Copyright Work-for-Hire Agreement, and Form Release for Photographs are simple enough that you should be able to use them without the advice of a lawyer in most situations. However, you should really hire a lawyer to draft more complicated agreements, especially if they involve somebody's services over a long period of time or any significant amount of money. Usually, businesspeople are able to work with only a few standard form agreements that they use to document the recurring business relationships that they enter. An agency agreement, in the case of an advertising agency, is an example of this sort of primary agreement.

If you hire a lawyer to draft the agreements you regularly use, you should be able to negotiate and use those basic agreements whenever you enter a new business relationship without incurring any legal fees. Further, the initial cost of the form agreements is amortized over the life of their use and will probably be recouped more than once by the legal fees you *don't* have to pay to extricate yourself from misunderstandings and to collect what is due you. Ask your lawyer to leave an "Additional Provisions" space in your form agreements or pay for a little instruction from your lawyer in drafting an addendum to the basic agreement whenever you encounter a situation that requires special language. But don't vary from your basic agreement unless there is definitely enough money involved to make special handling of the client or supplier desirable. Otherwise, you end up with as many different agreements as you have clients and your office manager (maybe that's you) will have to remember all the variations from standard procedure.

Many creative people assume that a written contract between people who know and trust each other is unnecessary and that having a lawyer prepare a written agreement in such a case is an avoidable expense. Neither of these assumptions is true. Even if you enter an agreement with another ethical person, a written contract is a necessity, for precision and for documentation. Even honest and knowledgeable businesspeople sometimes fail to communicate to each other all the terms of their agreement. Putting an agreement in writing lets both parties "see" their agreement and provides an opportunity for them to negotiate points of the agreement they have previously omitted from their discussions. Further, a written agreement serves to document the terms of the agreement throughout the life of the business arrangement. Human memory is fallible; even honest people can forget the precise terms of their agreements if they're not written down. And a written agreement can be crucial to proving the existence of the agreement if one of the parties dies, or is fired, or moves away.

And remember that no lawyer can include any provision in any written agreement that will compel ethical conduct from a dishonest person. The best any lawyer can do is to include provisions in a written agreement that prescribe penalties for failure to abide by the terms of the contract, and even this will not ensure that a dishonest person does not act dishonestly. Your best protection against truly dishonest people is to avoid entering agreements with them, since a true renegade has little fear of lawsuits, and in any event, having to go to court to obtain what you were due under the terms of the agreement you made is expensive, time-consuming, and frustrating.

Generally, the more complex the terms of the agreement and the longer its duration, the more it needs to be documented in writing. The very fact that an agreement is in writing can eliminate or lessen the likelihood of disputes. Further, while it may be good business practice to reduce most agreements to writing, some sorts of agreements are not valid or enforceable unless they're in writing. For example, almost universally in English-speaking countries, contracts that may not be performed within a year must be in writing as well as contracts for the sale of goods worth more than $500. And the copyright statute requires transfers and exclusive licenses of copyrights to be in writing. It also provides that nothing an independent contractor creates can be a work-for-hire unless there is a written agreement to that effect signed by both the independent contractor and the person who employed him or her.

All of these are good reasons for consulting a lawyer when you enter into an agreement of any importance. A good lawyer who is familiar with your business can not only help you define and document your agreement, but can advise you concerning the law that governs your business relationship and suggest contract provisions that can help you reach your goals and avoid disputes.

And need we discuss the importance of care in signing documents other people offer you? Consulting a lawyer can be just as important, or even more important, when the contract was drafted by lawyers for the other party. The old saw about never signing an agreement you haven't read is as true as ever, but what you really want to avoid is ever signing an agreement that you *don't understand*. Almost any agreement that requires a written document to memorialize it is important enough to examine carefully before signing. And this probably means having a lawyer review it for you. You should remember that in any business agreement there are actually two sorts of possible written contracts documenting the relationship— their version and your version. This is especially true when the contracting parties are not equal in power, such as when a freelancer is presented with an agreement drafted by lawyers for a large agency. Having your own lawyer in a situation like this can help you feel less like David confronting Goliath.

People tend to get very excited about the money terms of an agreement—who gets paid what and when—and not excited enough about other provisions of the same agreement. Terms in one part of an agreement can modify those in another part of the same agreement. This means that the whole story of who gets paid what and when can be controlled by paragraphs remote from the one that promises you a 15 percent royalty. A skillful lawyer who knows your business can often tweak several paragraphs in an offered agreement to allow you advantages that you didn't know you needed and wanted. These advantages can be just as important—or more important, especially in an agreement involving your creative work—than those outlining the payments due you. Your lawyer can explain complex contract provisions to you and, by negotiating on your behalf, turn the offered agreement into one that allows you more control, gets you paid more quickly, and is generally more favorable than the un-negotiated contract you were originally offered. But your lawyer *must* be familiar with your business before he or she can do the job you need. If you take your contract to a lawyer who says, "Just how long is a copyright these days, anyway?" it's time to consult another lawyer.

Copyrights and trademarks and the personal services of writers and illustrators and photographers are intangible, but they are valuable. This means that the business arrangements surrounding them must be in writing, on paper, and in contracts.

Breaking an Agreement

Sometimes creative people figure that signing agreements is no big deal—that they can simply sue to get out of the contracts they sign if they become unhappy with the people on the other end of them. This is a very dangerous notion. First of all, you can't sue someone just because you feel like it. If you try, your lawyer will tell you to sit down, quit waving your contract, and say slowly and clearly what exactly it is that the other party to the contract has done to breach that contract.

Then your lawyer will give you the third degree. "Has the other person failed to do something promised in the contract? Has that person done something that is prohibited by the contract? Which provision of your contract leads you to believe that you have grounds to sue? Are you aware that your failure to live up to the promises you made in paragraphs 7 through 9 would allow the other party to your contract to retaliate with a countersuit against you if you file suit? Have you considered the implications of paragraph 12 of the agreement, which requires you to give written notice of any claimed breach and allow the other party to the agreement to try to 'cure' the default that you claim has occurred? Do you understand that paragraph 13 of the agreement requires that you bring your suit in the courts of Peoria, Illinois, where the other contracting party maintains its home office? Do you realize that you could become liable for the attorney fees of the person you want to sue if you bring suit and lose?" Your lawyer will end this distressing discussion with the question all lawyers ask all clients before they lift their expensive fountain pens to begin work: "How do you expect to pay my fees?"

Get the picture? Not a pretty one, is it? But it is realistic. It may be that the first lawyer you hate, if you decide to bring suit, is your own, because he or she may have to tell you some home truths about the agreement you signed so cavalierly last year when you still thought you were bulletproof.

Even if you can find a reason to sue and can afford it, and even if you win your suit, you may not get what you want. Judges don't give plaintiffs what they ask for just because they ask. And there are many more likely results of a lawsuit involving a contract than that the contract is declared null and void. One of the most common remedies judges use when someone is unhappy with a contract is "reformation"; this means the judge orders the contract to be altered in some way to cure the inequity the plaintiff complains about. Another result is that the defendant is ordered to pay the plaintiff money damages to compensate the plaintiff for whatever the defendant did wrong. A third remedy is "specific performance," which is the name for what a court orders when it requires the defendant to do what he or she promised to do in the contract. Each of these remedies can give plaintiffs some relief in situations that have become uncomfortable, but none of them gives a plaintiff what he may really want, which is never to have to lay eyes on the defendant again. The law respects the right of adults to enter contracts, presumes that people mean what they agree to in contracts, and hesitates to allow one party to a contract to change her mind and back out of an enforceable agreement. If the law takes seriously your power to enter binding agreements, shouldn't you?

If you approach any contract with care and patience, you should avoid most of the tangles that contracts can cause. Remember, if a business arrangement involves your being paid for your work or paying someone else, it's worth a written contract.

◆ ◆ ◆

Advertising Agency Agreements

The booklet *A Client's Guide to Agency/Client Contracts,* available from the American Association of Advertising Agencies (the AAAA) for $35, is an annotated compendium of various sample contract provisions that agencies and clients may adapt for use in their individual contracts. Explanatory notes accompany each contract provision. Provisions cover such areas as agency services, agency compensation, billing practices, exclusivity, indemnification, term and termination, general provisions, and signatures. The AAAA also publishes *Various Provisions in Agency-Client Agreements,* which contains an assortment of provisions taken from contracts provided by AAAA members and covers such topics as mutually exclusive arrangements, confidentiality, sequential liability, compensation, terminations, and more. Available only to AAAA members, this publication is $10.

Another good discussion of an advertising agency agreement (with comprehensive commentary on its provisions), called the Sample Agreement for Advertising Services, appears in a booklet called *Guidelines for Advertiser/Agency Contracts* by Elhanan C. Stone. Published by and available from the Association of National Advertisers for $22.50, the booklet includes discussions of agency services, compensation for different services, billing and estimating procedures, auditing and accounting, terminating an agreement, ownership of materials, relationships with independent contractors, and conflicts of interest.

These short booklets can teach you, and/or your lawyer, what standard provisions are customary in agency agreements, what those provisions do, and which provisions are desirable from the viewpoint of the client and from that of the agency. Consult the Trade Associations Resources section in the appendix of this book to find out how to order a copy of each booklet, for your own edification and for your files.

◆ ◆ ◆

Appendix

Federal Trade Commission Resources

Besides ensuring that advertising is fair, the Federal Trade Commission is charged with enforcing numerous statutes and rules that have to do with particular industries and their practices.

The FTC's guidelines for complying with the Children's Online Privacy Protection Act are reproduced below:

How to Comply with the Children's Online Privacy Protection Rule

The Children's Online Privacy Protection Act becomes effective April 21, 2000. The regulations apply to the online collection of personal information from children under 13. They spell out what a Web site operator must include in a privacy policy, when and how to seek verifiable consent from a parent, and what responsibilities an operator has to protect children's privacy and safety online.

The Federal Trade Commission staff prepared this guide to help you comply with the new requirements for protecting children's privacy online and understand the FTC's enforcement authority.

Who Must Comply

If you operate a commercial Web site or an online service directed to children under 13 that collects personal information from children or if you operate a general audience Web site and have actual knowledge that it collects personal information from children, you must comply with the Children's Online Privacy Protection Act.

To determine whether a Web site is directed to children, the FTC will consider several factors, including the subject matter; visual or audio content; the age of models on the site; language; whether advertising on the Web site is directed to children; information regarding the age of the actual or intended audience; and whether a site uses animated characters or other child-oriented features.

To determine whether an entity is an "operator" with respect to information collected at a site, the FTC will consider who owns and controls the information; who pays for the collection and maintenance of the information; what the pre-existing contractual relationships are in connection with the information; and what role the Web site plays in collecting or maintaining the information.

Personal Information

The Children's Online Privacy Protection Act and Rule apply to individually identifiable information about a child that is collected online, such as full name, home address, e-mail address, telephone number, or any other information that would allow someone to identify or contact the child. The Act and Rule also cover other types of information—for example, hobbies, interests and information collected through cookies or other types of tracking mechanisms—when they are tied to individually identifiable information.

Basic Provisions

Privacy Notice Placement

An operator must post a link to a notice of its information practices on the home page of its Web site or online service and at each area where it collects personal information from children. An operator of a general audience site with a separate children's area must post a link to its notice on the home page of the children's area.

The link to the privacy notice must be clear and prominent. Operators may want to use a larger font size or a different color type on a contrasting background to make it so. A link in small print at the bottom of the page— or a link that is indistinguishable from other links on your site—is not considered clear and prominent.

Content

The notice must be clearly written and understandable; it should not include any unrelated or confusing materials. It must state the following information:

- The name and contact information (address, telephone number, and e-mail address) of all operators collecting or maintaining children's personal information through the Web site or online service. If more than one operator is collecting information at the site, the site may select and provide contact information for only one operator who will respond to all inquiries from parents about the site's privacy policies. Still, the names of all the operators must be listed in the notice.

- The kinds of personal information collected from children (for example, name, address, e-mail address, hobbies, etc.) and how the information is collected—directly from the child or passively, say, through cookies.
- How the operator uses the personal information. For example, is it for marketing back to the child? Notifying contest winners? Allowing the child to make the information publicly available through a chat room?
- Whether the operator discloses information collected from children to third parties. If so, the operator also must disclose the kinds of businesses in which the third parties are engaged; the general purposes for which the information is used; whether the third parties have agreed to maintain the confidentiality and security of the information; and that the parent has the option to agree to the collection and use of the child's information without consenting to the disclosure of the information to third parties.
- That the operator may not require a child to disclose more information than is reasonably necessary to participate in an activity as a condition of participation.
- That the parent can review the child's personal information, ask to have it deleted, and refuse to allow any further collection or use of the child's information. The notice also must state the procedures for the parent to follow.

Direct Notice to Parents

Content

The notice to parents must contain the same information included on the notice on the Web site. In addition, an operator must notify a parent that it wishes to collect personal information from the child; that the parent's consent is required for the collection, use, and disclosure of the information; and how the parent can provide consent. The notice to parents must be written clearly and understandably, and must not contain any unrelated or confusing information. An operator may use any one of a number of methods to notify a parent, including sending an e-mail message to the parent or a notice by postal mail.

Verifiable Parental Consent

Before collecting, using, or disclosing personal information from a child, an operator must obtain verifiable parental consent from the child's parent. Until April 2002, the FTC will use a sliding scale approach to parental consent in which the required method of consent will vary based on how the operator uses the child's personal information. That is, if the operator uses the information for internal purposes, a less rigorous method of consent is required. If the operator discloses the information to others, the situation presents greater dangers to children, and a more reliable method of consent is required. The sliding scale approach will sunset in April 2002 subject to a Commission review planned for October 2001.

Internal Uses

Operators may use e-mail to get parental consent for all internal uses of personal information, such as marketing back to a child based on his or her preferences or communicating promotional updates about site content, as long as they take additional steps to increase the likelihood that the parent has, in fact, provided the consent. For example, operators might seek confirmation from a parent in a follow up e-mail, or confirm the parent's consent by letter or phone call.

Public Disclosures

When operators want to disclose a child's personal information to third parties or make it publicly available (for example, through a chat room or message board), the sliding scale requires them to use a more reliable method of consent, including:

- getting a signed form from the parent via postal mail or facsimile;
- accepting and verifying a credit card number;
- taking calls from parents, through a toll-free telephone number staffed by trained personnel;
- e-mail accompanied by digital signature;
- e-mail accompanied by a PIN or password obtained through one of the verification methods above.

But in the case of a monitored chat room, if all individually identifiable information is stripped from postings before it is made public—and the information is deleted from the operator's records—an operator does not have to get prior parental consent.

Disclosures to Third Parties

An operator must give a parent the option to agree to the collection and use of the child's personal information without agreeing to the disclosure of the information to third parties. That is, a parent can grant consent to allow his/her child to participate in activities on the site without consenting to the disclosure of the child's information to third parties.

Exceptions

The regulations include several exceptions that allow operators to collect a child's e-mail address without getting the parent's consent in advance. These exceptions cover many popular online activities for kids, including contests, online newsletters, homework help and electronic postcards. Prior parental consent is not required when:

- an operator collects a child's or parent's e-mail address to provide notice and seek consent;
- an operator collects an e-mail address to respond to a one-time request from a child and then deletes it;
- an operator collects an e-mail address to respond more than once to a specific request—say, for a subscription to a newsletter. In this case, the operator must notify the parent that it is communicating regularly with the child and give the parent the opportunity to stop the communication before sending or delivering a second communication to a child;
- an operator collects a child's name or online contact information to protect the safety of a child who is participating on the site. In this case, the operator must notify the parent and give him or her the opportunity to prevent further use of the information;
- an operator collects a child's name or online contact information to protect the security or liability of the site or to respond to law enforcement, if necessary, and does not use it for any other purpose.

October 2001/April 2002

Come October 2001, the Commission will seek comment from interested parties to determine whether technology has progressed as expected and whether secure electronic methods are widely available and affordable. Subject to the Commission's review, the sliding scale will expire in April 2002. Until then, operators are encouraged to use the more reliable methods of consent for all uses of children's personal information.

New Notice for Consent

An operator is required to send a new notice and request for consent to parents if there are material changes in the collection, use, or disclosure practices to which the parent had previously agreed. Take the case of the operator who got parental consent for a child to participate in contests that require the child to submit limited personal information, but who now wants to offer the child chat rooms. Or, consider the case of the operator who wants to disclose the child's information to third parties who are in materially different lines of business from those covered by the original consent—for example, marketers of diet pills rather than marketers of stuffed animals. In these cases, the Rule requires new notice and consent.

Timing

The Rule covers all personal information collected after April 21, 2000, regardless of any prior relationship an operator has had with a child. For example, if an operator collects the name and e-mail address of a child before April 21, 2000, but plans to seek information about the child's street address after that date, the later collection would trigger the Rule's requirements. In addition, come April 21, 2000, if an operator continues to offer activities that involve the ongoing collection of information from children—like a chat room—or begins to offer such activities for the first time, notice and consent are required for all participating children regardless of whether the children had already registered at the site.

Access Verification

At a parent's request, operators must disclose the general kinds of personal information they collect from children (for example, name, address, telephone number, e-mail address, hobbies), as well as the specific information collected from children who visit their sites. Operators must ensure they are dealing with the child's parent before they provide access to the child's specific information. They can use a variety of methods to verify the parent's identity, including:

- obtaining a signed form from the parent via postal mail or facsimile;
- accepting and verifying a credit card number;
- taking calls from parents on a toll-free telephone number staffed by trained personnel;
- e-mail accompanied by digital signature;
- e-mail accompanied by a PIN or password obtained through one of the verification methods above.

Revoking and Deleting

At any time, a parent may revoke his/her consent, refuse to allow an operator to further use or collect their child's personal information, and direct the operator to delete the information. In turn, the operator may terminate any service provided to the child, but only if the information at issue is reasonably necessary for the child's participation in that activity. For example, an operator may require children to provide their e-mail addresses to participate in a chat room so the operator can contact a youngster if he is misbehaving in the chat room. If, after giving consent, a parent asks the operator to delete the child's information, the operator may refuse to allow the child to participate in the chat room in the future. If other activities on the Web site do not require the child's e-mail address, the operator must allow the child access to those activities.

Safe Harbors

Industry groups or others can create self-regulatory programs to govern participants' compliance with the Children's Online Privacy Protection Rule. These guidelines must include independent monitoring and disciplinary procedures and must be submitted to the Commission for approval. The Commission will publish the guidelines and seek public comment in considering whether to approve the guidelines. An operator's compliance with Commission-approved self-regulatory guidelines will serve as a "safe harbor" in any enforcement action for violations of the Rule.

Enforcement

Once the Rule becomes effective (April 2000), the Commission may bring enforcement actions and impose civil penalties for violations in the same manner as for other Rules under the FTC Act. In the meantime, the Commission also retains authority under Section 5 of the FTC Act to examine information practices in use before the Rule's effective date for deception and unfairness. In interpreting Section 5 of the FTC Act, the Commission has determined that a representation, omission or practice is deceptive if it is likely to:

• mislead consumers; and
• affect consumers' behavior or decisions about the product or service.

Specifically, it is a deceptive practice under Section 5 to represent that a Web site is collecting personal identifying information from a child for one reason (say, to earn points to redeem a premium) when the information will be used for another reason that a parent would find material —and when the Web site does not disclose the other reason clearly or prominently.

In addition, an act or practice is unfair if the injury it causes, or is likely to cause, is:

• substantial;
• not outweighed by other benefits; and
• not reasonably avoidable.

For example, it is likely to be an unfair practice in violation of Section 5 to collect personal identifying information from a child, such as e-mail address, home address, or phone number, and sell or otherwise disclose that information to a third party without giving parents adequate notice and a chance to control the collection and use of the information.

For More Information

If you have questions about complying with the Children's Online Privacy Protection Act, visit the FTC online at *www.ftc.gov*. Click on "Privacy Initiatives." Or, call the FTC's Consumer Response Center toll-free at 1-877-FTC-HELP (382-4357), or write Consumer Response Center, Federal Trade Commission, 600 Pennsylvania Avenue, NW, Washington DC 20580.

To assist compliance of the businesses they regulate, the FTC also publishes many pamphlets and guides outlining the requirements applicable to certain activities in the marketplace and to the advertising and selling of certain products and services. The titles of some of the more useful of those publications are listed below, including those designed to educate consumers and businesspeople. Whether you are wearing your "cautious consumer" hat or your "serious businessperson" hat, or both, you will find them informative. Just reading the titles is educational! In addition to the listed publications, the FTC publishes other speeches, policy statements, regulations, federal consumer-protection laws, FTC staff reports, and the transcripts of FTC workshops. These may also be useful to you, depending on how regulated your business activities are and whether you have regular access to a lawyer who can advise you regarding the government's regulation of your industry. You can find all these publications on the FTC Web site, at *www.ftc.gov*.

The FTC Web site is useful, but it probably contains far more information than you ever wanted—or needed—about the activities and pronouncements of the Federal Trade Commission. However, because it is organized logically and indexed for ease of reference, you can learn only about topics that interest you and leave the rest to others. And reading the publications of the FTC *is* a useful expenditure of your time. Think of it this way: You can either find out how to stay on the right side of FTC regulations now, or find out later, when your ads or marketing practices get you in trouble. You choose.

The publications listed below are, like all the information listed on the FTC Web site, divided by topic. Any of these publications may be printed out in text form; most may also be printed in PDF form. Remember that you can order copies of the publications themselves directly from the FTC by using the address at the end of this section.

Order or print off the Web site some of the following useful information, designed by your government to help keep you out of trouble.

FTC Publications for Consumers and Businesses

Advertising

PUBLICATIONS FOR CONSUMERS

Advertising and Marketing on the Internet: The Rules of the Road
Auction Guides: Not So Hot Properties
Eco-Speak: A User's Guide to the Language of Recycling Alert
"Free" and "Low-Cost" PC Offers. Go Figure. Alert
FTC Explains "Made in USA" Standard to Confirm Consumer
      Confidence Alert
Infomercials
Long Distance Deals
Making Sense of Long Distance Advertising
Now Consumers Can Tell It to the FTC—Toll-Free Alert
Project Mailbox III: Catch the Bandit in Your Mailbox Campaign
Sorting out "Green" Advertising Claims
Take the "Bait" out of Rebates Alert
Tips for Making Environmental Marketing Claims on Mail
Toy Ads on Television

PUBLICATIONS FOR BUSINESSES

A Business Checklist for Direct Marketers
Advertising and Marketing on the Internet: The Rules of the Road
Advertising Consumer Leases
Businessperson's Guide to the Mail and Telephone Order
      Merchandise Rule
Complying with the "Made in USA" Standard
Dietary Supplements: An Advertising Guide for Industry
Down . . . But Not Out: Advertising and Labeling of Feather and
      Down Products
Environmental Marketing Claims
Frequently Asked Advertising Questions: A Guide for Small Business
How to Advertise Consumer Credit: Complying with the Law
How to Comply with the Children's Online Privacy Protection Rule
In the Loupe: Advertising Diamonds, Gemstones and Pearls
In-FUR-mation Alert: How to Comply with the Fur Products
      Labeling Act
Making Environmental Marketing Claims on Mail
Project Mailbox III: Catch the Bandit in Your Mailbox Campaign
Screening Advertisements: A Guide for the Media
Selling on the Internet: Prompt Delivery Rules Alert

Threading Your Way through the Labeling Requirements under the
     Textile and Wool Acts
Voluntary Guidelines for Providers of Weight Loss Products or Services
Wedding Gown Labels: Unveiling the Requirements
When Yellow Pages Invoices Are Bogus Alert
Y2K? Y2Care: Communicating Product Compliance to Customers Alert

GUIDES
Dietary Supplements: An Advertising Guide for Industry
FTC Guide Concerning the Use of Endorsements and Testimonials
FTC Guide Concerning the Use of the Word "Free"
FTC Guides against Deceptive Pricing
Guides for Private Vocational and Distance Education Schools
Guides for the Household Furniture Industry
Guides for the Jewelry, Precious Metals, and Pewter Industries
Refractive Eye Surgery Advertising: Guidance for Marketers

POLICY STATEMENTS
Enforcement Policy Statement on Food Advertising
Enforcement Policy Statement on U.S. Origin Claims ("Made in USA")
FTC Policy Statement on Comparative Advertising
FTC Policy Statement on Deception
FTC Policy Statement on Unfairness
FTC Policy Statement Regarding Advertising Substantiation
Joint FCC/FTC Policy Statement for the Advertising of Dial-Around
     and Other Long-Distance Services to Consumers
"Made in USA" Standard

Automobiles

PUBLICATIONS FOR CONSUMERS
66 Ways to Save Money
Auction Guides: Not So Hot Properties
Auto Service Contracts
Buying a New Car
Buying a Used Car
Buying a Used Car Alert
Car Ads: Reading between the Lines
Consider the Alternatives: Alternative Fueled Vehicles and Alternative
     Vehicle Fuels
"Gas-Saving" Products
How to Be Penny Wise, Not Pump Fuelish Alert

Keys to Vehicle Leasing
Look Before You Lease Alert
The Low-Down on High Octane Gasoline
Now Consumers Can Tell It to the FTC—Toll-Free Alert
Renting a Car
Saving Money at the Pump Brief
Taking the Scare out of Auto Repair
Tips for Buying a Used Car
Vehicle Repossession

PUBLICATIONS FOR BUSINESSES
A Dealer's Guide to the Used Car Rule
How to Comply with the FTC Fuel Rating Rule
Labeling Alternative Fueled Vehicles
Labeling Alternative Fuels

Children's Issues

PUBLICATIONS FOR CONSUMERS
Entertainment Ratings: Pocket Guide
How to Be Web Ready
How to Protect Kids' Privacy Online
Now Consumers Can Tell It to the FTC—Toll-Free Alert
Protecting Kids from the Sun
Ready, Set . . . Credit
The Real Deal: Playing the Buying Game
$cholarship $cams Campaign
Site-Seeing on the Internet: A Consumer's Guide to Travel in Cyberspace
Traveling in Cyberspace? Be Savvy! Campaign

PUBLICATIONS FOR BUSINESSES
900 Numbers: Advertising to Children
How to Comply with the Children's Online Privacy Protection Rule

Credit

PUBLICATIONS FOR CONSUMERS
66 Ways to Save Money
Ads Promising Debt Relief May Be Offering Bankruptcy Alert
Advance-Fee Loan Scams Campaign
Automatic Debit Scams

Avoiding Credit and Charge Card Fraud
Building a Better Credit Record
Choosing and Using Credit Cards
Cosigning a Loan
Credit and ATM Cards: What to Do If They're Lost or Stolen
Credit and Divorce
Credit and Your Consumer Rights
Credit Card Blocking
Credit Card Loss Protection Offers: They're the Real Steal
Credit Repair: Getting Back in the Black Campaign
Credit Repair: Help Yourself First Alert
Credit Repair: Self-Help May Be Best
Credit Rules Bookmark
Credit Scoring
Easy Credit? Not So Fast. The Truth about Advance-Fee Loan Scams
Electronic Banking
Equal Credit Opportunity
Fair Credit Billing
Fair Credit Reporting
Fair Credit Reporting Act (as amended) Campaign
Fair Debt Collection
Fiscal Fitness: Choosing a Credit Counselor
Getting a Loan: Your Home as Security
Getting Credit When You're Over 62
Getting Purse-onal Alert
Gold and Platinum Cards
Guide to Online Payments
High-Rate, High-Fee Loans (Section 32 Mortgages)
Home Equity Credit Lines
Home Equity Scams: Borrowers Beware!
Home Financing Primer
How to Dispute Credit Report Errors
Identity Crisis . . . What to Do If Your Identity Is Stolen Alert
Identity Theft: Identity Thieves Can Ruin Your Good Name
ID Theft Web Site
ID Theft: When Bad Things Happen to Your Good Name
Just When You Thought It Was Safe . . . Advance-Fee Loan "Sharks" Alert
Knee Deep in Debt
Looking for the Best Mortgage?
Mortgage Discrimination
Mortgage Servicing
NCPWeek-ly: Credit Fraud—Know the Rules, Use the Tools
Need a Loan? Think Twice about Using Your Home as Collateral Alert

Negative Credit Can Squeeze a Job Search
New ID? Bad IDea: File Segregation Exposed
Now Consumers Can Tell It to the FTC—Toll-Free Alert
Payday Loans=Costly Cash
Ready, Set . . . Credit
Refinancing Your Home
Reverse Mortgages
Second Mortgage Financing
Secured Credit Card Marketing Scams
The Credit Practices Rule
Using Ads to Shop for Home Financing
Utility Credit
Year 2000 Consumer Update: Banking
Y2K? Y2Care: Preparing Your Personal Finances for the
    Year 2000 Alert
Y2K? Y2Care: Protecting Your Finances from Y2K
    Scam Artists Alert

PUBLICATIONS FOR BUSINESSES
Advertising Consumer Leases
Complying with the Credit Practices Rule
Consumer Reports: What Insurers Should Know about Them
Credit Reports: What Information Providers Need to Know
Fair Credit Reporting Act (as amended) Campaign
Getting Business Credit Alert
How to Advertise Consumer Credit: Complying with the Law
How to Write Readable Credit Forms
Using Consumer Reports: What Employers Need to Know
Y2K? Y2 Care: 7 Steps to a Successful Transition for Consumer
    Financial Service Providers Alert

RULES AND ACTS
Consumer Leasing Act
Credit Repair Organizations Act
Electronic Fund Transfer Act
Equal Credit Opportunity Act
Fair Credit and Charge Card Disclosure Act—Fair Credit Billing Act
Fair Credit Reporting Act (FCRA) (as amended, November 1999)
Fair Credit Reporting Act—Home Page
Fair Debt Collection Practices Act (FDCPA) (as amended)
Fair Debt Collection Practices Act—Home Page
Federal Deposit Insurance Corporation Improvement Act of 1991
Home Ownership and Equity Protection Act

Identity Theft and Assumption Deterrence Act
Information about the Opt-out Provisions of the FCRA
Notices of Rights and Duties under the FCRA (July 1, 1997)
Truth in Lending Act

Diet, Health, and Fitness

PUBLICATIONS FOR CONSUMERS
Aging Parents and Adult Children Together (A/PACT)
Avoiding the Muscle Hustle: Tips for Buying Exercise Equipment
     Campaign
Avoiding the Muscle Hustle Brief
Eye Wear
Fraudulent Health Claims
Generic Drugs: Saving Money at the Pharmacy
Health Spas: Exercise Your Rights
Home-Use Tests for HIV Can Be Inaccurate, FTC Warns
Indoor Tanning
Infertility Services
Lotions and Potions: The Bottom Line about Multilevel
     Marketing Plans
The Muscle Hustle: Test Your Exercise I.Q. Brief
Now Consumers Can Tell It to the FTC—Toll-Free Alert
Paunch Lines: Weight Loss Claims Are No Joke for Dieters Alert
Project Waistline Campaign
Protecting Kids from the Sun
Pump Fiction: Tips for Buying Exercise Equipment
Setting Goals for Healthy Weight Loss
Sound Advice on Hearing Aids
Sunscreens
The Skinny on Dieting
The Truth about Impotence Treatment Claims Alert
Viatical Settlements: A Guide for People with Terminal Illnesses
Virtual Health "Treatments" Campaign
Virtual "Treatments" Can Be Real-World Deceptions Alert
Vision Correction Procedures
Who Cares: Sources of Info about Health Care Products and Services

PUBLICATIONS FOR BUSINESSES
Dietary Supplements: An Advertising Guide for Industry
Voluntary Guidelines for Providers of Weight Loss Products
     or Services

GUIDES
Refractive Eye Surgery Advertising: Guidance for Marketers

E-Commerce and the Internet

PUBLICATIONS FOR CONSUMERS
Don't Get Burned by a Pyramid Scheme Campaign
Entertainment Ratings: Pocket Guide
"Free" and "Low-Cost" PC Offers. Go Figure. Alert
FTC Names Its Dirty Dozen: 12 Scams Most Likely to Arrive via Bulk
    E-mail Alert
Going Shopping? Go Global! A Guide for E-Consumers Alert
Guide to Online Payments
How to Be Web Ready
How to Protect Kids' Privacy Online
ID Theft: When Bad Things Happen to Your Good Name
International Lottery Scams Alert
Internet Auctions: A Guide for Buyers and Sellers
Internet Auctions: Secrets of Success Alert
Medical Billing Business Opportunity Schemes
'Net Based Business Opportunities: Are Some Flop-portunities?
'Net Based Business Opportunities: Beware of Flop-portunities Alert
Now Consumers Can Tell It to the FTC—Toll-Free Alert
Online Investment Opportunities: 'Net Profit or 'Net Gloss? Alert
Online Investment Opportunities: 'Net Profit or 'Net Gloss? Campaign
Problems with Online Holiday Purchase? Alert
Safe Shopping Tips (Holiday Shopping Tips)
Shop Safely Online
Site-Seeing on the Internet: A Consumer's Guide to Travel in Cyberspace
Take the "Bait" out of Rebate Alert
Traveling in Cyberspace? Be Savvy! Campaign
Trouble @ the In-Box
Trouble @ the In-Box Alert
Unsolicited Mail, Telemarketing and E-mail: Where to Go to "Just Say
    No" Alert

PUBLICATIONS FOR BUSINESSES
Advertising and Marketing on the Internet: The Rules of the Road
BBB-Online: Code of Online Business Practices
Electronic Commerce: Selling Internationally. A Guide for Business Alert
How to Comply with the Children's Online Privacy Protection Rule
Internet Auctions: A Guide for Buyers and Sellers

Selling on the Internet: Prompt Delivery Rules Alert
Web site Woes: Avoiding Web Service Scams Alert

Environment

PUBLICATIONS FOR CONSUMERS
Consider the Alternatives: Alternative Fueled Vehicles and Alternative
      Vehicle Fuels
Eco-Speak: A User's Guide to the Language of Recycling Alert
Energy Efficient Light Bulbs: A Bright Idea
Energy Guide to Home Heating and Cooling
Energy Guide to Major Home Appliances
"Gas-Saving" Products
The Low-Down on High Octane Gasoline
Now Consumers Can Tell It to the FTC—Toll-Free Alert
Rebuilding Your Home after a Disaster
Sorting Out "Green" Advertising Claims
Tips for Making Environmental Marketing Claims on Mail
Water Testing Scams
Year 2000 Consumer Updates—Air Travel in the Year 2000

PUBLICATIONS FOR BUSINESSES
Complying with the FTC's Appliance Labeling Rule
Environmental Marketing Claims
How to Comply with the FTC Fuel Rating Rule
Labeling Alternative Fueled Vehicles
Labeling Alternative Fuels
Making Environmental Marketing Claims on Mail

GUIDES
Guides for the Use of Environmental Marketing Claims (Green Guides)

Franchise and Business Opportunities

PUBLICATIONS FOR CONSUMERS
Answering the Knock of a Business "Opp" Alert
Consumer Guide to Buying a Franchise
Could Biz Opp Offers Be Out for Your Coffers?
Franchise and Business Opportunities
The Gifting Club "Gotcha"
Going to Display Rack and Ruin

Lotions and Potions: The Bottom Line about Multilevel Marketing Plans
Medical Billing Business Opportunity Schemes
Multilevel Marketing Plans
'Net Based Business Opportunities: Are Some Flop-portunities?
'Net Based Business Opportunities: Beware of Flop-portunities
Now Consumers Can Tell It to the FTC—Toll-Free Alert
Project Trade Name Games Campaign
The Seminar Pitch: A Real Curve Ball
Thinking of Buying a Business Opportunity?
Wealth Building Scams
Work-at-Home Schemes

GUIDES
Your Legal Rights: Guide to the FTC Franchise Rule

At Home

PUBLICATIONS FOR CONSUMERS
66 Ways to Save Money
Aging Parents and Adult Children Together (A/PACT)
Auction Guides: Not So Hot Properties
Avoiding Home Equity Scams Alert
Cooling off Rule
Energy Guide to Home Heating and Cooling
Energy Guide to Major Home Appliances
Entertainment Ratings: Pocket Guide
Getting a Loan: Your Home as Security
The Gifting Club "Gotcha"
High-Rate, High-Fee Loans (Section 32 Mortgages)
Home Equity Credit Lines
Home Equity Loans: The Three-Day Cancellation Rule Alert
Home Equity Scams: Borrowers Beware!
Home Financing Primer
Home Improvement: Tools You Can Use Campaign
Home Sweet Home Improvement
Home Water Treatment Units
How to Be Web Ready
How to Buy a Manufactured Home
How to Protect Kids' Privacy Online
ID Theft: When Bad Things Happen to Your Good Name
Internet Auctions: A Guide for Buyers and Sellers
Lawn Service Contracts

Looking for the Best Mortgage?
Mortgage Discrimination
Mortgage Servicing
Need a Loan? Think Twice about Using Your Home as
     Collateral Alert
Now Consumers Can Tell It to the FTC—Toll-Free Alert
Problems with Online Holiday Purchase? Alert
Project Mailbox III: Catch the Bandit in Your Mailbox Campaign
Rebuilding Your Home After a Disaster
Refinancing Your Home
Reverse Mortgages
Reverse Mortgages—Cashing In on Home Ownership Alert
Safe Shopping Tips (Holiday Shopping Tips)
Second Mortgage Financing
Shop Safely Online
Shopping by Phone: A One-Stop Guide to Consumer Protection
Shopping by Phone or Mail
Take the "Bait" out of Rebates Alert
Thinking about a Home Improvement? Don't Get Nailed Alert
Time-share Resales
Time-share Tips
Using Ads to Shop for Home Financing
Wash Daze: Laundry Gadgets Won't Lighten the Load Alert

PUBLICATIONS FOR BUSINESSES
Down . . . But Not Out: Advertising and Labeling of Feather and
     Down Products
Internet Auctions: A Guide for Buyers and Sellers
Project Mailbox III: Catch the Bandit in Your Mailbox Campaign
Threading Your Way through the Labeling Requirements under the
     Textile and Wool Acts

GUIDES
Guides for the Household Furniture Industry

Investments

PUBLICATIONS FOR CONSUMERS
$100K a Year? Mmmmm . . . Brief
Answering the Knock of a Business "Opp" Alert
Consumer Guide to Buying a Franchise
Costly Coupon Scams

Could Biz Opp Offers Be out for Your Coffers?
Don't Get Burned . . . by a Pyramid Scheme Campaign
FCC License Auctions Alert
Franchise and Business Opportunities
Get-Rich-Quick and Self-Employment Schemes Campaign
The Gifting Club "Gotcha"
Going to Display Rack and Ruin
How to Avoid Losing Your Money to Investment Frauds Alert
International Lottery Scams Alert
Investing in Rare Coins Alert
Investment Risks
IRS Does Not Approve IRA Investments Alert
Lights! Camera! Rip-Off! How to Tell When a Scam Is Born Alert
Looking for the Best Mortgage?
Make Huge Profits with Amazing No-Risk Investments Brief
Medical Billing Business Opportunity Schemes
Multilevel Marketing Plans
'Net Based Business Opportunities: Are Some Flop-portunities?
'Net Based Business Opportunities: Beware of Flop-portunities Alert
Now Consumers Can Tell It to the FTC—Toll-Free Alert
Online Investment Opportunities: 'Net Profit or 'Net Gloss? Alert
Online Investment Opportunities: 'Net Profit or 'Net Gloss? Campaign
Profits in Pyramid Schemes? Don't Bank on It Alert
Project Mailbox III: Catch the Bandit in Your Mailbox? Campaign
Project Trade Name Games Campaign
Psst . . . Wanna Buy a Bridge? Campaign
The Seminar Pitch: A Real Curve Ball
So You've Got a Great Idea? Brief
So You've Got a Great Idea? Campaign
Taxpayers with IRA's: FYI
Telecommunication Scams Using FCC Licenses
Test Your Investment IQ
Time-share Resales
Time-share Tips
Trouble @ the In-Box
Viatical Settlements: A Guide for People with Terminal Illnesses
Wealth Building Scams
Work-at-Home Schemes
Y2K? Y2Care: Preparing Your Personal Finances for the Year 2000 Alerts

PUBLICATIONS FOR BUSINESSES
Y2K? Y2Care: 7 Steps to a Successful Transition for Consumer Financial
    Service Providers Alert

Pay-Per-Call Services

PUBLICATIONS FOR CONSUMERS
"900" Numbers: FTC Rule Helps Consumers
Cramming: Mystery Phone Charges
International Telephone Number Scams
International Telephone Number Scams Alert
Long Distance Deals
Making Sense of Long Distance Advertising
Now Consumers Can Tell It to the FTC—Toll-Free Alert
Phone, E-Mail, and Pager Messages May Signal Costly Scams Alert
Toll-Free Telephone Number Scams

PUBLICATIONS FOR BUSINESSES
Complying with the 900-Number Rule

Products and Services

PUBLICATIONS FOR CONSUMERS
After a Disaster: Hiring a Contractor Alert
Aging Parents and Adult Children Together (A/PACT)
All That Glitters . . . How to Buy Jewelry
Auction Guides: Not So Hot Properties
Avoiding the Muscle Hustle: Tips for Buying Exercise Equipment
      Campaign
Beloved . . . Bejeweled . . . Be Careful: What to Know Before You Buy
      Jewelry Alert
Buying Time: The Facts about Pre-Paid Phone Cards
Caring for Your Clothes
Caskets and Burial Vaults
Choosing a Career or Vocational School
Closet Cues: Care Labels and Your Clothes
Clothing Care Symbol Guide
Cramming: Mystery Phone Charges
Eco-Speak: A User's Guide to the Language of Recycling Alert
Electronic Checkout Scanners Campaign
Energy Efficient Light Bulbs: A Bright Idea
Entertainment Ratings: Pocket Guide
Focus on Phone Leasing
"Free" and "Low-Cost" PC Offers. Go Figure. Alert
FTC Explains "Made in USA" Standard to Confirm Consumer
      Confidence Alert

Funerals: A Consumer Guide
The Gifting Club "Gotcha"
Green Card Lottery Scams Alert
Grocery Store Rain Checks
Help Wanted . . . Finding a Job
Home Improvement: Tools You Can Use Campaign
Home Sweet Home Improvement
Home Water Treatment Units
Home-Use Tests For HIV Can Be Inaccurate, FTC Warns
How to Right a Wrong
If You've Got "The Look" . . . Look Out! Avoiding Modeling Scams
Infomercials
Internet Auctions: A Guide for Buyers and Sellers
It's Your Call: Shopping in the New Telecommunications Marketplace
Kitchen Gadgets Offer Food for "Thaw-t" Alert
Lawn Service Contracts
Layaway Purchase Plans
Long Distance Deals
Lotions and Potions: The Bottom Line about Multilevel Marketing Plans
Making Sense of Long Distance Advertising
Making Sure the Scanned Price Is Right
The Muscle Hustle: Test Your Exercise I.Q. Brief
Negative Option Plans for Books, Records, Videos
Now Consumers Can Tell It to the FTC—Toll-Free Alert
Personal Emergency Response Systems
Petal Pushers: Is Your 'Local' Florist Really Long-Distance? Alert
Problems with Online Holiday Purchase? Alert
Project CLEAN Campaign
Pump Fiction: Tips for Buying Exercise Equipment
Rebuilding Your Home After a Disaster
Resolving Consumer Disputes: Mediation and Arbitration
A Rose Is a Rose Is a Ruse? Campaign
Safe Shopping Tips (Holiday Shopping Tips)
Service Contracts
So You've Got a Great Idea? Brief
So You've Got a Great Idea? Campaign
Solving Consumer Problems
Spotting Sweet-Sounding Promises of Fraudulent Invention Promotion
     Firms Alert
Take the "Bait" out of Rebates Alert
Thinking about a Home Improvement? Don't Get Nailed Alert
Tips for Making Environmental Marketing Claims on Mail
Tobacco Products

Toy Ads on Television
Unordered Merchandise
Viatical Settlements: A Guide for People with Terminal Illnesses
Warranties
Wash Daze: Laundry Gadgets Won't Lighten the Load Alert
Water Testing Scams
Who Cares: Sources of Information about Health Care Products
    and Services
Y2K? Y2Care: Consumer Electronic Products Alert
Y2K? Y2Care: Information-Technology and Home Office Products Alert
Year 2000 Consumer Updates: Air Travel in the Year 2000

PUBLICATIONS FOR BUSINESSES
A Businessperson's Guide to Federal Warranty Law
Businessperson's Guide to the Mail and Telephone Order Merchandise Rule
Calling It Cotton: Labeling and Advertising Cotton Products
Complying with the FTC's Appliance Labeling Rule
Complying with the Funeral Rule
Complying with the "Made in USA" Standard
Down . . . But Not Out: Advertising and Labeling of Feather and
    Down Products
Environmental Marketing Claims
Five Steps to Avoiding Office Supply Scams Alert
Good Pricing Practices? SCAN DO
How to Comply with the Children's Online Privacy Protection Rule
In the Loupe: Advertising Diamonds, Gemstones and Pearls
In-FUR-mation Alert—How to Comply with the Fur Products
    Labeling Act
Internet Auctions: A Guide for Buyers and Sellers
Labeling Alternative Fueled Vehicles
Labeling Alternative Fuels
Measuring Up! Good Packaging Practices for Dairy Products
Project BOSS: Banish Office Supply Scams
Selling on the Internet: Prompt Delivery Rules Alert
Threading Your Way through the Labeling Requirements under the
    Textile and Wool Acts
Website Woes: Avoiding Web Service Scams Alert
Wedding Gown Labels: Unveiling the Requirements
Writing a Care Label: How to Comply with Amended Care
    Labeling Rule
Writing Readable Warranties
Y2K? Y2Care: Communicating Product Compliance to Your
    Customers Alert

GUIDES
Guides for the Household Furniture Industry
Guides for the Jewelry, Precious Metals, and Pewter Industries

Scholarships, Employment, and Job Placement

PUBLICATIONS FOR CONSUMERS
Choosing a Career or Vocational School
Coping with a Temporary Loss of Income
Federal and Postal Job Scams: Tip-offs to Rip-offs Alert
Get-Rich-Quick and Self-Employment Schemes Campaign
Help Wanted . . . Finding a Job
Medical Billing Business Opportunity Schemes
Now Consumers Can Tell It to the FTC—Toll-Free Alert
OUCH . . . Students Getting Stung Trying to Find $$$ for College Alert
Scholarship Scams Campaign

PUBLICATIONS FOR BUSINESSES
Raising Funds? What to Know about Hiring a Professional

GUIDES
Guides for Private Vocational and Distance Education Schools

Telemarketing

PUBLICATIONS FOR CONSUMERS
66 Ways to Save Money
Advance-Fee Loan Scams Campaign
Aging Parents and Adult Children Together (A/PACT)
Are You a Target of . . . Telephone Scams?
Automatic Debit Scams
Avoid a School Break Bust Alert
Border-Line Scams Are the Real Thing Alert
Charitable Donation$: Give or Take?
Easy Credit? Not So Fast. The Truth about Advance-Fee Loan Scams
FTC Names Its Dirty Dozen: 12 Scams Most Likely to Arrive Via Bulk
    E-mail Alert
ID Theft: When Bad Things Happen to Your Good Name
International Lottery Scams Alert
It's Your Call: Shopping in the New Telecommunications Marketplace
Just When You Thought It Was Safe . . . Advance-Fee Loan "Sharks" Alert

Magazine Subscription Scams
Now Consumers Can Tell It to the FTC—Toll-Free Alert
Operation False Alarm Campaign
Operation Missed Giving Campaign
Prize Offers
Project Know Fraud: Telemarketing Fraud
Project Mailbox III: Catch the Bandit in Your Mailbox Campaign
Public Safety Fund-Raising Appeals: Make Your Donations Count Alert
Putting Cold Calls on Ice Alert
Reloading Scams: Double Trouble for Consumers
A Rose Is a Rose Is a Ruse? Campaign
Spread the Word about Telemarketing Fraud Campaign
Straight Talk about Telemarketing
Telemarketing Fraud: What You Need to Know. Project Know Fraud
Telemarketing Recovery Scams
Telemarketing Travel Fraud
Toll-Free Telephone Number Scams
Traveler's Advisory: Get What You Pay For Alert
Unsolicited Mail, Telemarketing and E-mail: Where to Go to "Just Say
    No" Alert
Y2K? Y2Care: New Consumer Alert Offers Tips for Protecting Your
    Finances from Year 2000 Scam Artists

PUBLICATIONS FOR BUSINESSES
Avoiding Office Supply Scams
Businessperson's Guide to the Mail and Telephone Order
    Merchandise Rule
Complying with the Telemarketing Sales Rule
Donating to Public Safety Fund-Raiser$
Five Steps to Avoiding Office Supply Scams Alert
Guidelines for Managers of Telemarketing Enterprises Who Sell
    Magazine Subscriptions
Project BOSS: Banish Office Supply Scams
Project Mailbox III: Catch the Bandit in Your Mailbox Campaign
Operation False Alarm Campaign
Operation Missed Giving Campaign
Raising Funds? What to Know about Hiring a Professional
Website Woes: Avoiding Web Service Scams Alert

How to Order Printed Copies of Publications

If you would prefer to have printed copies of any of the publications listed
above, you may order them directly from the FTC. Send your name,

address, and telephone and fax numbers to the address below; include your list of requested publications and an indication of the number of copies of each you need.

Consumer Response Center
Federal Trade Commission
Room H-130
600 Pennsylvania Avenue, N.W.
Washington, DC 20580-0001

You may also fax your request to: (202) 326-2572.

Other Federal Agencies

Advertising for any kind of product or service is regulated by the Federal Trade Commission, but other federal agencies also regulate the marketing of certain products. Sometimes jurisdiction over the advertising and sale of one sort of product is shared by more than one of these other agencies. If you create advertising or publicity materials for any of these products, contact the agency that regulates such advertising for that product to request copies of the regulations by which you must abide and for publications explaining those regulations. Much of this information is available to be printed out from the Web sites for the agencies, the addresses for which are given below. Note that this list of agencies that regulate advertising and the list of products and services they regulate is not exhaustive.

Bureau of Alcohol, Tobacco and Firearms (BATF)
Web site: *www.atf.treas.gov*
Alcoholic beverages

Consumer Product Safety Commission (CPSC)
Web site: *www.cpsc.gov/search/cpscQueryhit.htm*
Bicycles
Consumer products
Flammable fabrics
Hazardous materials and poisons
Refrigerators
Toys

Department of Agriculture
Web site: *www.usda.gov*
Eggs and egg products
Fruits and vegetables
Meat and meat products
Poultry and poultry products
Seeds

Department of Commerce
Web site: *www.doc.gov*
Consumer products
Fire detection and fire extinguishing devices
Fruits and vegetables
Seafood

Department of Energy
Web site: *www.doe.gov*
Air conditioners
Dishwashers
Heaters and heating devices (such as furnaces)
Ovens, ranges, and microwave ovens
Refrigerators and freezers
Stereos
Televisions
Washers and dryers
Water heaters

Department of Housing and Urban Development (HUD)
Web site: *www.hud.gov*
Apartments
Land and real estate
Mobile homes

Department of Transportation (DOT)
Web site: *www.dot.gov*
Boats
Motorized vehicles
Tires
Airlines, bus companies, and other carriers

Department of the Treasury
Web site: *www.treas.gov*
Alcoholic beverages
Imported goods
Tobacco products

Environmental Protection Agency (EPA)
Web site: *www.epa.gov/epahome/search.html*
Engines
Fuels and fuel additives
Insect and rodent traps and repellents
Insecticides and pesticides
Motorized vehicles
Noise-emitting devices
Poisons

Federal Reserve Board (FRB)
Web site: *www.bog.frb.fed.us/general.htm*

Food and Drug Administration (FDA)
Web site: *www.fda.gov*
Authorized by Congress to enforce the Federal Food, Drug, and Cosmetic
Act and several other public health laws, the agency monitors, among other
activities, the advertising and marketing of:
Food and non-alcoholic beverages
Biological products
Cosmetics
Medicines and medical devices (such as hearing aids)
Radiation-emitting consumer products (such as microwave ovens)
Feed and drugs for pets and farm animals

Securities and Exchange Commission (SEC)
Web site: *www.sec.gov*

Internal Revenue Service (IRS):
Web site: *www. irs.gov*
Some political advertising

U.S. Postal Service
Web site: *www.usps.gov/environ/webpages/search.htm*

Better Business Bureau Programs and Guidelines

According to the Better Business Bureau (BBB), "fostering public confidence in truthful advertising was the primary concern that led to the formation of the organizations that today are called Better Business Bureaus" and "the monitoring of advertising remains a key part of the BBB's overall mission." For advertisers and those who create advertising, the programs of the Better Business Bureau can be extremely useful tools for staying on the right side of the Federal Trade Commission and the other government agencies, both state and national, that regulate advertising.

Better Business Bureau Advertising Review Programs

Local Better Business Bureaus regularly monitor advertising for truth and accuracy, as well as for compliance with local, state, and federal regulations relating to advertising. When possibly questionable advertising is noted, the advertiser is contacted and requested to substantiate the claims that are being made, and to voluntarily comply with the guidelines.

The national Council of Better Business Bureaus (CBBB) administers what the chairman of the Federal Trade Commission called "the best example of self-regulation in the country." This is the joint effort of the three units of the Council of Better Business Bureaus that monitor national advertising with the voluntary participation of advertisers. These three units are the National Advertising Division (NAD), the Children's Advertising Review Unit (CARU), and the National Advertising Review Board (NARB). Working in concert with the NARB, the NAD investigates questions of truth and accuracy in national commercial advertising. The CARU reviews advertising directed at children under the age of twelve for compliance with CARU's Self-Regulatory Guidelines for Children's Advertising. The three units also review, evaluate, investigate, and resolve complaints about such ads, which come largely from competitors, but also from consumers and trade associations. "National advertising" is defined as "any paid commercial message, in any medium (including labeling), if it has the purpose of inducing a sale or other commercial transaction or persuading the audience of the value or usefulness of a company, product or service; if it is disseminated nationally or to a substantial portion of the United States, or is test market advertising prepared for national campaigns, and if the content is controlled by the advertiser."

The final case decisions of NAD, CARU, and NARB are published in *NAD Case Reports*. This publication, issued ten times a year, is one of the best ways advertisers can educate themselves about acceptable, and unacceptable, advertising practices. The reports it contains dissect and analyze advertising claims in great detail. Participation in the review process is voluntary for advertisers, and the NAD has no enforcement powers, but advertisers usually heed the NAD's judgments, since any advertiser that refuses to voluntarily modify an ad that is deemed to be untruthful or inaccurate, or fails to abide by the CARU Guidelines, is likely to be reported by the NAD to the FTC, which takes the NAD's judgments and recommendations very seriously. Individual copies of *NAD Case Reports* are $100 each; an annual subscription is $1,000. The NAD's decisions are also now available on CD; this is an excellent research tool and a good resource for developing advertising. Call or write the National Advertising Division to inquire about a subscription to *NAD Case Reports* or to buy the comprehensive CD (which is also available from the Association of National Advertisers— see the Trade Association Resources section of this appendix to order from The Association of National Advertisers).

National Advertising Division
Council of Better Business Bureaus, Inc.
845 Third Avenue
New York, NY 10022
(212) 754-1320
www.bbb.org

Whether you create ads that are disseminated nationally or published and aired only by local or regional publications and broadcasters, if you read and abide by the two Better Business Bureau advertising codes reproduced below (by permission of the Council of Better Business Bureaus), your ads will likely escape the notice of local, state, or federal regulators. Read and use both the Better Business Bureau Code of Advertising and the CARU Self-Regulatory Guidelines for Children's Advertising to make sure your ads escape the sort of attention you'd rather avoid.

Better Business Bureau Code of Advertising

Foreword

These basic advertising standards are issued for the guidance of advertisers, advertising agencies, and advertising media.

It is not possible to cover fully the wide variety of advertising practices by specific standards in a code of this type, which is designed to apply to the offering of all goods and services. Where the Better Business Bureau has developed specific industry advertising codes, it is recommended that industry members adhere to them. If specific questions arise which are not covered or involve advertising directed to children, it is recommended that *Do's and Don'ts in Advertising* (a comprehensive two volume loose-leaf compendium published by the Council of Better Business Bureaus) be consulted. Advertisers, agencies, and media should also be sure that they are in compliance with local, state, and federal laws and regulations governing advertising.

Adherence to the provisions of this Code will be a significant contribution toward effective self-regulation in the public interest.

Basic Principles

1. The primary responsibility for truthful and non-deceptive advertising rests with the advertiser. Advertisers should be prepared to substantiate any claims or offers made before publication or broadcast and, upon request, present such substantiation promptly to the advertising medium or the Better Business Bureau.
2. Advertisements which are untrue, misleading, deceptive, fraudulent, falsely disparaging of competitors, or insincere offers to sell shall not be used.
3. An advertisement as a whole may be misleading although every sentence separately considered is literally true. Misrepresentation may result not only from direct statements but by omitting or obscuring a material fact.

1. Comparative Price, Value, and Savings Claims

Advertisers may offer a price reduction or saving by comparing their selling price with:

- their own former selling price,
- the current selling price of identical merchandise sold by others in the market area, or
- the current selling price of comparable merchandise sold by the advertiser or by others in the market area.

When any one of these comparisons is made in advertising, the claim should be based on the following criteria and the advertising should make clear to which of the above the comparative price or savings claim relates.

a.   Comparison with own former selling price

(1) The former price should be the actual price at which the advertiser has been currently offering the merchandise immediately preceding the sale, on a regular basis, and for a reasonably substantial period of time.

(2) Offering prices, as distinguished from actual former selling prices, have frequently been used as a comparative to deceptively imply

a saving. In the event few or no sales were made at the advertised comparative price, the advertiser should make sure that the higher price does not exceed the advertiser's usual and customary retail markup for similar merchandise, is not an inflated or exaggerated price, and is one at which the merchandise was openly and actively offered for sale, for a reasonably substantial period of time, in the recent, regular course of business, honestly and in good faith.

(3) Descriptive terminology often used by advertisers includes: "regularly," "was," "you save $_____," and "originally." If the word "originally" is used and the original price is not the last previous price, that fact should be disclosed by stating the last previous price, or that intermediate markdowns have been taken, e.g., "originally $400, formerly $300, now $250"; "originally $400, intermediate markdowns taken, now $250."

b. Comparison with current price of identical merchandise sold by others

(1) The comparative price should not exceed the price at which representative principal retail outlets in the market area have been selling the identical merchandise immediately preceding the advertiser's offer, on a regular basis and for a reasonably substantial period of time. Such comparisons should be substantiated by the advertiser immediately prior to making any advertised comparisons.

(2) Descriptive terminology often used by advertisers includes: "selling elsewhere at $_____." (Refers to market area cited in (1) above.)

c. Comparison with current price of comparable merchandise sold by the advertiser or by others

(1) The comparative price should not exceed the price at which the advertiser or representative principal retail outlets in the market area have been selling the comparable merchandise immediately preceding the advertiser's sale, on a regular basis and for a reasonably substantial period of time. Such comparisons should be substantiated by the advertiser immediately prior to making any advertised comparisons.

(2) In all such cases, the advertiser should make certain that comparable merchandise is similar in all respects and of at least like grade and quality.

(3) Descriptive terminology often used by advertisers includes: "comparable value," "compares with merchandise selling at $____," "equal to merchandise selling for $____."

d. List prices

"List price," "manufacturer's list price," "reference price," "suggested retail price," and similar terms have been used deceptively to state or imply a saving which was not, in fact, the case. A list price may be advertised as a comparative to the advertised sales price only to the extent that it is the actual selling price currently charged by the advertiser or by representative principal retailers in the market area where the claim is made.

Such a comparison should be substantiated by the advertiser immediately prior to making any advertised comparison.

e. "Imperfects," "irregulars," "seconds"

No comparative price should be used in connection with an imperfect, irregular, or second article unless it is accompanied by a clear and conspicuous disclosure that such comparative price applies to the price of the article, if perfect. The comparative price advertised should be based on

(1) the price currently charged by the advertiser for the article without defects, or
(2) the price currently charged by representative principal retailers in the trade area for the article without defects, and the advertisement should disclose which basis of comparison is being used.

f. "Factory to you," "factory direct," "wholesaler," "wholesale prices"

The terms "factory to you," "factory direct," "wholesaler," "wholesale prices" and others of similar import have been the subject of great abuse in advertising. They imply a significant saving from the actual price at which identical merchandise is currently being offered by representative principal retailers in the market area, or where identical merchandise is not being offered, from comparable values in the market area. Such terms should not be used unless the implied savings can be substantiated and the terms meet all of the requirements below.

(1) The terms "factory to you," "direct from maker," "factory outlet" and the like should not be used unless all advertised merchandise is actually manufactured by the advertiser or in factories owned or controlled by the advertiser.

(2) The terms "wholesaler," "wholesale outlet," "distributor" and the like should not be used unless the advertiser actually owns and operates or directly and absolutely controls a wholesale or distribution facility which primarily sells products to retailers for resale.

(3) The terms "wholesale price," "at cost," and the like should not be used unless they are the current prices which retailers usually and customarily pay when they buy such merchandise for resale.

g. Sales

(1) The unqualified term "sale" may be used in advertising only if there is a significant reduction from the advertiser's usual and customary price of the merchandise offered and the sale is for a limited period of time. If the sale exceeds thirty days, advertisers should be prepared to substantiate that the offering is indeed a valid reduction and has not become their regular price.

(2) Time limit sales should be rigidly observed. For example, merchandise offered in a "one-day sale," "three-day sale," "this week only, sale" should be taken off "sale" and revert to the regular price immediately following expiration of the stated time.

(3) Introductory sales should be limited to a stated time period, and the selling price should be increased to the advertised regular price immediately following termination of the stated period.

(4) Advertisers may currently advertise future increases in their own prices on a subsequent date provided that they do, in fact, increase the price to the stated amount on that date and maintain it for a reasonably substantial period of time thereafter.

h. "Emergency" or "distress" sales

Emergency or distress sales, including but not limited to bankruptcy, liquidation, and going out of business sales, should not be advertised unless the stated or implied reason is a fact, should be limited to a stated period of time, and should offer only such merchandise as is affected by the emergency. "Selling out," "closing out sale," and similar terms should not be used unless the concern so advertising is actually going out of business. The unqualified term "liquidation sale" means that the advertiser's entire business is in the process of actually being liquidated prior to actual closing. Advertisers should conform with the requirements of applicable local, state, and federal laws.

i. "Up to" savings claims

Savings or price reduction claims covering a group of items with a range of savings should state both the minimum and maximum savings without undue or misleading display of the maximum. The number of items available at the maximum savings should comprise a significant percentage, typically 10%, of all the items in the offering, unless local or state law requires otherwise.

j. Lowest price, underselling claims

Despite an advertiser's best efforts to ascertain competitive prices, the rapidity with which prices fluctuate and the difficulty of determining prices of all sellers at all times preclude an absolute knowledge of the truth of generalized underselling/lowest price claims. Advertisers should have proper substantiation for all claims prior to dissemination; unverifiable underselling claims should be avoided.

k. Price equaling, meeting competitors' prices

Advertisements which set out company policy of matching or bettering competitors' prices may be used, provided the terms of the offer are specific and in good faith and provided the terms of the offer are not unrealistic or unreasonable. Advertisers should be aware that such claims can create an implicit obligation to adjust prices generally for specific merchandise upon a showing that the advertiser's price for that merchandise is not as low as or lower than a competitor's, in order to preserve the accuracy of the advertised claims.

An advertisement which expresses a policy of matching or bettering competitors' prices should conspicuously and fully disclose any material and significant conditions which apply and specify what evidence a consumer must present to take advantage of the offer. Such evidence should not place an unrealistic or unreasonable burden on the consumer.

2. "Free"

a. The word "free" may be used in advertising whenever the advertiser is offering an unconditional gift. If receipt of the "free" merchandise or service is conditional on a purchase:

- the advertiser must disclose this condition clearly and conspicuously together with the "free" offer (not by placing an asterisk or symbol next to "free" and referring to the condition(s) in a footnote);
- the normal price of the merchandise or service to be purchased must not have been increased nor its quantity or quality reduced; and
- the "free" offer must be temporary; otherwise, it would become a continuous combination offer, no part of which is free.

b.   In a negotiated sale no "free" offer of another product or service should be made where:

- the product or service to be purchased usually is sold at a price arrived at through bargaining, rather than at a regular price; or
- there may be a regular price but other material factors such as quantity, quality, or size are arrived at through bargaining.

3.   "Cents-off" Sales

The principles stated in the standard dealing with "free" should be followed in the advertising of "cents-off" sales.

4.   Trade-in Allowances

Any advertised trade-in allowance should be an amount deducted from the advertiser's current selling price without a trade-in. That selling price must be clearly disclosed in the advertisement. It is misleading to offer a fixed and arbitrary allowance regardless of the size, type, age, condition, or value of the article traded in, for the purpose of disguising the true retail price or creating the false impression that a reduced price or a special price is obtainable only by such trade-in.

5.   Credit

Whenever a specific credit term is advertised, it should be available to all respondents unless qualified as to respondents' credit acceptability. All credit terms must be clearly and conspicuously disclosed in the advertisement, as required by the federal Truth in Lending Act and applicable state laws.

The Truth in Lending Act and Regulation Z which implements the Act, as well as Regulation M which covers consumer leasing, contain important provisions that affect any advertising to aid or promote the extension of consumer credit and should be carefully reviewed by every advertiser.

a.   Open-end credit

The requirements for advertising open-end credit under Regulation Z are complex. Therefore, advertisers are advised to consult Section

226.16 of the Regulation for details on terms triggering disclosure, prescribed terminology and information that must be disclosed.

b.   Closed–end credit

Advertisers are advised to consult Section 226.24 of Regulation Z for details of closed–end credit advertising. If an advertisement of closed–end credit contains any of the following triggering terms, three specific disclosures must also be stated, clearly and conspicuously. The triggering terms are:

- the amount or percentage of any down payment;
- the number of payments or period of repayment;
- the amount of any payment, expressed either as a percentage or as a dollar amount; or
- the amount of any finance charge.

The three disclosures are:

(1) the amount or percentage of the down payment;
(2) the terms of repayment; and
(3) the "annual percentage rate," using that term spelled out in full. If the rate may be increased after consummation of the credit transaction, that fact must be disclosed.

c.   "Easy credit," "liberal terms"

The terms "easy credit," "easy credit terms," "liberal terms," "casy pay plan," and other similar phrases relate to credit worthiness as well as to the terms of sale and credit repayment, and should be used only when:

(1) consumer credit is extended to persons whose ability to pay or credit rating is below typical standards of credit worthiness;
(2) the finance charges and annual percentage rate do not exceed those charged to persons whose credit rating has been determined and who meet generally accepted standards of credit worthiness;
(3) the down payment is as low and the period of repayment of the same duration as in consumer credit extensions to those of previously determined credit worthiness; and
(4) the debtor is dealt with fairly on all conditions of the transaction including the consequences of a delayed or missed payment.

d.   "No credit rejected"

The words "no credit rejected" or words of similar import should not be used unless true, since they imply that consumer credit will be extended to anyone regardless of the person's credit worthiness or financial ability to pay.

6.   Extra Charges

Whenever a price is mentioned in advertising, any extra charges should also be disclosed in immediate conjunction with the price (e.g., delivery, installation, assembly, excise tax, postage, and handling).

7.   Bait Advertising and Selling

A "bait" offer is an alluring but insincere offer to sell a product or service which the advertiser does not intend to sell. Its purpose is to switch consumers from buying the advertised merchandise or service, in order to sell something else, usually at a higher price or on a basis more advantageous to the advertiser.

   a. No advertisement should be published unless it is a bona fide offer to sell the advertised merchandise or service.
   b. The advertising should not create a false impression about the product or service being offered in order to lay the foundation for a later "switch" to other, more expensive products or services, or products of a lesser quality at the same price.
   c. Subsequent full disclosure by the advertiser of all other facts about the advertised article does not preclude the existence of a bait scheme.
   d. An advertiser should not use nor permit the use of the following bait scheme practices:

   • refusing to show or demonstrate the advertised merchandise or service; disparaging the advertised merchandise or service, its warranty, availability, services and parts, credit terms, etc.;
   • selling the advertised merchandise or service and thereafter "unselling" the customer to make a switch to other merchandise or service;
   • refusing to take orders for the advertised merchandise or service or to deliver it within a reasonable time;
   • demonstrating or showing a defective sample of the advertised merchandise; or
   • having a sales compensation plan designed to penalize salespersons who sell the advertised merchandise or service.

e. An advertiser should have on hand a sufficient quantity of advertised merchandise to meet reasonably anticipated demands, unless
the advertisement discloses the number of items available or states
"while supplies last." If items are available only at certain branch-
es, their specific locations should be disclosed. The use of
"rainchecks" is no justification for inadequate estimates of reasonably anticipated demand.

f. Actual sales of the advertised merchandise or service may not preclude the existence of a bait scheme since this may be merely an
attempt to create an aura of legitimacy. A key factor in determining the existence of "bait" is the number of times the merchandise
or service was advertised compared to the number of actual sales
of the merchandise or service.

8.   Warranties (or Guarantees)

a. When the term "warranty" (or "guarantee") is used in product
advertising, the following disclosure should be made clearly and
prominently: a statement that the complete details of the warranty
can be seen at the advertiser's store prior to sale, or in the case of
mail or telephone order sales, are available free on written request.

b. (1) "satisfaction guarantee," "money back guarantee," "free trial
offer," or similar representations should be used in advertising
only if the seller or manufacturer refunds the full purchase
price of the advertised product at the purchaser's request.

(2) When "satisfaction guarantee" or similar representations are used
in advertising, any material limitations or conditions that apply
to the guarantee should be clearly and prominently disclosed.

c. When the term "lifetime," "life" or similar representations are used
in advertising to describe the duration of the warranty or guarantee, the advertisement should clearly and prominently disclose the
life to which the representation refers.

d. Sellers or manufacturers should advertise that a product is war-
ranted or guaranteed only if the seller or manufacturer promptly
and fully performs its obligations under the warranty or guarantee.

e. Advertisers should make certain that any advertising of warranties
complies with the Consumer Products Warranty Act, effective July
4, 1975, relevant Federal Trade Commission requirements, and any
applicable state and local laws.

9.   Layout and Illustrations

The composition and layout of advertisements should be such as to mini-
mize the possibility of misunderstanding by the reader. For example, prices,
illustrations, or descriptions should not be so placed in an advertisement as

to give the impression that the price or terms of featured merchandise apply to other merchandise in the advertisement when such is not the fact. An advertisement should not be used which features merchandise at a price or terms boldly displayed, together with illustrations of higher-priced merchandise, so arranged as to give the impression that the lower price or more favorable terms apply to the other merchandise, when such is not the fact.

10. Asterisks

An asterisk may be used to impart additional information about a word or term which is not in itself inherently deceptive. The asterisk or other reference symbol should not be used as a means of contradicting or substantially changing the meaning of any advertising statement. Information referenced by asterisks should be clearly and prominently disclosed.

11. Abbreviations

Commonly known abbreviations may be used in advertising. However, abbreviations not generally known to or understood by the general public should be avoided.

For example, "deliv. Extra" is understood to mean that there is an extra charge for delivery of the merchandise. "New Battery, $25 W.T.," is not generally understood to mean "with trade-in."

12. Use or Condition Disclosures

a.   "Used," "secondhand," etc.

A product previously used by a consumer should be clearly and conspicuously described as such, e.g., "used," "secondhand," "pre-owned," "repossessed," "rebuilt," "reconditioned."

b.   "Rebuilt," "reconditioned"

(1) The term "rebuilt" should be used only to describe products that have been completely disassembled, reconstructed, repaired and refinished, including replacement of parts.

(2) The term "reconditioned" should be used only to describe products that have received such repairs, adjustments, or finishing as were necessary to put the product in satisfactory condition without rebuilding.

c.   "As is"

When merchandise is offered on an "as is" basis, i.e., in the condition in which it is displayed at the place of sale, the words "as is" should be indicated in any advertising and on the bill of sale. An advertiser also may describe the condition of the merchandise if so desired.

d.   "Second," "irregular," "imperfect"

If merchandise is defective or rejected by the manufacturer because it falls below specifications, it should be advertised by terms such as "second," "irregular," or "imperfect."

e.   "Discontinued"

Merchandise should not be described as "discontinued," "discontinued model," or by words of similar import unless the manufacturer has, in fact, discontinued its manufacture, or the retail advertiser will discontinue offering it entirely after clearance of existing inventories. If discontinuance is only by the retailer, the advertising should indicate that fact, e.g., "we are discontinuing stocking these items."

13. Superiority Claims-Comparatives-Disparagement

a.   Truthful comparisons using factual information may help consumers make informed buying decisions, provided:

(1) all representations are consistent with the general rules and prohibitions against false and deceptive advertising;
(2) all comparisons that claim or imply, unqualifiedly, superiority to competitive products or services are not based on a selected or limited list of characteristics in which the advertiser excels while ignoring those in which the competitors excel;
(3) the advertisement clearly discloses any material or significant limitations of the comparison; and
(4) the advertiser can substantiate all claims made.

b.   Advertising which deceptively or falsely disparages a competitor or competing products or services should not be used.

14. Superlative Claims-Puffery

Superlative statements, like other advertising claims, are objective (factual) or subjective (puffery):

• objective claims relate to tangible qualities and performance values of a product or service which can be measured against accepted standards or tests. As statements of fact, such claims can be proved or disproved and the advertiser should possess substantiation.

- subjective claims are expressions of opinion or personal evaluation of the intangible qualities of a product or service. Individual opinions, statements of corporate pride, and promises may sometimes be considered puffery and not subject to test of their truth and accuracy. Subjective superlatives which tend to mislead should be avoided.

15. Testimonials and Endorsements

In general, advertising which uses testimonials or endorsements is likely to mislead or confuse if:

- it is not genuine and does not actually represent the current opinion of the endorser;
- it is not quoted in its entirety, thereby altering its overall meaning and impact;
- it contains representations or statements which would be misleading if otherwise used in advertising;
- while literally true, it creates deceptive implications;
- the endorser is not competent or sufficiently qualified to express an opinion concerning the quality of the product or service being advertised or the results likely to be achieved by its use;
- it is not clearly stated that the endorser, associated with some well-known and highly-regarded institution, is speaking only in a personal capacity, and not on behalf of such an institution, if such be the fact;
- broad claims are made as to endorsements or approval by indefinitely large or vague groups, e.g., "the homeowners of America," "the doctors of America";
- an endorser has a pecuniary interest in the company whose product or service is endorsed and this is not made known in the advertisement.

Advertisers should consult Federal Trade Commission Guides on Testimonials and Endorsements for detailed guidance.

16. Rebate

"The terms "rebate," "cash rebate," or similar terms may be used only when payment of money will be made by the retailer or manufacturer to a purchaser after the sale, and the advertising should make clear who is making the payment.

17. Company Name or Trade Style

No words should be used in a company name or trade style which would mislead the public either directly or by implication. For example, the words "factory" or "manufacturer" should not be used in a company name unless the advertiser actually owns and operates or directly and absolutely controls the manufacturing facility that produces the advertised products. Similarly, the term "wholesale" or "wholesaler" should not be used in a company name unless the advertiser actually owns and operates or directly and absolutely controls a wholesale or distribution facility which primarily sells products to retailers for resale.

18. Contests and Games of Chance

a. If contests are used, the advertiser should publish clear, complete, and concise rules and provide competent impartial judges to determine the winners.

b. No contest, drawing, or other game of chance that involves the three elements of prize, chance, and consideration should be conducted since it constitutes a lottery and is in violation of federal statutes.

c. The Federal Trade Commission has rendered various decisions on contests and games of chance relating to disclosure of the number of prizes to be awarded and the odds of winning each prize, and issued a trade regulation rule for games of chance in the food retailing and gasoline industries. Advertisers should make certain any contest conforms to FTC requirements as well as any applicable local and state laws.

19. Claimed Results

Claims as to energy savings, performance, safety, efficacy, results, etc. which will be obtained by or realized from a particular product or service should be based on recent and competent scientific, engineering, or other objective data.

20. Unassembled Merchandise

When advertised merchandise requires partial or complete assembly by the purchaser, the advertising should disclose that fact, e.g., "unassembled," "partial assembly required."

A Better Business Bureau Publication
Supported by Business in the Interest of Consumers
Published by:
Council of Better Business Bureaus, Inc.
4200 Wilson Blvd.
Arlington, VA 22203

Children's Advertising Review Unit
Self Regulatory Guidelines for Children's Advertising

The Children's Advertising Review Unit (CARU) of the Council of Better Business Bureaus was established in 1974 by the National Advertising Review Council (NARC) to promote responsible children's advertising and to respond to public concerns. The NARC is a strategic alliance of the advertising industry and the Council of Better Business Bureaus (CBBB). Its Board of Directors comprises key executives from the CBBB, the American Association of Advertising Agencies (AAAA), the American Advertising Federation (AAF), and the Association of National Advertisers (ANA). The NARC Board sets policy for CARU's self-regulatory program, which is administered by the CBBB and is funded directly by members of the children's advertising industry.

CARU's Academic and Business Advisory Boards, composed of leading experts in education, communication, and child development as well as prominent industry leaders, advise on general issues concerning children's advertising and assist in revisions of the Guidelines.

The basic activity of CARU is the review and evaluation of child-directed advertising in all media. When children's advertising is found to be misleading, inaccurate, or inconsistent with the Guidelines, CARU seeks changes through the voluntary cooperation of advertisers.

CARU provides a general advisory service for advertisers and agencies and also is a source of informational material for children, parents, and educators. CARU encourages advertisers to develop and promote the dissemination of educational messages to children consistent with the Children's Television Act of 1990. In addition, CARU maintains a clearinghouse for research on children's advertising and has published an annotated bibliography.

Principles

Six basic Principles underlie CARU's Guidelines for advertising directed to children under 12:

1. Advertisers should always take into account the level of knowledge, sophistication, and maturity of the audience to which their message is primarily directed. Younger children have a limited

capacity for evaluating the credibility of information they receive. They also may lack the ability to understand the nature of the information they provide. Advertisers, therefore, have a special responsibility to protect children from their own susceptibilities.

2. Realizing that children are imaginative and that make-believe play constitutes an important part of the growing up process, advertisers should exercise care not to exploit unfairly the imaginative quality of children. Unreasonable expectations of product quality or performance should not be stimulated either directly or indirectly by advertising.

3. Recognizing that advertising may play an important part in educating the child, advertisers should communicate information in a truthful and accurate manner and in language understandable to young children with full recognition that the child may learn practices from advertising which can affect his or her health and well-being.

4. Advertisers are urged to capitalize on the potential of advertising to influence behavior by developing advertising that, wherever possible, addresses itself to positive and beneficial social behavior, such as friendship, kindness, honesty, justice, generosity, and respect for others.

5. Care should be taken to incorporate minority and other groups in advertisements in order to present positive and pro-social roles and role models wherever possible. Social stereotyping and appeals to prejudice should be avoided.

6. Although many influences affect a child's personal and social development, it remains the prime responsibility of the parents to provide guidance for children. Advertisers should contribute to this parent-child relationship in a constructive manner.

These Principles embody the philosophy upon which CARU's mandate is based. The Principles, and not the Guidelines themselves, determine the scope of our review. The Guidelines effectively anticipate and address many of the areas requiring scrutiny in child-directed advertising, but they are illustrative rather than limiting. Where no specific Guideline addresses the issues of concern to CARU, it is these broader Principles that CARU applies in evaluating advertising directed to the uniquely impressionable and vulnerable child audience.

Interpretation of the Guidelines

Because children are in the process of developing their knowledge of the physical and social world, they are more limited than adults in the experience and skills required to evaluate advertising and to make purchase decisions. For these reasons, certain presentations and techniques which may be appropriate for adult-directed advertising may mislead children if used in child-directed advertising.

The function of the Guidelines is to delineate those areas that need particular attention to help avoid deceptive advertising messages to children. The intent is to help advertisers deal sensitively and honestly with children and is not meant to deprive them, or children, of the benefits of innovative advertising approaches.

The Guidelines have been kept general in the belief that responsible advertising comes in many forms and that diversity should be encouraged. The goal in all cases should be to fulfill the spirit as well as the letter of the Guidelines and the Principles on which they are based.

Scope of the Guidelines

The Guidelines apply to advertising addressed to children under 12 years of age in all media, including print, broadcast, and cable television, radio, video, point-of-sale, and online advertising and packaging. CARU interprets this as including fund-raising activities and sponsor identifications on non-commercial television and radio. One section applies to adult-directed advertising only when a potential child-safety concern exists (see Safety, below).

Product Presentations and Claims

Children look at, listen to, and remember many different elements in advertising. Therefore, advertisers need to examine the total advertising message to be certain that the net communication will not mislead or misinform children.

1. Copy, sound, and visual presentations should not mislead children about product or performance characteristics. Such characteristics may include, but are not limited to, size, speed, method of operation, color, sound, durability, and nutritional benefits.
2. The advertising presentation should not mislead children about benefits from use of the product. Such benefits may include, but are not limited to, the acquisition of strength, status, popularity, growth, proficiency, and intelligence.
3. Care should be taken not to exploit a child's imagination. Fantasy, including animation, is appropriate for younger as well as older children. However, it should not create unattainable performance expectations nor exploit the younger child's difficulty in distinguishing between the real and the fanciful.
4. The performance and use of a product should be demonstrated in a way that can be duplicated by the child for whom the product is intended.

5. Products should be shown used in safe ways, in safe environments, and in safe situations.
6. What is included and excluded in the initial purchase should be clearly established.
7. The amount of product featured should be within reasonable levels for the situation depicted.
8. Representation of food products should be made so as to encourage sound use of the product with a view toward healthy development of the child and development of good nutritional practices. Advertisements representing mealtime should clearly and adequately depict the role of the product within the framework of a balanced diet. Snack foods should be clearly represented as such, and not as substitutes for meals.
9. In advertising videos, films, and interactive software, advertisers should take care that only those which are age-appropriate are advertised to children. If an industry rating system is available, the rating label should be prominently displayed.
10. Portrayals of violence and presentations that could frighten or provoke anxiety in children should be avoided.
11. If objective claims are made in an advertisement directed to children, the advertiser should be able to supply adequate substantiation.

Sales Pressure

Children are not as prepared as adults to make judicious, independent purchase decisions. Therefore, advertisers should avoid using extreme sales pressure in advertising presentations to children.

1. Children should not be urged to ask parents or others to buy products. Advertisements should not suggest that a parent or adult who purchases a product or service for a child is better, more intelligent, or more generous than one who does not. Advertising directed toward children should not create a sense of urgency or exclusivity, for example, by using words like "now" and "only."
2. Benefits attributed to the product or service should be inherent in its use. Advertisements should not convey the impression that possession of a product will result in more acceptance of a child by his or her peers. Conversely, it should not be implied that lack of a product will cause a child to be less accepted by his or her peers. Advertisements should not imply that purchase and use of a product will confer upon the user the prestige, skills, or other special qualities of characters appearing in advertising.
3. All price representations should be clearly and concisely set forth. Price minimizations such as "only" or "just" should not be used.

Disclosures and Disclaimers

Children have a more limited vocabulary and less developed language skills than adolescents and adults. They read less well, if at all, and rely more on information presented pictorially than verbally. Simplified wording, such as "You have to put it together" instead of "Assembly required," significantly increases comprehension.

1. All information that requires disclosure for legal or other reasons should be in language understandable by the child audience. Disclaimers and disclosures should be clearly worded, legible and, prominent. When technology permits, both audio and video disclosures are encouraged, as is the use of demonstrative disclosures.
2. Advertising for unassembled products should clearly indicate that they need to be put together to be used properly.
3. If any item essential to use of the product is not included, such as batteries, this fact should be disclosed clearly.
4. Information about products purchased separately, such as accessories or individual items in a collection, should be disclosed clearly to the child audience.
5. If television advertising to children involves the use of a toll-free telephone number, it must be clearly stated, in both audio and video disclosures, that the child must get an adult's permission to call.

a. In print or online advertising, this disclosure must be clearly and prominently displayed.
b. In radio advertising, the audio disclosure must be clearly audible.

6. If an advertiser creates or sponsors an area in cyberspace, either through an online service or a Web site, the name of the sponsoring company and/or brand should be prominently featured, (including, but not limited to wording such as "The . . . Playground", or "Sponsored by . . .").
7. If videotapes, CD-ROMs, DVDs, or software marketed to children contain advertising or promotions (e.g. trailers) this fact should be clearly disclosed on the packaging, and the advertising itself should be separated from the program and clearly designated as advertising.

Comparative Claims

Advertising which compares the advertised product to another product may be difficult for young children to understand and evaluate. Comparative claims should be based on real product advantages that are understandable to the child audience.

1. Comparative advertising should provide factual information. Comparisons should not falsely represent other products or previous versions of the same product.
2. Comparative claims should be presented in ways that children understand clearly.
3. Comparative claims should be supported by appropriate and adequate substantiation.

Endorsement and Promotion by Program or Editorial Characters

Studies have shown that the mere appearance of a character with a product can significantly alter a child's perception of the product. Advertising presentations by program/editorial characters may hamper a young child's ability to distinguish between program/editorial content and advertising.

1. All personal endorsements should reflect the actual experiences and beliefs of the endorser. Celebrities and real-life authority figures may be used as product endorsers, presenters, or testifiers. However, extra care should be taken to avoid creating any false impression that the use of the product enhanced the celebrity's performance.
2. An endorser represented, either directly or indirectly, as an expert must possess qualifications appropriate to the particular expertise depicted in the endorsement.
3. Program personalities, live or animated, should not be used to sell products, premiums, or services in or adjacent to programs primarily directed to children in which the same personality or character appears.
4. Products derived from or associated with program content primarily directed to children should not be advertised during or adjacent to that program.
5. In print media primarily designed for children, a character or personality associated with the editorial content of a publication should not be used to sell products, premiums, or services in the same publication.
6. For print and interactive electronic media in which a product-, service-, or product/service-personality is featured in the editorial content (e.g., character-driven magazines or Web sites, product-driven magazines or Web sites, and club newsletters) guideline 4 does not specifically apply. In these instances, advertising content should nonetheless be clearly identified as such.

Premiums, Promotions, and Sweepstakes

The use of premiums, promotions, and sweepstakes in advertising has the potential to enhance the appeal of a product to a child. Therefore, special attention should be paid to the advertising of these marketing techniques to guard against exploiting children's immaturity.

Premiums

1. Children have difficulty distinguishing product from premium. If product advertising contains a premium message, care should be taken that the child's attention is focused primarily on the product. The premium message should be clearly secondary.
2. Conditions of a premium offer should be stated simply and clearly. "Mandatory" statements and disclosures should be stated in terms that can be understood by the child audience.

Kids' Clubs

In advertising to children, care should be taken not to mislead them into thinking they are joining a club when they are merely making a purchase or receiving a premium. Before an advertiser uses the word "club," certain minimum requirements should be met. These are:

1. Interactivity—The child should perform some act constituting an intentional joining of the club and receive something in return. Merely watching a television program or eating in a particular restaurant, for example, does not constitute membership in a club.
2. Continuity—There should be an ongoing relationship between the club and the child member, for example, in the form of newsletter or activities, at regular intervals.
3. Exclusivity—The activities or benefits derived from membership in the club should be exclusive to its members, and not merely the result of purchasing a particular product.

Please see the Data Collection section of the Guidelines for Interactive Electronic Media for special considerations when fulfilling these requirements in the interactive media.

Sweepstakes and Contests

In advertising sweepstakes to children, care should be taken not to produce unrealistic expectations of the chances of winning, or inflated expectations of the prize(s) to be won. Therefore:

1. The prize(s) should be clearly depicted.
2. The "odds" for winning should be clearly disclosed in language clearly understandable to the child audience, for instance, "Many will enter, a few will win." In appropriate media, disclosures must be included in the audio portion.
3. All prizes should be appropriate to the child audience.
4. Alternate means of entry should be disclosed.

5. Online contests should not require the child to provide more information than is necessary and should be limited where possible to information including the child's and parent's e-mail addresses. Per the Data Collection section of the Guidelines, parents should be contacted and receive direct notification when a child enters a contest, to provide offline contact information to fulfill the contest (e.g. verify winner eligibility and send prize).

Safety

Imitation, exploration, and experimentation are important activities to children. They are attracted to commercials in general and may imitate product demonstrations and other actions without regard to risk. Many childhood accidents and injuries occur in the home, often involving abuse or misuse of common household products.

1. Products inappropriate for use by children should not be advertised directly to children. This is especially true for products labeled, "Keep out of the reach of children." Additionally, such products should not be promoted directly to children by premiums or other means. Medications, drugs, and supplemental vitamins should not be advertised to children.
2. Advertisements for children's products should show them being used by children in the appropriate age range. For instance, young children should not be shown playing with toys safe only for older children. Such inappropriate products or promotions include displaying or knowingly linking to the URL of a Web site not in compliance with CARU's Guidelines.
3. Adults should be shown supervising children when products or activities could involve a safety risk.
4. Advertisements should not portray adults or children in unsafe situations, or in acts harmful to themselves or others. For example, when athletic activities (such as bicycle riding or skateboarding) are shown, proper precautions and safety equipment should be depicted.
5. Advertisements should avoid demonstrations that encourage dangerous or inappropriate use or misuse of the product. This is particularly important when the demonstration can be easily reproduced by children and features products accessible to them.

Guidelines for Interactive Electronic Media (e.g. Internet and Online Services)

The guidelines contained in this section highlight issues unique to Internet and online advertising to children under 13. They are to be read within the broader context of the overall Guidelines, which apply to advertising in all media. For these purposes, the term "advertisers" also refers to any person who operates a commercial Web site located on the Internet or an online service. Although CARU's Self-Regulatory Guidelines for Children's Advertising address advertising directed to children under 12 years of age, in order to harmonize with the Federal Trade Commission's ("FTC") final rule implementing the Children's Online Privacy Protection Act of 1998 ("the Rule"), the guidelines contained in the section on Data Collection below apply to Web sites directed to children under 13 years of age.

Just as these new media are rapidly evolving, so in all likelihood will this section of the Guidelines. Advances in technology, increased under-standing of children's use of the medium, and the means by which these current guidelines are implemented will all contribute to the evolution of the "Interactive Electronic Media" section. CARU's aim is that the Guidelines will always support "notice", "choice," and "consent" as defined by the FTC, and reflect the latest developments in technology and its appli-cation to children's advertising.

Further, these children's Guidelines must be overlaid on the broader, and still developing industry standards, government statutory provisions and definitions for protecting and respecting privacy preferences. These indus-try standards include disclosure of what information is being collected and its intended uses, and the opportunity for the consumer to withhold con-sent for its collection for marketing purposes. Thus, in the case of Web sites directed to children that collect personal information from children, rea-sonable efforts, taking into consideration available technology, should be made to establish that notice is offered to, and choice exercised by a parent or guardian.

The availability of hyperlinks between sites can allow a child to move seamlessly from one to another. However there is no way to predict where the use of successive links on successive pages will lead. Therefore, advertis-ers who maintain sites for children should not knowingly link their sites to pages of other sites that do not comply with CARU's Guidelines.

In keeping with CARU's Principle regarding respecting and fostering the parents' role in providing guidance for their children, advertisers who communicate with children through e-mail should remind and encourage parents to check and monitor their children's use of e-mail and other online activities regularly.

To respect the privacy of parents, information collected and used for the sole purpose of obtaining verifiable parental consent or providing notice should not be maintained in retrievable form by the site if parental consent is not obtained after a reasonable time.

The following guidelines apply to online activities which are inten-tionally targeted to children under 13, or where the Web site knows the visitor is a child. In child-directed sites or general interest sites with areas designed for children, age screening methods should determine whether verifiable parental consent or direct parental notification is necessitated per the Data Collection section of the Guidelines. Care should be taken so that screening questions do not encourage children to provide inaccurate information to avoid obtaining parental permission. For purposes of this section, these activities include making a sale or collecting data, and do not include the use of "spokescharacters" or branded environments for informational or entertainment purposes, which are addressed in the "Endorsement" and "Disclosure" sections of the Guidelines.

Making a Sale

Advertisers who transact sales with children online should make reasonable efforts in light of all available technologies to provide the person responsible for the costs of the transaction with the means to exercise control over the transaction. If there is no reasonable means provided to avoid unauthorized purchases of goods and services by children, the advertiser should enable the person responsible to cancel the order and receive full credit without incurring any charges. Advertisers should keep in mind that under existing state laws, parents may not be obligated to fulfill sales contracts entered into by their young children.

1. Children should always be told when they are being targeted for a sale.
2. If a site offers the opportunity to order or purchase any product or service, either through the use of a "click here to order" button or other on-screen means, the ordering instructions must clearly and prominently state that a child must have a parent's permission to order.
3. In the case of an online means of ordering, there should be a clear mechanism after the order is placed allowing the child or parent to cancel the order.

Data Collection

The ability to gather information, for marketing purposes, to tailor a site to a specific interest, etc., is part of the appeal of the interactive media to both the advertiser and the user. Young children however, may not understand the nature of the information being sought, nor its intended uses. The solicitation of personally identifiable information from children (e.g., full names, addresses, e-mail addresses, phone numbers) triggers special privacy and security concerns.

Therefore, in collecting information from children under 13 years of age, advertisers should adhere to the following principles:

1. In all cases, the information collection or tracking practices and information uses must be clearly disclosed, along with the means of correcting or removing the information. The disclosure notice should be prominent and readily accessible before any information is collected. For instance, in the case of passive tracking, the notice should be on the page where the child enters the site. A heading such as "Privacy," "Our Privacy Policy," "Note to Parents," or similar designation which allows an adult to click on to obtain additional information on the site's information collection and tracking practices and information uses is acceptable.

2. When personal information (such as e-mail addresses or screen names associated with other personal information) will be publicly posted so as to enable others to communicate directly with the child online, or when the child will be able otherwise to communicate directly with others, the company must obtain prior verifiable parental consent.

3. When personal information will be shared or distributed to third parties, except for parties that are agents or affiliates of the company or provide support for the internal operation of the Web site and that agree not to disclose or use the information for any other purpose, the company must obtain prior verifiable parental consent.

4. When personal information is obtained for a company's internal use, and there is no disclosure, verifiable parental consent may be obtained through the use of e-mail coupled with some additional steps to provide assurance that the person providing the consent is the parent. [The acceptability of this method for acquiring verifiable parental consent will sunset pursuant to the Rule and is intended to provide the industry the opportunity to develop seamless digital methods of securing verifiable parental consent through technological innovation.]

5. When online contact information is collected and retained to respond directly more than once to a child's specific request (such as an e-mail newsletter or contest) and will not be used for any other purpose, the company must directly notify the parent of the nature and intended uses and permit access to the information sufficient to permit a parent to remove or correct the information.

In furtherance of the above principles, advertisers should adhere to the following guidelines:

1. Before asking children for personal information about themselves or others, advertisers should remind children to ask a parent for per-

mission to answer the information gathering questions (e.g., "You must ask your Mom or Dad if you can answer these questions").

2. The advertiser should disclose, in language easily understood by a child, why the information is being requested (e.g., "We'll use your name and e-mail to enter you in this contest and also add it to our mailing list") and whether the information is intended to be shared, sold, or distributed outside of the collecting advertiser company.

3. If information is collected from children through passive means (e.g., navigational tracking tools, browser files, etc.) this should be disclosed to the child and the parent along with what information is being collected.

4. Advertisers should encourage the child to use an alias (e.g., "Bookworm," "Skater," etc.), first name, nickname, initials, or other alternative to full names or screen names which correspond with an e-mail address, for any activities which will involve public posting.

5. If the information is optional, and not required to engage in an activity, that fact should be clearly disclosed in language easily understood by a child (e.g., "You don't have to answer to play the game"). The advertiser should clearly disclose what use it will make of this information, if provided, as in guideline 2 above, and should not require a child to disclose more personal information than is reasonably necessary to participate in the online activity (e.g., play a game, enter a contest, etc.).

6. The interactivity of the medium offers the opportunity to communicate with children through electronic mail. While this is part of the appeal of the medium, it creates the potential for a child to receive unmanageable amounts of unsolicited e-mail. If an advertiser communicates with a child by e-mail, there should be an opportunity with each mailing for the child or parent to choose by return e-mail to discontinue receiving mailings.

Guidelines for the Advertising of 900/976 Teleprograms to Children

These guidelines, promulgated in 1989, have been superseded by a prohibition by the Federal Trade Commission that pay-per-call services cannot be directed to children under 12, unless the service is a "bona fide educational service." Likewise, ads for 900-number services cannot be directed to children under 12, unless the service is a bona fide educational service per section 308.3 (d)(I) of the Rule Pursuant to the Telephone Disclosure and Dispute Resolution Act of 1992. This portion of CARU's guidelines may be found as a reference on CARU's Web site at *www.caru.org*.

The Children's Advertising Guidelines have been in existence since 1972 when they were published by the Association of National Advertisers, Inc. to encourage truthful and accurate advertising sensitive to the special nature of children. Subsequently, the advertising community established CARU to serve as an independent manager of the industry's self-regulatory program. CARU edited and republished the Self-Regulatory Guidelines for Children's Advertising in 1975, and revised them in 1977, 1983, 1991, and 1995. In 1996 CARU edited its Guidelines to include a new section addressing the Internet. The latest revisions, in 1999, deal expressly with data collection and privacy on the Internet. The assistance of CARU's Academic and Business Advisory Committees, and of other children's advertisers, their agencies and trade associations has been invaluable.

Trade Association Resources

Advertising industry trade associations can offer valuable information to both agencies and their clients. The Association of National Advertisers, Inc. says it is "the only organization exclusively dedicated to serving the interests of corporations that advertise and market their products and services in the United States." The American Association of Advertising Agencies, Inc. is a national organization of advertising agencies. These organizations offer a wealth of resources to advertisers and agencies. To introduce yourself to each, check out their easy-to-navigate Web sites. And consider ordering copies of the publications concerning advertising law that are listed here.

Association of National Advertisers, Inc.
708 Third Avenue
New York, NY 10017–4270
(212) 697–5950
Web site: *www.ana.net*

Along with numerous other publications on a variety of topics of interest to advertisers, the following publications relating to advertising law are available from the ANA. (Note: The descriptions of the publications listed are those of the ANA.)

NAD/CARU/NARB Case Reports (1972–1998) (CD-ROM)
By NAD/CARU/NARB
How much and what kind of data is required to substantiate an advertising claim? Now marketers and advertisers can purchase one comprehensive database with all of the published decisions from the advertising industry's self-regulatory forum: the National Advertising Division (NAD) and Children's Advertising Review Unit (CARU) of the Council of Better Business Bureaus, and decisions on appeals to the National Advertising Review Board (NARB). Filled with hundreds of advertising case studies, it includes discussions of critical legal issues such as: the adequacy of claim support, in-depth analysis of what constitutes sufficient and reliable scientific data, and thorough evaluations of the design and value of consumer perceptions studies for use as evidence.

This ready-to-run CD-ROM is easy to use on both PCs and MACs. It can be searched using company and/or product names, product types, case citations or by the legal and factual issues involved in a case. In minutes, you can access the full text of every published decision along with a detailed description of the evidence provided and the legal principles on which decisions were based. This is a must for marketers or legal professionals responsible for substantiating advertising claims. (Note: A CD–ROM update for the year 1999 will be furnished at no additional cost for CDs purchased in 1999. Subsequent updates will be available at a nominal cost.)

Published by: The National Advertising Division (NAD), The Children's Advertising Review Unit (CARU), and The National Advertising Review Board (NARB).

Price: $52

Please Be Ad-vised (Third Edition)
By Douglas J. Wood, Esq.
Most advertising and marketing executives cannot claim a mastery of advertising and marketing law; yet it is an area we deal in almost every day. *Please Be Ad-vised* is considered the industry's legal reference guide for advertising and marketing professionals. It is a comprehensive and practical tool for avoiding legal blunders. In addition to summaries of dozens of legal issues, the book provides sample legal forms for everything from ownership and protection of creative work to agency–client relationships. It also includes a standard contract for developing Web sites and FAST standards for interactive media.

Other topics included are copyright and trademark infringement, working with production companies, contracts and employment agreements, rules of comparative advertising, government regulation, talent unions, and negotiating with employees.

Published by: The Association of National Advertisers, Inc. (ANA).

Price: $59.95

Guidelines for Advertiser/Agency Contracts
By Elhanan C. Stone
In *Guidelines for Advertiser/Agency Contracts,* the process of formalizing a contract with an advertising agency is clearly explained. The study covers agency services, compensation for different services, billing and estimating procedures, auditing and accounting, terminating an agreement, ownership of materials, relationships with independent contractors, and conflicts of interest.

Published by: The Association of National Advertisers, Inc. (ANA).

Price: $22.50

American Association of Advertising Agencies, Inc.
405 Lexington Avenue
New York, NY 10174–1801
(212) 682–2500
Web site: *www.aaaa.org*

Along with numerous other publications on a variety of topics of interest to both agencies and advertisers, the following publications relating to advertising law are available from the AAAA. (Note: The descriptions of the publications listed are those of the AAAA.)

Protection against Damage Claims
Alerts AAAA members to certain kinds of legal risks characteristic of the agency business and describes procedures to help reduce agency exposure. 32 pages. ©1987. Revised 1992.

Members Only: $10

A Client's Guide to the Law and Advertising
The first section of this booklet examines the effect of the Federal Trade Commission and other federal bodies on advertising, as well as the industry's own mechanism for dealing with suspect advertising before government gets involved. The second section analyzes certain kinds of legal risks that are characteristic of the advertising business—and describes some procedures that can reduce both agency and advertising exposure to such risks. Includes the Standards of Practice of the American Association of Advertising Agencies.

Members: $15
Non-Members: $35

A Client's Guide to Agency/Client Contracts
An annotated compendium of various sample contract provisions that agencies and clients may select from and adapt for use in their individual contracts. Explanatory notes accompany each contract provision, making this booklet especially user-friendly. Provisions cover such areas as agency services, agency compensation, billing practices, exclusivity, indemnification, term and termination, general provisions, and signatures.

Members: $15
Non-Members: $35

Various Provisions in Agency-Client Agreements
Provisions taken from contracts provided by AAAA members. Covers such topics as mutually exclusive arrangements, confidentiality, sequential liability, compensation, terminations, and more. ©1996. Revised 1998.

Members Only: $10

To place an order for an AAAA publication, please contact Amy Espinal *(amy@aaaa.org)* at (212) 850-0777.

In addition to AAAA information and resources, other advertising and marketing trade associations can be easily accessed from the AAAA Web site. Depending on your professional activities, you might find the programs or publications of one of these other organizations helpful. The AAAA site links to the following organizations via its Advertising and Media-Related Associates Web Directory:

The Advertising Council
Advertising Educational Foundation (AEF)
Advertising Mail Marketing Association (AMMA)
Advertising Research Foundation (ARF)
Agricultural Publishers Association (APF)
American Advertising Federation (AAF)
American Business Press (ABP)
American Marketing Association (AMA)
Association for Interactive Marketing (AIM)
Association of Directory Marketing (ADM)
Association of Directory Publishers (ADP)
Association of Independent Commercial Producers (AICP)
Association of Local TV Stations (ALTV)
Association of National Advertisers (ANA)
Audit Bureau of Circulations (ABC)
Business Marketing Association
Business Publications Audit of Circulation, Inc. (BPA)
Cable and Telecommunications Marketing Association (CTMA)
CableTelevision Advertising Bureau (CAB)
Canadian Business Press (CBP)
Certified Audit of Circulations (CAC)
Coalition for Advertising Supported Information and Entertainment (CASIE)
Direct Marketing Association (DMA)
Interactive Services Association (ISA)
International Advertising Association (IAA)

International Reciprocal Trade Association (IRTA)
Internet Advertising Bureau (IAB)
Magazine Publishers of America (MPA)
Marketing Research Association (MRA)
National Agri-Marketing Association (NAMA)
National Association of Broadcasters (NAB)
National Cable Television Association (NCTA)
New York New Media Association (NYNMA)
Newspaper Association of America (NAA)
Outdoor Advertising Association of America (OAAA)
Promotion Marketing Association of America
Promotional Products Association International
Radio Advertising Bureau (RAB)
Television Bureau of Advertising (TVB)
Yellow Pages Publishers Association (YPPA)

The Web pages for these organizations are linked to the AAAA site: *www.aaaa.org/resources/related/index.html.*

Copyright Office Resources

Free Publications on Copyright

The following publications on copyright are available from the Copyright Office. These publications are short and well written, and they're free. Use the numbers of the titles to order the circulars you want.

TITLE	NUMBER
Copyright Basics	Circular 1
Copyright Notice	Circular 3
Copyright Fees	Circular 4
Obtaining Access to and Copies of Copyright Office Records and Deposits	Circular 6
"Best Edition" of Published Copyrighted Works for the Collections of the Library of Congress	Circular 7b
Mandatory Deposit of Copies or Phonorecords for the Library of Congress	Circular 7d
Works-Made-for-Hire under the 1976 Copyright Act	Circular 9
Recordation of Transfers and Other Documents	Circular 12
Copyright Registration for Derivative Works	Circular 14
Renewal of Copyright	Circular 15
Duration of Copyright	Circular 15a
Extension of Copyright Terms	Circular 15t
Reproductions of Copyrighted Works by Educators and Librarians	Circular 21
How to Investigate the Copyright Status of a Work	Circular 22
Ideas, Methods, or Systems	Circular 31
Blank Forms and Other Works Not Protected by Copyright	Circular 32
Computing and Measuring Devices	Circular 33
Copyright Protection Not Available for Names, Titles, or Short Phrases	Circular 34
Copyright Registration for Works of the Visual Arts	Circular 40
Deposit Requirements for Registration of Claims to Copyright in Visual Arts Materials	Circular 40a
Copyright Claims in Architectural Works	Circular 41
Cartoons and Comic Strips	Circular 44
Copyright Registration for Motion Pictures, Including Video Recordings	Circular 45
Copyright Registration for Musical Compositions	Circular 50
Copyright Registration for Multimedia Works	Circular 55
Copyright Registration for Sound Recordings	Circular 56
Copyright Registration of Musical Compositions and Sound Recordings	Circular 56a
Copyright Registration for Computer Programs	Circular 61
Copyright Registration for Online Works	Circular 66

Other circulars and copies of regulations, etc. are available. For a list of all available publications, ask for Circular 2, Publications on Copyright, which is also free.

Copyright Registration Forms

Regular Registration Forms

There are four primary sorts of copyright registration forms, each for a different sort of work. They are:

- **Form PA,** for registration of works of the **P**erforming **A**rts, including dramas, music, and lyrics
- **Form TX,** for registration of nondramatic literary (**TeX**tual) works, including fiction and nonfiction, books, short stories, poems, collections of poetry, essays, articles in serials, and computer programs
- **Form VA,** for registration of works of the **V**isual **A**rts, including pictorial, graphic, and sculptural works
- **Form SR,** for registration of the copyrights in **S**ound **R**ecordings, including records, tapes, CDs, and all other forms of phonorecords

Short Forms

Short versions of some copyright registration forms are now available. They are: **Short Form PA; Short Form TX;** and **Short Form VA.** These short forms are used to register the same sorts of works as the longer forms but they request minimal information and the instructions for filling them out are brief. They are, however, just as effective for registering claims to copyright as the longer registration forms. Note, however, that the short copyright registration forms may be used only if all of the following circumstances apply:

1. By a living author who is the only author of his or her work if that author is the sole owner of the copyright in the work
2. By an author who is not filing anonymously
3. If the work is completely new in the sense that it does not contain material that has been previously published or registered or that is in the public domain
4. If the work is not a work-made-for-hire

If all these conditions are not met, you must use one of the standard registration forms, which remain in use for registration applications where the short forms are inappropriate. The registration fee remains the same whether the standard form or the short form is used.

Copyright Registration Forms via the Internet

It is now possible to fill out copyright registration forms on the Copyright Office Web site. You must still print out your registration form (in two-sided form, on a single sheet) and send the completed form to the Copyright Office with your registration fee and specimens of the registered work, but this is a much more efficient system than ordering the registration form, filling it out by hand or typewriter, and only then returning it to the Copyright Office. The Copyright Office Web site includes information on many copyright topics and will also allow you to link to other copyright-related resources on the Internet. The Web site address is *www.loc.gov/copyright*.

Obtaining Forms and Publications

The copyright registration forms, copyright publications, and information on copyright offered by the Copyright Office are now available through several channels.

Information via the Internet

Through the Copyright Office's Web site, you can read any of more than thirty Copyright Office publications on copyright or download copyright registration forms. The Copyright Office Web site address is *www.loc.gov/copyright*. This site includes information on many copyright topics and will also allow you to link to other copyright-related resources on the Internet.

You can also subscribe to the Copyright Office's free electronic mailing list. NewsNet issues periodic e-mail messages to alert subscribers to various copyright-related subjects of interest. To subscribe, send an e-mail to *listserv@rs8.loc.gov*. In the body of your message, say: "Subscribe US Copyright." To let you know that your message has been received, you will receive a standard message indicating that your NewsNet subscription has been accepted.

Information via Fax-on-Demand

Copyright Office circulars and announcements are also available by fax. Call (202) 707-2600 from any touchtone telephone, key in your fax number and the numbers of the documents you want, and those documents will be sent to your fax machine. You can request that the list of available documents be faxed to you if you don't know the numbers of the ones you want. Copyright application forms are not available by fax.

Information by Telephone

To speak to a Copyright Information Specialist, call (202) 707-3000 between 8:30 A.M. and 5 P.M. EST Monday through Friday except holidays;

recorded information is available twenty-four hours a day and seven days a week. (The Copyright Office offers very good information and publications on copyright, but it does not give legal advice and will not advise callers regarding copyright infringement or bringing an infringement suit, disputes over copyright ownership, publishing agreements, or collecting royalties. Only a lawyer can furnish this sort of advice.)

To order free copyright registration forms, call the Forms and Publications Hotline at (202) 707-9100, twenty-four hours a day, and leave a recorded message.

Information by Mail

To order Copyright Office circulars or copyright registration forms by mail, write:

Library of Congress
Copyright Office
Publications Section, LM-455
101 Independence Avenue, S.E.
Washington, DC 20559-6000

U.S. Trademark Registration

Almost the only useful, reliable information on trademark registration for anyone but a lawyer is the pamphlet *Basic Facts about Trademarks,* available from the U.S. Patent and Trademark Office without charge. This booklet contains all the information necessary to federally register a trademark, along with the necessary forms and instructions. The bad news is that anyone but a trademark lawyer may have a hard time preparing a trademark registration application using this booklet. This is not because it's badly written or incomplete, but because the regulations that apply to everyone who wants to register a trademark are complex and particular and can frustrate even lawyers. Read it for the information it contains and to convince yourself that you need to know more to register your trademark than you can find out from any booklet. Then call a trademark lawyer, who won't be learning how to file a registration application by practicing on yours.

You can order a free copy of *Basic Facts about Trademarks* by calling the Trademark Office's Public Information Line at (703) 308-HELP.

State Trademark Registration

In addition to the registrations granted by the federal government to trademarks in use in interstate commerce, every state registers trademarks in use in that state. It is much easier for a mark to qualify for state registration than federal registration. State registration is also much cheaper—in most states the filing fee is $20 or less.

In most states, the division of state government that grants trademark registrations and maintains records concerning registered marks is called the Department of State or the Office of the Secretary of State. Sometimes it is further named the Corporations Division or the Trademark Division. With a little detective work in the phone directory for the city in which your state capitol is located, you ought to be able to find the address and phone number for this division of government in your state.

If you call this office, you will be sent a short form to fill out to apply for trademark registration. The few questions asked are easy to answer, especially if you refer to the instructions that will be sent with it. All states require that marks be currently in use in the state before registration is granted. If you are currently using your trademark in the state where you apply for registration, your registration will probably be sent to you within a few weeks after you return your application.

State trademark registration offers pretty good protection for trademarks used only or almost only within that state. A registration puts you on record as the owner of your mark and will prevent registration of at least identical marks for the same products or services within the state. A state registration also has the advantage of notifying marketers outside the state that you are currently using your trademark, since state registrations are consulted for and reported in trademark searches conducted by those who plan to market products or services nationally. This has the effect of warning people away from your mark.

A state trademark registration is a very good start toward protecting your rights in your mark, even if you offer a product or service only within your state and do not plan immediately to market it outside the state. When you do expand your marketing area outside the state, make note of the date of the first advertisement or sale of your product or service outside the state, keep a record of the date in your file for your trademark, and consider applying for federal trademark registration, especially if the interstate activity for your mark was not just a one-time or occasional event.

Form Nonexclusive License of Copyright

Although exclusive licenses of copyright must be in writing, it is not necessary that *nonexclusive* licenses of copyright be written. However, a written nonexclusive license is an excellent idea, if for no other reason than that the parties to the agreement will have, in a written license, documentation of the duration and scope of the license as well as of other important terms of their agreement. This form agreement allows the author of a work to license it to another person or a company on a nonexclusive basis—that is, others may be granted the same rights to use the copyright.

Nonexclusive License of Copyright

This agreement is made between Aaron Bowers[1] (hereinafter referred to as "the Author"[2]) and Ace Advertising Agency[3] (hereinafter referred to as "the Licensee"), with reference to the following facts:

That the Author, an independent contractor,[4] is the creator of and owner of the copyright in a certain unpublished[5] drawing (hereinafter referred to as "the Work"), which may be more fully described as follows:

a three-by-five-inch pen-and-ink portrait of the mythical character Paul Bunyan,[6] a photocopy[7] of which is attached hereto and made a part of this agreement by this reference.

The Author and the Licensee agree as follows:

1. That the Author hereby grants to the Licensee the nonexclusive right to reproduce, publish, prepare derivative works of and from, combine with other materials, display publicly, and otherwise use and exploit the Work[8] for a period of thirty-six (36)[9] months from the date written below.

2. That, during the term of this License of Copyright, the Licensee shall have the nonexclusive right to exercise the rights granted herein throughout the United States and Canada.[10]

3. That the Licensee shall have the right to crop, edit, alter, or otherwise modify the Work to the extent that the Licensee, in the sole discretion of the Licensee, deems necessary to suit it to such uses as the Licensee may choose to make of the Work.[11]

4. That the Licensee will pay to the Author the sum of Five Hundred Dollars ($500), which amount it is agreed will constitute Author's only compensation for the grant of rights made herein.[12]

5. That the Author warrants that he or she is the owner of copyright in the Work and possesses full right and authority to convey the rights herein conveyed. The Author further warrants that the Work does not infringe the copyright in any other work and does not invade any privacy, publicity, trademark, or other rights of any other person.[13] The Author further agrees to indemnify and hold the Licensee harmless in any litigation in which a third party challenges any of the warranties made by the Author in this paragraph if any such litigation results in a judgment adverse to the Author in a court of competent jurisdiction;[14] and

6. That this agreement shall be governed by the laws of the State of Tennessee[15] applicable to contracts made and to be performed therein and shall be construed according to the Copyright Law of the United States, Title 17, Section 101, et seq., United States Code; and

7. That this agreement shall enure to the benefit of and bind the parties and their respective heirs, representatives, successors, and assigns.[16]

In witness whereof, the Author and the Licensee have executed this document in two (2) counterpart originals[17] as of[18] the first day of December, 2001.[19]

_____ [20]   _____ [21]
Author   Licensee

_____ [22]   _____ [23]
Address   Address

_____   _____

_____ [24]   By: _____ [25]
Social Security Number   _____ [26]

                                     Title

_____

[1] Insert the name of the author of the work. If two or more people created the work as co-authors, insert all their names here and add enough spaces for their signatures, etc., at the end of the agreement.

[2] If you want to be more specific, use "Photographer," "Writer," "Songwriter," "Composer," "Illustrator," etc.; use the same designation throughout the document everywhere the word "Author" appears here. If two or more people created the work as coauthors, use the following language: "(hereinafter jointly referred to as 'the Author')."

[3] Insert the name of the person or company to whom the copyright in the work is being licensed.

[4] This form license agreement is inappropriate for use by anyone who is *not* an independent contractor. The works created by employees as part of their jobs are works-for-hire; no written agreement is necessary to document the work-for-hire situation in such a circumstance because the relationship of the employee and employer determines, as a matter of law, the ownership of the copyright in any work created on the job by the employee. However, even someone who works at a full-time job is an independent contractor with regard to any activity outside his or her job responsibilities. This language makes clear that the Author is not an employee of the Licensee.

[5] If the Work has been published, use language similar to the following to specify the year of first publication of the Work: "a certain drawing, first published in 2001." One of the three elements of copyright notice is the year date of first publication of the work.

[6] Insert a detailed description of the Work sufficient to allow the parties to the license and everyone else to determine just which particular work, out of all similar works, is the subject of the license, i.e., "a photograph of three-year-old twin girls, each holding a black Labrador puppy," "a poem titled 'Midsummer's Eve,'" "a musical composition titled 'Wind Dance,'" "an essay titled 'High Hopes,'" "a non-fiction magazine article titled 'Trends in Consumer Electronics Purchases,'" etc.

[7] If it is practicable, attach a copy of the Work, similar to the sort of copies required for registration of copyright, to each original of the Nonexclusive License of Copyright document. If it is not practicable to do so, omit this language and use a much more detailed description of the Work or use photographs (for three-dimensional works such as sculptures) or other identifying material, such as the script for a film, and change the language describing the attached materials.

[8] These are the exclusive rights of copyright given to copyright owners by the U.S. copyright statute and the copyright statutes of other countries. However, since this is a nonexclusive license, the Author may also grant the right to other parties to exercise these rights; further, the Author retains the right to exercise these rights simultaneously with any licensee.

[9] When they draft agreements, lawyers traditionally use both words and figures to specify important numbers and sums of money one party must pay the other. This is done to diminish the possibility that a typographical error will lead to a misunderstanding of some important provision of the agreement, such as its duration, or the underpayment of one party or overpayment by the other. This is a good practice to adopt in modifying this form agreement for your own use. The period of the license may be as short or as long (up to a maximum of the remainder of the term of copyright protection for the Work) as the parties wish. Use "for the full term of copyright protection" to license the copyright for the remainder of the term of copyright protection; otherwise, specify the number of months or years the license will endure.

[10] Specify the territory to which the license applies. If the Author's intent is to grant a nonexclusive license for the entire world, use this language: "That the Licensee shall have the nonexclusive right to exercise the rights granted herein throughout the world...."

[11] Unless permission to alter the work is given by the author of the work, anyone who significantly modifies it may be legally liable to the author for distorting his or her work. The right to alter a work may be important to an advertising agency or company that intends to use the work in various formats. This paragraph may be omitted if the Author objects to any modification of the Work. Or, any such modification may be made dependent upon the prior written approval of the Author: "That the Licensee shall not have the right to crop, edit, alter, or otherwise modify the work without the prior written consent of the Author to any such modification." Ordinarily, nonexclusive licensees, as opposed to those who acquire ownership of the copyright in a work they want to use or the exclusive right to use it, are granted only limited rights to alter a work unless that work is of no real artistic importance to the author.

[12] If payment is to be made in installments, use language similar to the following: "That the Licensee will pay to the Author the sum of Ten Thousand Dollars ($10,000), which amount it is agreed will constitute the Author's only compensation for the grant of rights made herein and which shall be paid according to the following schedule: Five Thousand Dollars ($5,000) shall be paid upon the execution of this agreement; Twenty-five Hundred Dollars ($2500) shall be paid on a date not later than thirty (30) days after the date of execution of this agreement; and Twenty-five Hundred Dollars ($2500) shall be paid on a date not later than sixty (60) days after the date of execution of this agreement." The phrase "only compensation" refers to the fact that this agreement does not provide for the periodic payment of royalties to the Author, as do many agreements in which authors license copyrights to others, such as book publishers or music publishers. This simple form Nonexclusive License of Copyright is inadequate to document a license of copyright made in return for the promise of the payment of royalties.

[13] This sort of provision is common in licenses of copyright to protect the person or company acquiring the license of copyright from lawsuits for infringement based on actions against the Author. This seems reasonable if you consider that licensees usually have no knowledge of the circumstances surrounding the creation of the work of others and need to make sure that they are buying only rights in copyrights, *not* lawsuits.

[14] This is called a "hold harmless" clause and is very common in book publishing, music publishing, and other agreements in which one party acquires rights in the copyright in a work created by an independent contractor. This is a fairly mild example of a "hold harmless" clause. Authors should expect to see provisions similar to those made in paragraph 5 of this agreement in any document that licenses a copyright for any substantial period of time; no licensee should agree to acquire a license of copyright unless the author of the work will make, in writing, promises similar to these in the document that grants the license of copyright.

[15] Insert here the name of the state where you live. It is an advantage to a litigant to be able to file or defend a suit in his or her home state. However, it may be that each party to the agreement will want any suit concerning it to be filed in his or her home state. This is a point of negotiation but, as a practical matter, the more powerful of the two parties to the agreement will prevail.

[16] This allows the Author to assign any sums due under the agreement to a third party or the estate of an Author who dies to collect any such sums on his or her behalf. It also permits the Licensee to, in turn, assign its nonexclusive license to another person or company. However, under some circumstances, especially those where the license is granted in return for the periodic payment of royalties, the author will not want the licensee to assign its nonexclusive license to any other party; the usual reason for this objection is that the author may not know and trust this secondary licensee and may have no confidence in the ability of any such secondary licensee to exploit the copyright in the licensed work. In such an event, add this language to limit the right of the licensee to assign the license of copyright to another entity: "However, the Licensee shall not attempt to convey any of the rights granted herein to the Licensee to any third party without the prior written consent of the Author."

[17] Specify how many original copies of the agreement (i.e., copies of the agreement, even if they are photocopies, that bear the original signatures of the parties).

[18] In agreements, "as of" means: "We are signing this agreement today, but we mean for it to take effect *as of* two weeks ago", or "next month." A date specified that is before or after the agreement is actually signed is referred to as the "effective date" of the agreement.

[19] If you want the agreement to become effective on the date it is signed, use that date here. If you want it to be effective as of a previous date, use that date. If you want to postpone the time when the agreement becomes operative until a later date, use that future date.

[20] Leave this space blank for the signature of the Author.

[21] Leave this space blank for the signature of the Licensee.

[22] Insert the Author's address here.

[23] Insert the Licensee's address here.

[24] Leave this space blank for the Author's Social Security Number. It may be necessary for the Licensee to file a report of the Licensee's payments to the Author with the Internal Revenue Service; if so, the Author's Social Security Number will be necessary for any such filings.

[25] Insert here the name of the person who is acting on behalf of his or her company when that company is the Licensee. If the Licensee is an individual, this line may be omitted.

[26] Insert here the title of the person who is acting on behalf of his or her company when that company is the Licensee. If the Licensee is an individual, this line may be omitted.

Form Exclusive License of Copyright

To be legally effective, exclusive licenses of copyright must be in writing and must be signed by at least the owner of the copyright licensed; this form agreement allows the author of a work to license it exclusively to another person or company.

Exclusive License of Copyright

This agreement is made between Natalie Wilson[1] (hereinafter referred to as "the Author"[2]) and Ace Advertising Agency[3] (hereinafter referred to as "the Licensee"), with reference to the following facts:

A. That the Author, an independent contractor,[4] is the creator of and owner of the copyright in a certain unpublished[5] drawing (hereinafter referred to as "the Work"), which may be more fully described as follows:

a three-by-five-inch pen-and-ink portrait of the mythical character Paul Bunyan,[6] a photocopy[7] of which is attached hereto and made a part of this agreement by this reference.

B. That the Work was completed during 2001.[8]

C. That the Author's date of birth is July 7, 1951.[9]

The Author and the Licensee agree as follows:

1. That the Author hereby grants to the Licensee the sole and exclusive right to reproduce, publish, prepare derivative works of and from, combine with other materials, display publicly, and otherwise use, control the use of, and exploit the Work[10] for a period of thirty-six (36)[11] months from the date written below.

2. That, during the term of this License of Copyright, the Licensee shall have the right to exercise the rights granted herein throughout the United States and Canada.[12]

3. That the Licensee shall have the right to crop, edit, alter, or otherwise modify the Work to the extent that the Licensee, in the sole discretion of the Licensee, deems necessary to suit it to such uses as the Licensee may choose to make of the Work.[13]

4. That the Licensee will pay to the Author the sum of Five Hundred Dollars ($500), which amount it is agreed will constitute Author's only compensation for the grant of rights made herein.[14]

5. That the Author warrants that he or she is the owner of copyright in the Work and possesses full right and authority to convey the rights herein conveyed. The Author further warrants that the Work does not infringe the copyright in any other work and does not invade any privacy, publicity, trademark, or other rights of any other person.[15] The Author further agrees to indemnify and hold the Licensee harmless in any litigation in which a third party challenges any of the warranties made by the Author in this paragraph if any such litigation results in a judgment adverse to the Author in a court of competent jurisdiction;[16] and

6. That this agreement shall be governed by the laws of the State of Tennessee[17] applicable to contracts made and to be performed therein and shall

be construed according to the Copyright Law of the United States, Title 17, Section 101, et seq., United States Code; and

   7. That this agreement shall enure to the benefit of and bind the parties and their respective heirs, representatives, successors, and assigns.[18]

   In witness whereof, the Author and the Licensee have executed this document in two (2) counterpart originals[19] as of [20] the first day of December, 2001.[21]

_____ [22]	_____ [23]
Author	Licensee
_____ [24]	_____ [25]
Address	Address

_____ [26]   By: _____ [27]
Social Security Number   _____ [28]
                                        Title

---

[1] Insert the name of the author of the work. If two or more people created the work as co-authors, insert all their names here and add enough spaces for their signatures, etc., at the end of the agreement.

[2] If you want to be more specific, use "Photographer," "Writer," "Songwriter," "Composer," "Illustrator," etc.; use the same designation throughout the document everywhere the word "Author" appears here. If two or more people created the work as coauthors, use the following language: "(hereinafter jointly referred to as 'the Author')."

[3] Insert the name of the person or company to whom the copyright in the work is being licensed.

[4] This form license agreement is inappropriate for use by anyone who is *not* an independent contractor. The works created by employees as a part of their jobs are works-for-hire; no written agreement is necessary to document the work-for-hire situation in such a circumstance because the relationship of the employee and employer determines, as a matter of law, the ownership of the copyright in any work created on the job by the employee. However, even someone who works at a full-time job is an independent contractor with regard to any activity outside his or her job responsibilities. This language makes clear that the Author is not an employee of the Licensee.

[5] If the Work has been published, use language similar to the following to specify the year of first publication of the Work: "a certain drawing, first published in 2001." One of the three elements of copyright notice is the year date of first publication of the work.

[6] Insert a detailed description of the Work sufficient to allow the parties to the license and everyone else to determine just which particular work, out of all similar works, is the subject of the license, i.e., "a photograph of three-year-old twin girls, each holding a black Labrador puppy," "a poem titled 'Midsummer's Eve,'" "a musical composition titled 'Wind Dance,'" "an essay titled 'High Hopes,'" "a non-fiction magazine article titled 'Trends in Consumer Electronics Purchases,'" etc.

[7] If it is practicable, attach a copy of the Work, similar to the sort of copies required for registration of copyright, to each original of the Exclusive License of Copyright document. If it is not

practicable to do so, omit this language and use a much more detailed description of the Work or use photographs (for three-dimensional works such as sculptures) or other identifying material, such as the script for a film, and change the language describing the attached materials.

[8]Specify the year during which the Work was finished by the Author. (The Copyright Office permits exclusive licensees to register with the Copyright Office their interests in the copyrights they license; the year date the Work was completed is required on any application for copyright registration.);

[9]Insert the correct date. (The author's date of birth is also required on any application for copyright registration.)

[10]These are the exclusive rights of copyright given to copyright owners by the U.S. copyright statute and the copyright statutes of other countries.

[11]When they draft agreements, lawyers traditionally use both words and figures to specify important numbers and sums of money one party must pay the other. This is done to diminish the possibility that a typographical error will lead to a misunderstanding of some important provision of the agreement, such as its duration, or the underpayment of one party or overpayment by the other. This is a good practice to adopt in modifying this form agreement for your own use. The period of the license may be as short or as long (up to a maximum of the remainder of the term of copyright protection for the Work) as the parties wish. Use "for the full term of copyright protection" to license the copyright for the remainder of the term of copyright protection; otherwise, specify the number of months or years the license will endure.

[12]Since a copyright owner may grant simultaneous exclusive licenses to a copyright in different geographic areas, specify the territory to which the license applies. If the Author's intent is to grant an exclusive license for the entire world, use this language: "That the Licensee shall have the right to exercise the rights granted herein throughout the world...."

[13]Unless permission to alter the work is given by the Author of the work, anyone who significantly modifies it may be legally liable to the Author for distorting his or her work. The right to alter a work may be important to an advertising agency or company that intends to use the work in various formats. This paragraph may be omitted if the Author objects to any modification of the Work. Or, any such modification may be made dependent upon the prior written approval of the Author: "That the Licensee shall not have the right to crop, edit, alter, or otherwise modify the work without the prior written consent of the Author to any such modification."

[14]If payment is to be made in installments, use language similar to the following: "That the Licensee will pay to the Author the sum of Ten Thousand Dollars ($10,000), which amount it is agreed will constitute the Author's only compensation for the grant of rights made herein and which shall be paid according to the following schedule: Five Thousand Dollars ($5,000) shall be paid upon the execution of this agreement; Twenty-five Hundred Dollars ($2500) shall be paid on a date not later than thirty (30) days after the date of execution of this agreement; and Twenty-five Hundred Dollars ($2500) shall be paid on a date not later than sixty (60) days after the date of execution of this agreement." The phrase "only compensation" refers to the fact that this agreement does not provide for the periodic payment of royalties to the Author, as do many agreements in which authors license copyrights to others, such as book publishers or music publishers. This simple form Exclusive License of Copyright is inadequate to document a license of copyright made in return for the promise of the payment of royalties; while the *license* provisions of this agreement are adequate for such an arrangement, agreements that provide for the payment of royalties universally make many other provisions necessary, such as a provision specifying the right of the author to occasionally examine the books of the Licensee.

[15]This sort of provision is common in licenses of copyright to protect the person or company acquiring the license of copyright from lawsuits for infringement based on actions against the

Author. This seems reasonable if you consider that licensees usually have no knowledge of the circumstances surrounding the creation of the work of others and need to make sure that they are buying only rights in copyrights, *not* lawsuits.

[16] This is called a "hold harmless" clause and is very common in book publishing, music publishing, and other agreements in which one party acquires rights in the copyright in a work created by an independent contractor. This is a fairly mild example of a "hold harmless" clause. Authors should expect to see provisions similar to those made in paragraph 5 of this agreement in any document that exclusively licenses a copyright for any substantial period of time; no licensee should agree to acquire an exclusive license of copyright unless the author of the work will make, in writing, promises similar to these in the document that grants the license of copyright.

[17] Insert here the name of the state where you live. It is an advantage to a litigant to be able to file or defend a suit in his or her home state. However, it may be that each party to the agreement will want any suit concerning it to be filed in his or her home state. This is a point of negotiation but, as a practical matter, the more powerful of the two parties to the agreement will prevail.

[18] This allows the Author to assign any sums due under the agreement to a third party or the estate of an Author who dies to collect any such sums on his or her behalf. It also permits the Licensee to, in turn, assign its exclusive license to another person or company. However, under some circumstances, especially those where the license is granted in return for the periodic payment of royalties, the author will not want the licensee to assign its exclusive license to any other party; the usual reason for this objection is that the author may not know and trust this secondary licensee and may have no confidence in the ability of any such secondary licensee to exploit the copyright in the work. In such an event, add this language to limit the right of the licensee to assign the license of copyright to another entity: "However, the Licensee shall not attempt to convey any of the rights granted herein to the Licensee by the Author to any third party without the prior written consent of the Author."

[19] Specify how many original copies of the agreement (i.e., copies of the agreement, even if they are photocopies, that bear the original signatures of the parties).

[20] In agreements, "as of" means: "We are signing this agreement today, but we mean for it to take effect *as of* two weeks ago", or "next month." A date specified that is before or after the agreement is actually signed is referred to as the "effective date" of the agreement.

[21] If you want the agreement to become effective on the date it is signed, use that date here. If you want it to be effective as of a previous date, use that date. If you want to postpone the time when the agreement becomes operative until a later date, use that future date.

[22] Leave this space blank for the signature of the Author.

[23] Leave this space blank for the signature of the Licensee.

[24] Insert the Author's address here.

[25] Insert the Licensee's address here.

[26] Leave this space blank for the Author's Social Security Number. It may be necessary for the Licensee to file a report of the Licensee's payments to the Author with the Internal Revenue Service; if so, the Author's Social Security Number will be necessary for any such filings.

[27] Insert here the name of the person who is acting on behalf of his or her company when that company is the Licensee. If the Licensee is an individual, this line may be omitted.

[28] Insert here the title of the person who is acting on behalf of his or her company when that company is the Licensee. If the Licensee is an individual, this line may be omitted.

Form Assignment of Copyright

To be legally effective, assignments of copyright must be in writing and must be signed by at least the owner of the copyright transferred; this form agreement is for use in transferring ownership of a copyright from the author of the work to another person or company.

Assignment of Copyright

This agreement is made between Megan Bowers[1] (hereinafter referred to as "the Author"[2]) and Ace Advertising Agency[3] (hereinafter referred to as "the Assignee"), with reference to the following facts:

A. That the Author, an independent contractor,[4] is the creator of and owner of the copyright in a certain unpublished[5] drawing (hereinafter referred to as "the Work"), which may be more fully described as follows:

a three-by-five-inch pen-and-ink portrait of the mythical character Paul Bunyan,[6] a photocopy[7] of which is attached hereto and made a part of this agreement by this reference.

B. That the Work was completed during 2001.[8]

C. That the Author's date of birth is July 7, 1951.[9]

The Author and the Assignee agree as follows:

1. That the Author hereby assigns, transfers, and conveys to the Assignee all[10] right, title, and interest in and to the Work described above[11] together with the copyright therein and the right to secure copyright registration therefor, in accordance with Sections 101, 204, and 205 of Title 17 of the United States Code, the Copyright Law of the United States. The above assignment, transfer, and conveyance includes, without limitation, any and all features, sections, and components of the Work, any and all works derived therefrom, the United States and worldwide copyrights therein, and any renewals or extensions thereof, and any and all other rights that the Author now has or to which he or she may become entitled under existing or subsequently enacted federal, state, or foreign laws, including, but not limited to, the following rights: to reproduce, publish, and display the Work publicly, to prepare derivative works of and from the Work, to combine the Work with other materials, and to otherwise use, exploit, and control the use of the Work.[12] The above assignment further includes any and all causes of action for infringement of the Work, past, present, and future, and any and all proceeds from such causes accrued and unpaid and hereafter accruing; and

2. That the Assignee shall have the right to crop, edit, alter, or otherwise modify the Work to the extent that the Assignee, in the sole discretion of the Assignee, deems necessary to suit it to such uses as the Assignee may choose to make of the Work.[13]

3. That the Assignee will pay to the Author the sum of Five Hundred Dollars ($500),[14] which amount it is agreed will constitute Author's only compensation for the grant of rights made herein.[15]

4. That the Author warrants that he or she is the owner of copyright in the Work and possesses full right and authority to convey the rights herein conveyed. The Author further warrants that the Work does not infringe the copyright in any other work and does not invade any privacy, publicity, trademark, or other rights of any other person.[16] The Author further agrees to indemnify and hold the Assignee harmless in any litigation in which a third party challenges any of the warranties made by the Author in this paragraph if any such litigation results in a judgment adverse to the Author in a court of competent jurisdiction;[17] and

5. That this agreement shall be governed by the laws of the State of Tennessee[18] applicable to contracts made and to be performed therein and shall be construed according to the Copyright Law of the United States, Title 17, Section 101, et seq., United States Code; and

6. That this agreement shall enure to the benefit of and bind the parties and their respective heirs, representatives, successors, and assigns.[19]

In witness whereof, the Author and the Assignee have executed this document in two (2) counterpart originals[20] as of[21] the first day of December, 2001.[22]

_____ [23]	_____ [24]
Author	Assignee
_____ [25]	_____ [26]
Address	Address
_____	_____
_____ [27]	By: _____ [28]
Social Security Number	_____ [29]
	Title

---

[1] Insert the name of the author of the work. If two or more people created the work as co-authors, insert all their names here and add enough spaces for their signatures, etc., at the end of the agreement.

[2] If you want to be more specific, use "Photographer," "Writer," "Songwriter," "Composer," "Illustrator," etc.; use the same designation throughout the document everywhere the word "Author" appears here. If two or more people created the work as coauthors, use the following language: "(hereinafter jointly referred to as 'the Author')."

[3] Insert the name of the person or company to whom the copyright in the work is being assigned or transferred.

[4] This form assignment agreement is inappropriate for use by anyone who is *not* an independent contractor. The works created by employees as a part of their jobs are works-for-hire; no written agreement is necessary to document the work-for-hire situation in such a circumstance because the relationship of the employee and employer determines, as a matter of law, the ownership of the copyright in any work created on the job by the employee. However, even someone who works at a full-time job is an independent contractor with regard to any activity outside his or her job responsibilities. This language makes clear that the Author is not

an employee of the Assignee. This is an important point because an author who does not create a work as part of his or her job responsibilities may terminate an assignment of the sort made in this agreement at the halfway point of copyright protection.

[5] If the Work has been published, use language similar to the following to specify the year of first publication of the Work: "a certain drawing, first published in 2001." One of the three elements of copyright notice is the year date of first publication of the work.

[6] Insert a detailed description of the Work sufficient to allow the parties to the license and everyone else to determine just which particular work, out of all similar works, is the subject of the license, i.e., "a photograph of three-year-old twin girls, each holding a black Labrador puppy," "a poem titled 'Midsummer's Eve,'" "a musical composition titled 'Wind Dance,'" "an essay titled 'High Hopes,'" "a non-fiction magazine article titled 'Trends in Consumer Electronics Purchases,'" etc.

[7] If it is practicable, attach a copy of the Work, similar to the sort of copies required for registration of copyright, to each original of the Assignment of Copyright document. If it is not practicable to do so, omit this language and use a much more detailed description of the Work or use photographs (for three-dimensional works such as sculptures) or other identifying material, such as the script for a film, and change the language describing the attached materials.

[8] Specify the year during which the Work was finished by the Author. (This year date is required on any application for copyright registration.)

[9] Insert the correct date. (The author's date of birth is also required on any application for copyright registration.)

[10] It is, of course, possible to convey by assignment less than the entire copyright in a work. If this is desired, use language similar to the following: "That the Author hereby assigns, transfers, and conveys to the Assignee Fifty Per Cent (50%) of the entire right, title, and interest in and to the Work described above …"

[11] This assignment language does not convey ownership in any physical object or objects that embody the Work, since copyright ownership is separate from ownership of copies of the Work. If the parties intend to convey both the copyright in the work and ownership of a physical object or objects (such as a sculpture or an original painting), a separate sales agreement should be drafted to provide for the sale of any such physical object or objects. (However, as a practical matter, implied in any transfer of copyright in a work that requires possession of a particular physical object, such as a computer diskette [if the work in which copyright is transferred is computer software] to allow the work to be copied is the promise that the author of the work will at least make available for copying any such necessary physical object.)

[12] These are the exclusive rights of copyright given to copyright owners by the U.S. copyright statute and the copyright statutes of other countries.

[13] Unless permission to alter the work is given by the Author of the work, anyone who significantly modifies it may be legally liable to the Author for distorting his or her work.

[14] When they draft agreements, lawyers traditionally use both words and figures to specify sums of money one party must pay the other. This is done to diminish the possibility that a typographical error will lead to the underpayment of one party or overpayment by the other. It is a good rule to follow in modifying this form agreement for your own use.

[15] If payment is to be made in installments, use language similar to the following: "That the Assignee will pay to the Author the sum of Ten Thousand Dollars ($10,000), which amount it is agreed will constitute the Author's only compensation for the grant of rights made herein and which shall be paid according to the following schedule: Five Thousand Dollars ($5,000) shall be paid upon the execution of this agreement; Twenty-five Hundred Dollars ($2500) shall be paid on a date not later than thirty (30) days after the date of execution of this agreement; and

Twenty-five Hundred Dollars ($2500) shall be paid on a date not later than sixty (60) days after the date of execution of this agreement." The phrase "only compensation" refers to the fact that this agreement does not provide for the periodic payment of royalties to the Author, as do many agreements in which authors transfer copyrights to others, such as book publishers or music publishers. This simple form Assignment of Copyright is inadequate to document a transfer of copyright made in return for the promise of the payment of royalties; while the *transfer* provisions of this assignment are adequate for such an arrangement, agreements that provide for the payment of royalties universally make many other provisions necessary, such as a provision specifying the right of the author to occasionally examine the books of the assignee.

[16] This sort of provision is common in assignments of copyright to protect the person or company acquiring the copyright from lawsuits for infringement based on actions against the Author. This seems reasonable if you consider that assignees usually have no knowledge of the circumstances surrounding the creation of the work of others and need to make sure that they are buying only copyrights, *not* lawsuits.

[17] This is called a "hold harmless" clause and is very common in book publishing, music publishing, and other agreements in which one party acquires the copyright in a work created by an independent contractor. This is a fairly mild example of a "hold harmless" clause. Authors should expect to see provisions similar to those made in paragraph 4 of this agreement in any document that transfers ownership of a copyright; no assignee should agree to buy a copyright unless the author of the work will make, in writing, promises similar to these in the document that transfers ownership of the copyright.

[18] Insert here the name of the state where you live. It is an advantage to a litigant to be able to file or defend a suit in his or her home state. However, it may be that each party to the agreement will want any suit concerning it to be filed in his or her home state. This is a point of negotiation but, as a practical matter, the more powerful of the two parties to the agreement will prevail.

[19] This allows the Author to assign any sums due under the agreement to a third party or the estate of an Author who dies to collect any such sums on his or her behalf. It also permits the Assignee to, in turn, assign ownership of the copyright in the Work to another person or company. However, under some circumstances, especially those where the assignment is made in return for the periodic payment of royalties, the author will not want the assignee to assign the copyright in the work to any other party; the usual reason for this objection is that the author may not know and trust this secondary assignee and may have no confidence in the ability of any such secondary assignee to exploit the copyright in the work. In such an event, add this language to limit the right of the assignee to assign the copyright to another entity: "However, the Assignee shall not attempt to convey any of the rights granted herein to the Assignee by the Author to any third party without the prior written consent of the Author."

[20] Specify how many original copies of the agreement (i.e., copies of the agreement, even if they are photocopies, that bear the original signatures of the parties).

[21] In agreements, "as of" means: "We are signing this agreement today, but we mean for it to take effect *as of* two weeks ago", or "next month." A date specified that is before or after the agreement is actually signed is referred to as the "effective date" of the agreement.

[22] If you want the agreement to become effective on the date it is signed, use that date here. If you want it to be effective as of a previous date, use that date. If you want to postpone the time when the agreement becomes operative until a later date, use that future date.

[23] Leave this space blank for the signature of the Author.

[24] Leave this space blank for the signature of the Assignee.

[25] Insert the Author's address here.

[26] Insert the Assignee's address here.

[27] Leave this space blank for the the Author's Social Security Number. It may be necessary for the Assignee to file a report of the Assignee's payments to the Author with the Internal Revenue Service; if so, the Author's Social Security Number will be necessary for any such filings.

[28] Insert here the name of the person who is acting on behalf of his or her company when that company is the Assignee. If the Assignee is an individual, this line may be omitted.

[29] Insert here the title of the person who is acting on behalf of his or her company when that company is the Assignee. If the Assignee is an individual, this line may be omitted.

Form Work-for-Hire Agreement

To be legally effective, work-for-hire agreements must be in writing and must be signed by both the creator of the specially-commissioned work and the person or company that commissioned the work.

Work-for-Hire Agreement

This agreement is made between Rob Wilson[1] (hereinafter referred to as "the Author"[2]) and Ace Advertising Agency[3] (hereinafter referred to as "the Commissioning Party"), with reference to the following facts:

A. That the Author, an independent contractor,[4] has prepared, at the instruction and under the direction of the Commissioning Party, a certain unpublished[5] drawing (hereinafter referred to as "the Work"), which may be more fully described as follows:

a three-by-five-inch pen-and-ink portrait of the mythical character Paul Bunyan,[6] a photocopy[7] of which is attached hereto and made a part of this agreement by this reference.

B. That the Work was completed during 2001.[8]

C. That the Author's date of birth is July 7, 1951.[9]

The Author and the Commissioning Party agree as follows:

1. That the Work, including every embodiment thereof, was specifically prepared for the Commissioning Party and constitutes a work-for-hire, as defined in Title 17, Section 101, et seq., United States Code, the Copyright Law of the United States. The Author acknowledges and agrees that the Commissioning Party is and will be considered the author of the Work for purposes of copyright and is the owner of all rights of copyright in and to the Work and that the Commissioning Party will have the exclusive right to exercise all rights of copyright specified in Title 17, Section 101, et seq., United States Code, the Copyright Law of the United States, for the full term of copyright and will be entitled to register the copyright in and to the Work in the Commissioning Party's name.

2. That the Commissioning Party will pay to the Author the sum of Five Hundred Dollars ($500),[10] which amount[11] it is agreed will constitute Author's entire fee and only compensation[12] for the Author's services in creating and preparing the Work and for the agreement made herein (excluding reimbursement for such reasonable expenses as may have been incurred by the Author in connection with the creation of the Work), within thirty (30) days after delivery to the Commissioning Party of all existing physical embodiments of the Work, with the exception of a limited number of copies of the Work which the Author may retain for the sole purpose of display in the Author's professional portfolio or place of business or for entry in shows or competitions.[13]

3. That this agreement shall be governed by the laws of the State of Tennessee[14] applicable to contracts made and to be performed therein and shall be construed according to the Copyright Law of the United States, Title 17, Section 101, et seq., United States Code; and

4. That this agreement shall enure to the benefit of and bind the parties and their respective heirs, representatives, successors, and assigns.[15]

In witness whereof, the Author and the Commissioning Party have executed this document in two (2) counterpart originals[16] as of[17] the first day of December, 2001.[18]

_____ [19]   _____ [20]
Author   Commissioning Party
_____ [21]   _____ [22]
Address   Address

_____   _____

_____ [23]   By: _____ [24]
Social Security Number   [25]

                                     Title

---

[1] Insert the name of the Author of the work. If two or more people created the work as coauthors, insert all their names here and add enough spaces for their signatures, etc., at the end of the agreement.

[2] In every other situation where the creator of a work conveys the copyright in the work to another party, that creator is forever considered the author of the work, even after the copyright is owned by someone else. With a work-for-hire, the entity that commissions the work is considered, for copyright purposes, the "author" of the work from the inception of the work. Therefore, in this work-for-hire agreement, it is preferable to use a term other than "Author" to designate the creator of the Work. The best approach is to refer to the creator by a name that describes his or her profession, i.e., use "Photographer," "Writer," "Songwriter," "Composer," etc. Use the same designation throughout the document to refer to the creator of the work. If two or more people created the work as coauthors, use the following language:"(hereinafter jointly referred to as 'the Songwriters')."

[3] Insert the name of the person or company that commissioned the Work.

[4] This form work-for-hire agreement is inappropriate for use by anyone who is *not* an independent contractor. The works created by employees as a part of their jobs are works-for-hire; no written agreement is necessary to document the work-for-hire situation in such a circumstance because the relationship of the employee and employer determines, as a matter of law, the ownership of the copyright in any work created on the job by the employee. However, even someone who works at a full-time job is an independent contractor with regard to any activity outside his or her job responsibilities.

[5] If the Work has been published, use language similar to the following to specify the year of first publication of the Work:"a certain drawing, first published in 2001." One of the three elements of copyright notice is the year date of first publication of the work.

[6] Insert a detailed description of the Work sufficient to allow the parties to the license and everyone else to determine just which particular work, out of all similar works, is the subject of the license, i.e., "a photograph of three-year-old twin girls, each holding a black Labrador puppy," "a poem titled 'Midsummer's Eve,'" "a musical composition titled 'Wind Dance,'" "an essay titled 'High Hopes,'" "a non-fiction magazine article titled 'Trends in Consumer Electronics Purchases,'" etc.

[7] If it is practicable, attach a copy of the Work, similar to the sort of copies required for registration of copyright, to each original of the Work-For-Hire Agreement document. If it is not practicable to do so, omit this language and use a much more detailed description of the Work or use photographs (for three-dimensional works such as sculptures) or other identifying material, such as the script for a film, and change the language describing the attached materials.

[8] Specify the year during which the Work was finished by the Author. (This year date is required on any application for copyright registration.)

[9] Insert the correct date. (The Author's date of birth is also required on any application for copyright registration.)

[10] When they draft agreements, lawyers traditionally use both words and figures to specify sums of money one party must pay the other. This is done to diminish the possibility that a typographical error will lead to the underpayment of one party or overpayment by the other. It is a good rule to follow in modifying this form agreement for your own use.

[11] If payment is to be made in installments, use language similar to the following: "That the Commissioning Party will pay to the Author the sum of Ten Thousand Dollars ($10,000), which amount it is agreed will constitute the Author's entire fee and only compensation for the Author's services in creating and preparing the Work and for the agreement made herein (excluding reimbursement for such reasonable expenses as may have been incurred by the Author in connection with the creation of the Work) and which shall be paid according to the following schedule: Five Thousand Dollars ($5,000) shall be paid upon the execution of this agreement; Twenty-five Hundred Dollars ($2500) shall be paid on a date not later than thirty (30) days after the date of execution of this agreement; and Twenty-five Hundred Dollars ($2500) shall be paid on a date not later than sixty (60) days after the date of execution of this agreement."

[12] The phrase "entire fee and only compensation" refers to the fact that this agreement does not provide for the periodic payment of royalties to the Author, as do some other agreements in which authors transfer copyrights to others, such as book publishers or music publishers. This Work-For-Hire Agreement is inappropriate for use in any such situation.

[13] Although the Commissioning Party will own the copyright in the Work, it is considerate to allow the Author of the Work to retain a few copies of the work, if that is possible. This courtesy to the Author does not diminish or endanger the rights of the Commissioning Party since ownership of a physical object that embodies a work conveys no rights in the copyright in the work. The Author can look at and show the retained copies of the Work, but cannot make any further copies or otherwise exercise any rights of copyright.

[14] Insert here the name of the state where you live. It is an advantage to a litigant to be able to file or defend a suit in his or her home state. However, it may be that each party to the agreement will want any suit concerning it to be filed in his or her home state. This is a point of negotiation but, as a practical matter, the more powerful of the two parties to the agreement will prevail.

[15] This allows the Author to assign any sums due under the agreement to a third party or the estate of an Author who dies to collect any such sums on his or her behalf.

[16] Specify how many original copies of the agreement (i.e., copies of the agreement, even if they are photocopies, that bear the original signatures of the parties).

[17] In agreements, "as of" means: "We are signing this agreement today, but we mean for it to take effect *as of* two weeks ago," or "next month." A date specified that is before or after the agreement is actually signed is referred to as the "effective date" of the agreement.

[18] If you want the agreement to become effective on the date it is signed, use that date here. If you want it to be effective as of a previous date, use that date. If you want to postpone the time when the agreement becomes operative until a later date, use that future date.

[19] Leave this space blank for the signature of the Author.

[20] Leave this space blank for the signature of the Commissioning Party.

[21] Insert the Author's address here.

[22] Insert the Commissioning Party's address here.

[23] Leave this space blank for the the Author's Social Security Number. It may be necessary for the Commissioning Party to file a report of the Commissioning Party's payments to the Author with the Internal Revenue Service; if so, the Author's Social Security Number will be necessary for any such filings.

[24] Insert here the name of the person who is acting on behalf of his or her company when that company is the Commissioning Party. If the Commissioning Party is an individual, this line may be omitted.

[25] Insert here the title of the person who is acting on behalf of his or her company when that company is the Commissioning Party. If the Commissioning Party is an individual, this line may be omitted.

Release for Photographs

I hereby grant to <u>Magellan Press, Inc.</u>[1] and its assigns, licensees, and successors the irrevocable and unlimited right and permission to use, publish, and disseminate my name and any of the photographs (hereinafter called "the Photographs) taken on <u>January 24, 2000</u>[2] by <u>Jimmy Hahn</u>[3] that include my image, <u>in a book, tentatively titled "Romantic San Francisco," to be published by Magellan Press, Inc.</u>[4] and in other print publishing projects and in all media in connection with that book or any other publishing projects, for advertising, trade, or any other lawful purpose. I further grant to Magellan Press, Inc. and its assigns, licensees, and successors the right to crop, modify, and otherwise alter the aforementioned Photograph or Photographs, including preparing composite or distorted representations, and to combine it or them with any written copy, photographs, or illustrations. I waive my right to inspect that Photograph or Photographs as so altered or combined with other elements.

In return for the grants made herein, I agree that I shall receive as my only compensation <u>one (1) copy of the book "Romantic San Francisco," when such book is published.</u>[5] However, I understand that, in the sole discretion of Magellan Press, Inc., that book may not contain any photograph of me.[6]

I understand that by signing this Release I am waiving any claim I might otherwise make for invasion of privacy or infringement of the right of publicity. Further, I represent that I have read this Release before signing it and understand its provisions.

I affirm and warrant that I have reached the age of majority and have full authority to make the grants herein contained.[7]

_____	_____
Signature	Date of Signature
_____	_____
Print Name[8]	Signature of Witness[9]
_____	_____
Mailing Address[10]	Address of Witness[11]
_____	_____
_____	_____

or

I am the parent or legal guardian of _____[12] a minor, and hereby make the grants and representations set out above on behalf of him or her.

_____	_____
Signature	Date of Signature
_____	_____
Print Name[13]	Signature of Witness[14]
_____	_____
Mailing Address[15]	Address of Witness[16]
_____	_____
_____	_____

---

[1] Insert name of advertising agency here. If no agency is involved, use the name of the photographer.

[2] Insert the date the photographs were taken.

[3] Insert the name of the photographer.

[4] Insert a broad description of the project that will include the photographs.

[5] In the case of this project, the models would be working for publicity and the chance of being featured in a book of photography. In the case of paid models, insert language such as "One Thousand Five Hundred Dollars ($1,500)."

[6] This language is necessary to make clear that the final decision whether the photograph including this model will be included in the book as published is a decision of the editor of the book and that no promise is made that the model will appear in the final book.

[7] This space for the model's signature should be used if the model is of legal age (sometimes this is 18, sometimes 21). If the model is not of legal age in the state where the photograph is taken, the parent or guardian of the model must sign in the subsequent signature space. In some cases, professional models have been declared "emancipated minors" by going to court and requesting to be treated as adults for purposes of pursuing a profession. However, never believe that a minor has been emancipated and is able to be treated as an adult in making binding contracts without credible proof, such as seeing the court decree yourself, that this is so.

[8] Get the model to print his or her name in order to file this release correctly in your files and also so that the model's name in any credit line in any publication of the photographs of this model may be correctly spelled.

[9] Get someone to witness the model's signature in order to avoid any later claim that the signature is not that of the model.

[10] It may never be necessary to communicate with the model, but having the model's address is a good idea.

[11] If you ever need to be able to call on the witness to the model's signature, you will need to know where to find him or her.

[12] Insert the name of the minor who is the model for the photographs.

[13] Get the parent or guardian to print his or her name so that you will have its correct spelling.

[14] Get someone to witness the parent's or guardian's signature in order to avoid any later claim that the signature is not that of the parent or guardian.

[15] It may never be necessary to communicate with the parent or guardian, but having the parent's or guardian's address is a good idea.

[16] If you ever need to be able to call on the witness to the parent's or guardian's signature, you will need to know where to find him or her.

Glossary

assignment of copyright Like a sale of a copyright, usually made in return for a lump sum payment or the promise of the payment of a share of the income produced by the work. In addition to assignment of an entire copyright, an author may also assign only part of a copyright. The copyright statute requires that the transfer of ownership of any copyright be made in a written document signed by the person assigning the ownership of the copyright to someone else; no verbal assignment of copyright is possible. Anyone who acquires any right of copyright by assignment can, in turn, sell that right to someone else unless the written assignment document provides otherwise. An assignment of copyright may also be referred to as a "transfer" of copyright. (Assignment of copyright is one of three ways that ownership of rights in copyright is transferred to someone besides the author of the copyrighted work; the other two are license and work-for-hire.)

author In the language of the U.S. copyright statute, the creator of any copyrightable work, whether that work is a piece of advertising copy, short story, book, photograph, illustration, movie script, play, painting, computer software program, musical composition, or other sort of work. The exception to this is work-for-hire; if a work is created as a work-for-hire, the employer of the creator of the copyright owns the copyright from the inception of the work and is considered the author of the work for purposes of copyright.

case law   Law that originates in the decisions of courts as opposed to written laws passed by state legislatures or the U.S. Congress, which are called "statutes."

cease and desist letter   A letter written by the lawyer for the plaintiff in a lawsuit telling the defendant to immediately cease certain specified actions that infringe the plaintiff's copyright or trademark or other right and thereafter desist from any further such actions. These letters are usually the first indication that a defendant receives that his or her actions may have violated the plaintiff's rights. Depending on the merits of the plaintiff's claims of infringement, a defendant will decide to comply with the plaintiff's demands and try to settle the dispute out of court or to fight the plaintiff's assertions of infringement in court.

copyright   The set of exclusive rights that are granted, initially to the creators of works eligible for copyright protection, by the various copyright statutes that exist in most countries. In the United States, copyright protection begins when a work is first "fixed" in a tangible form and endures, in the case of a work created by an individual, until seventy years after the death of the creator.

copyright infringement   The unauthorized exercise of any of the exclusive rights reserved by law to copyright owners. The most usual sort of copyright infringement lawsuit claims that the defendant is guilty of unauthorized copying from the plaintiff's work. In this situation, copyright infringement is judged by a three-part circumstantial evidence test: (1) Did the accused infringer have access to the work that is said to have been infringed, in order to make copying possible? (2) Is the defendant actually guilty of *copying* from the plaintiff's work part of the plaintiff's protectable expression? And (3) Is the accused work substantially similar to the work the plaintiff says was copied? Coincidental creation of a work similar to an existing copyrighted work, without copying, is not infringement.

copyright notice   The three elements that legally serve to give notice to the world that a copyright owner is claiming ownership of a particular work. Copyright notice consists of three parts: the word "copyright" or the © symbol (or, for sound recordings, the ℗symbol), the year of first publication of the work, and the name of the copyright owner. No formalities are required to use copyright notice, and although it is no longer required to secure copyright protection, use of copyright notice does confer certain valuable procedural benefits (in a copyright infringement lawsuit) on the copyright owner.

copyright registration   The registration of a claim to ownership of a copyright, made in Washington, D.C., in the U.S. Copyright Office, a division of the Library of Congress. Copyright registration enhances the rights an author gains automatically by the act of creating a copyrightable work but does not, of itself, create these rights. The Copyright Office prescribes a specific form for the registration of copyright in each particular variety of work. Form TX is used for the registration of "literary" works, that is works, other than dramatic works, that consist primarily of TeXtual matter. Form PA is used to register copyrights in works of the Performing Arts, including plays, songs, and movies. Form SR is used to register the copyrights in Sound Recordings. There are other forms for other sorts of works; the names of the major varieties of copyright registration forms and the sort of works to be registered with each are listed in the Copyright Office Resources section of the appendix of this book.

defendant   The person or company whose actions are complained of in a lawsuit. In criminal trials, a defendant is presumed innocent until proven guilty. In civil lawsuits, such as a suit for copyright or trademark infringement or infringement of someone's privacy or right of publicity, no such presumption is made. Nothing is presumed about the actions of either the defendant or the plaintiff (the person or company that files the suit) until it is proven to the court. This means that even an innocent defendant is in the same position as a plaintiff, i.e., the defendant must prove his or her innocence just as the plaintiff must try to prove the truth of the allegations made in the complaint.

defenses   The arguments a defendant in a lawsuit makes in self-defense. The most important and the most commonly used defense in copyright infringement suits is the defense of "fair use," which is the argument that the complained-of

actions by the defendant are allowable under the law as a
permitted use of the plaintiff's work. In suits for libel, truth is
a defense, i.e., if the statement made by the defendant that
harmed the plaintiff can be demonstrated to be true, the
statement is not libel and the defendant is not liable for damages to the defendant.

exclusive rights of copyright   Those rights pertaining to a
copyright that may be exercised only, or exclusively, by the
owner of that copyright. Under the U.S. copyright statute,
the creator of a copyrighted work has the exclusive right to
copy or reproduce the work, to prepare alternate or "derivative" versions of the work, to distribute and sell copies of the
work, and to perform or display the work publicly. Usually
these rights may not be exercised by anyone other than the
author of the work or a person to whom he or she has sold
or licensed one or more of these "exclusive rights."

Federal Trade Commission   The Federal Trade Commission
(FTC) is the federal agency that enforces the Federal Trade
Commission Act, which is a federal law that regulates, among
other things, advertising. The Federal Trade Commission Act
prohibits unfair methods of commercial competition and
unfair or deceptive trade practices and empowers the FTC to
initiate proceedings to stop such methods or practices. Acting
on complaints from either consumers or competitors, or on
its own initiative, the FTC can, after an investigation, enter a
"cease and desist order" against any company that has
arguably transgressed its regulations. A cease and desist order
is in the nature of an injunction that prohibits an accused
false advertiser from further dissemination of specified
offending ads. Monetary penalties may be levied against companies that fail to abide by FTC cease and desist orders. In
addition to cease and desist orders, the FTC can ask, in federal court, for a whole laundry list of other remedies,
including preliminary and permanent injunctions, civil and
criminal penalties, and various forms of consumer relief, such
as corrective advertising, refunds, and invalidation of contracts
with affected consumers. Either before or after the FTC files
a complaint in federal court, the FTC and the advertiser that
is the subject of the FTC's investigation can enter a "consent
decree," which is like a settlement agreement.

injunction A court order that directs the enjoined party to do something or, more typically, to cease doing something and to refrain from doing it in future. Plaintiffs in trademark infringement suits typically seek injunctions to stop defendants from continuing to infringe the plaintiff's copyrights. The scope of an injunction and whether a litigant's motion for one is granted is at the discretion of the judge who hears the suit. A temporary injunction is usually granted at the same time a suit is filed and endures only ten days. A preliminary injunction is granted by a judge after hearing arguments for and against the injunction from both the plaintiff and the defendant and usually lasts until the end of the lawsuit, when it may ripen into a permanent injunction by means of a paragraph to that effect in the judge's order rendering his or her decision.

intent-to-use application Since November of 1989, marketers may file what is called an "intent-to-use" application to register a trademark with the U.S. Patent and Trademark Office, as opposed to a "use-based" application, which was formerly the only sort of registration application that was allowed. Application for registration may be made before actual use of a new trademark, so long as the trademark owner has a "bona fide intent" to begin to use the mark in interstate commerce within six months of the date the registration application is filed. The period of time for beginning use of the mark may be extended, in six-month increments and upon making the proper filings, to a total period of thirty-six months. Registration may then be granted after use of the mark is made in interstate commerce. This system allows a company to claim ownership of a mark by filing an intent-to-use application to register it; when a second company conducts a trademark search to ascertain the availability of the mark, the first company's application will appear in the search report and warn the second company away from the mark. Further, intent-to-use applications confer one other important benefit not formerly available: when a registration is eventually granted to an intent-to-use applicant, the date the applicant filed the registration application is deemed to be the date the applicant's rights in the mark commenced. This has the effect of "backdating" the applicant's rights to a date prior to the date of actual use of the mark, which was formerly the date ownership rights commenced.

libel   U.S. statutes generally provide that libel is: (1) a false statement (2) that is "of and concerning" the plaintiff; (3) that is published to a third party (4) that is made as a statement of fact (i.e., is not just someone's opinion) (5) that causes harm to the plaintiff by injuring her or his reputation or subjecting her or him to shame and ridicule in the community and (6) that is the result of some omission or fault of the defendant.

likelihood of confusion   The test courts apply in determining infringing similarity between trademarks. If consumers are likely to confuse the new mark with the older, established trademark because of the similarity of the marks, gauged by comparing the appearance, sound, and meaning of the two marks, likelihood of confusion is said to exist.

patent   A patent is a monopoly granted by the U.S. Patent Office for a limited time to the creator of a new invention. A utility patent may be granted to a process; a machine; a manufacture; a composition of matter; or an improvement of an existing idea that falls into one of these categories. For example, a utility patent would be granted to the inventor of a new industrial or technical process or a new chemical composition. Utility patents endure twenty years after the application for a patent was filed. Plant patents are issued for new asexually or sexually reproducible plants and last seventeen years from the date of issue. Design patents are granted for ornamental designs used for nonfunctional aspects of manufactured items; a design patent lasts for fourteen years from the date it is issued. An inventor must meet very strict standards before the Patent Office will grant a patent for his or her invention. A patent holder earns the exclusive right to make, use, and sell the invention for which the patent was granted. Any unauthorized manufacture, use, or sale of the patented invention within this country during the term of the patent is infringement.

plaintiff   In a civil lawsuit, the person or company that files a lawsuit to complain of the actions of the defendant that the plaintiff believes violate the plaintiff's rights.

public domain   Primarily, works for which copyright protection has expired. The U.S. copyright statute is based on the assumption that creative people will be encouraged to be creative if they are given exclusive control for a period of time over the use of their works. After that control ends, the public benefits from the right to make unlimited use of the previously protected creations. When a work falls into the public domain, the work has become available for use in any way by anyone. Besides works for which copyright protection has expired, the other major category of public domain works is works created by officers or employees of the U.S. government as part of their government jobs, which are in the public domain because the government has chosen not to claim copyright in works created at the taxpayers' expense.

puffery   Puffery is flattering, sometimes exaggerated sales rhetoric that consumers are not likely to rely upon when making a purchase. It is not actionable under either Section 43(a) or by the FTC because it does not amount to a materially misleading statement.

right of privacy   The right of privacy is the right of every U.S. citizen to be left alone, to live a life uninterrupted by intrusions into private matters or living areas, and to be free from unwilling exposure to public scrutiny or participation in the commercial process. There are four kinds of invasion of privacy. (1) "False light" invasion of privacy is the placing of someone in a "false light" before the public, usually by publishing a photograph or story that portrays that person in a misleading way that is offensive to him or her. (2) "Intrusion" invasion of privacy involves some invasion of a person's private space or solitude. The invasion of privacy does not have to result from a *physical* invasion of private space; eavesdropping on private conversations and taking photos of someone through a window with a long-range lens are examples of this sort of invasion of privacy. (3) "Public disclosure of private facts" invasion of privacy involves the publication of true but private information about an individual, such as details about the person's sex life or health or finances. (4) "Misappropriation" invasion of privacy is the unauthorized use of a person's name or likeness for commercial purposes, such as in an ad, and represents the most common sort of privacy lawsuit involving advertising creative people.

right of publicity   The infringement of someone's "right of publicity" consists of the exploitation of someone's name or

image in some commercial context without his or her permission. Unlike invasion of privacy, which is related to the
right of private people to be left alone, the right of publicity
is more in the nature of a property right of a famous person
to exclusively exploit his or her own fame. The right of publicity is really the "flip side" of the right of privacy, since a
violation of someone's right of publicity is a violation of his
or her right to be the only one to make use of the "publicity value" of his or her name and a private individual's name
usually has no such publicity value.

Section 43(a)   Section 43(a) of the Lanham Act, the federal
trademark statute, allows people who feel they have been
harmed by misrepresentations made in someone else's advertising to sue for false advertising. Usually the people who feel
they have been harmed and who sue are the competitors of
the company that places the allegedly false ad, and usually
they sue for significant false claims made about the advertised
products. However, Section 43(a) also allows suits to be
brought because of false claims made about the products of
the *competitors* of the advertiser.

settlement   Either the termination of a dispute or lawsuit by
mutual agreement of the plaintiff and the defendant or the
sum of money that is often paid, as an incentive to reach such
an agreement, to the plaintiff by the defendant in lieu of any
award of damages a court could make. The majority of lawsuits are settled before trial. The contract that embodies the
agreement reached, in addition to providing for a payment to
the plaintiff in settlement of the dispute or suit, may include
promises by one party to do or in the future to refrain from
doing something. A settlement agreement in an action
brought by the Federal Trade Commission against a company accused of false advertising is called a "consent order."

term of copyright   The period during which copyright protection endures for a copyrightable work. For any work created after December 31, 1977, copyright protection begins
the moment the work is first fixed in a tangible form. How
long it lasts depends to a large extent on who created it and
under what circumstances. Under ordinary circumstances,
copyright protection lasts for the remainder of the life of the
author of the work plus seventy years; if two or more authors

jointly create a work, copyright protection will endure until seventy years after the last of the authors dies. If a work is created as a work-for-hire, anonymously, or under a fictitious name, the term of copyright will either be one hundred and twenty years from the date the work was created or ninety-five years from the date it is published, whichever period expires first.

trademark   A word, phrase, sound, or symbol that represents in the marketplace the commercial reputation of a product or service. The Lanham Act, which is the U.S. federal statute governing unfair competition and trademarks, defines a trademark as "any word, name, symbol or device or any combination thereof adopted and used by a manufacturer or merchant to identify his goods and distinguish them from those manufactured or sold by others." A word or symbol qualifies as a trademark when it is actually used in commerce to identify the goods of a particular manufacturer or merchant and when it functions to identify and distinguish those goods from those of others. In this country, trademark ownership accrues by virtue of use of a trademark rather than by registration, although trademark registration significantly enhances the rights of trademark owners. Roughly speaking, trademark owners acquire rights in their marks commensurate with the duration and scope of their use of them. Service marks are trademarks that name services.

Trademark Dilution Act of 1995   A federal law that formalizes and makes a part of the federal trademark statute a principle of trademark law that had been available as a ground for suit in only about half the states. The act allows the owners of an existing "famous" trademark to ask the court to enjoin the use of the same mark by another company—even if there is no likelihood of confusion between the marks—on the ground that the defendant's use of the mark, even for non-competing goods or services, "dilutes" the distinctive quality of the famous mark. "Dilution" is defined in the act as "the lessening of the capacity of a famous mark to identify and distinguish goods or services, regardless of the presence or absence of 1) competition between the owner of the famous mark and other parties, or 2) likelihood of confusion, mistake, or deception."

trademark directory   A trademark directory lists trademarks
that are registered and therefore already in use by someone
else. Marks are listed alphabetically, according to the category of product or service they name or designate. A trademark
directory is most useful in the case of marks that consist sole-
ly of words. A trademark directory only short-circuits further
pursuit of unavailable marks; it cannot finally clear a mark for
use. For this, a full trademark search is necessary.

trademark infringement   The use of a trademark without
permission of the trademark owner or the use of a trademark
that is confusingly similar to a trademark owned by someone
else. Trademark infringement is judged by the "sight, sound,
and meaning test." That is, the new mark is compared to the
established trademark for similarities of appearance, sound,
and meaning. If the two marks are so similar that the average
consumer is likely to confuse the products or services the
marks name, or to believe that they are somehow related, the
new name infringes the older mark. Intent is immaterial in
evaluating most trademark infringement cases. In other
words, use of a trademark that is confusingly similar to an
established trademark will create problems whether or not it
was an intentional effort to trade on the good commercial
reputation of the established mark.

trademark registration   The registration of a claim to ownership of a trademark, made in Washington, D.C. in the U.S.
Patent and Trademark Office, a division of the Department of
Commerce. Trademark registration enhances the rights an
owner gains by virtue of the use of a trademark but does not
of itself create those rights. Among other advantages, a federal registrant is presumed to have rights in the registered mark
superior to anyone else except prior users of the mark and is
entitled to use the ® symbol (or another prescribed form of
federal trademark notice) that signifies federal trademark registration. While it is possible to register a trademark both with
the state governments in the states where it is used *and* in the
(federal) U.S. Patent and Trademark Office if it is used in
interstate or international commerce, federal registration
rather than state registration is generally sought by trademark
owners who can qualify for it because it confers much
greater benefits than state trademark registration. Trademark
registration is difficult and usually requires the services of a

lawyer experienced in trademark law, unlike copyright registration, which is usually readily granted after a registration process that is simple enough that copyright owners can usually accomplish it themselves.

trademark search   A survey of data on existing trademarks performed by a trademark search service in order to clear a proposed trademark for use or, alternately, eliminate it from consideration because it is determined to infringe an established mark. Most marks are cleared for use by "full" trademark searches, which are searches of U.S. federal and state trademark registrations as well as of data regarding valid but unregistered marks. The results of trademark searches are reported in trademark search reports and are interpreted in trademark search opinion letters.

unregistrable trademarks   Names (or design marks) for products or services that, because of certain inherent characteristics, are deemed by the U.S. trademark statute to be unworthy of registration. The ten statutory grounds for denial by the U.S. Patent and Trademark Office of an application to register a name or design as a trademark are: the mark is confusingly similar to a trademark that is already federally registered; the word or, more usually, symbol for which registration is sought does not function as a trademark, that is, does not act in the marketplace to identify the source of the goods or services to which it is applied; the mark is "immoral, deceptive, or scandalous"; the mark disparages or falsely suggests a connection with persons, institutions, beliefs, or national symbols, or brings them into contempt or disrepute; the mark consists of or simulates the flag or coat of arms or other insignia of the United States or of a state or municipality or a foreign nation; the mark is the name, portrait, or signature of a particular living individual who has not given his or her consent for use of the mark, or is the name, signature, or portrait of a deceased president of the United States during the life of his or her surviving spouse, unless that spouse has given consent to use of the mark; the mark is "merely descriptive" of the goods or services it names; the mark is "deceptively misdescriptive" of the goods or services it names; the mark is "primarily geographically descriptive or deceptively misdescriptive" of the goods or services it names; and the mark is primarily a surname.

work   In the language of the U.S. copyright statute, any copy-rightable product of the imagination, whether it is a book, poem, photograph, painting, poem, play, musical composition, movie, or other sort of work.

work-for-hire   A work created by an independent contractor (a freelancer) if the work falls into one of nine categories of specially commissioned works named in the U.S. copyright statute and both the independent contractor and the person who commissions the creation of the work agree in writing that it is to be considered a work-for-hire, or a work that is created by an employee as part of his or her full-time job. Works-made-for-hire belong to the employers of the people who create them, and those employers are considered the authors of those works for copyright purposes from the inception of the works. (Work-for-hire is one of three ways that ownership of rights in copyright are transferred to someone besides the author of the copyrighted work; the other two are assignment of copyright and license of copyright.)

Index

Allworth Books

The Copyright Guide, Revised Edition by Lee Wilson (softcover, 6 × 9, 192 pages, $18.95)

The Trademark Guide by Lee Wilson (softcover, 6 × 9, 192 pages, $18.95)

The Patent Guide: A Friendly Guide to Protecting and Profiting from Patents by Carl W. Battle (softcover, 6 × 9, 224 pages, $18.95)

Legal Guide for the Visual Artist, Fourth Edition by Tad Crawford (softcover, 8½ × 11, 272 pages, $19.95)

Business and Legal Forms for Illustrators, Revised Edition with CD-ROM by Tad Crawford (softcover, 8½ × 11, 192 pages, $24.95)

Business and Legal Forms for Graphic Designers, Revised Edition with CD-ROM by Tad Crawford (softcover, 8½ × 11, 240 pages, $24.95)

Business and Legal Forms for Fine Artists, Revised Edition with CD-ROM by Tad Crawford (softcover, 8½ × 11, 144 pages, $19.95)

Licensing Art and Design, Revised Edition by Caryn R. Leland (softcover, 6 × 9, 128 pages, $16.95)

Mastering 3D Animation by Peter Ratner (softcover, includes CD-ROM, 8 × 9⅞, 480 pages, $35.00)

Design Connoisseur: An Eclectic Collection of Imagery and Type by Steven Heller and Louise Fili (softcover, 7½ × 9⅜, 208 pages, $19.95)

Graphic Design and Reading: Explorations of an Uneasy Relationship edited by Gunnar Swanson (softcover, 6¾ × 9⅞, 256 pages, $19.95)

The Soul of the New Consumer: The Attitudes, Behaviors, and Preferences of E-Customers by Laurie Windham with Ken Orton (hardcover, 6 × 9, 320 pages, $24.95)